Critical Essays on
SIR WALTER SCOTT: THE WAVERLEY NOVELS

CRITICAL ESSAYS
ON
BRITISH LITERATURE

Zack Bowen, General Editor
University of Miami

Critical Essays on
SIR WALTER SCOTT:
The Waverley Novels

edited by

HARRY E. SHAW

G. K. Hall & Co.
An Imprint of Simon & Schuster Macmillan
New York

Prentice Hall International
London   Mexico City   New Delhi   Singapore   Sydney   Toronto

G. K. Hall & Co.
An Imprint of Simon & Schuster Macmillan
1633 Broadway
New York, New York 10019

Library of Congress Cataloging-in-Publication Data

Critical essays on Sir Walter Scott : the Waverly novels / edited by Harry E. Shaw.
   p.   cm. — (Critical essays on British literature)
   Includes bibliographical references and index.
   ISBN 0-7838-0005-3 (alk. paper)
   1. Scott, Walter, Sir, 1771–1832. Waverly novels.   2. Historical fiction. Scottish—History and criticism.   3. Scotland—In literature I. Shaw, Harry E., 1946–   .   II. Series.
PR5322.W43c74   1996
823'.7—dc20   96-34274
                                                           CIP

The paper used in this publication meets the minimum requirements of American National Standard for Information Sciences—Permanence of Paper for Printed Library Materials. ANSI Z3948-1984. ⊚™
10 9 8 7 6 5 4 3 2 1

Printed in the United States of America

For my parents

Contents

INDIVIDUAL NOVELS

General Editor's Note

◆

The Critical Essays on British Literature series provides a variety of approaches to both classical and contemporary writers of Britain and Ireland. The formats of the volumes in the series vary with the thematic designs of individual editors and with the amount and nature of existing reviews and criticism, augmented, where appropriate, by original essays by recognized authorities. It is hoped that each volume will be unique in developing a new overall perspective on its particular subject.

Harry Shaw's introduction discusses the early and later Scott depicted by biographers: The first leading a middle-class, wholesome country life, and the second the increasingly wealthy (until his business reverses) Laird of Abbotsford Manor ensconced in his castle. The latter's reverence for the past and for valor rewarded with land and property formed the basis for his Tory political outlook that irritated critics of a more progressive political persuasion. Thus Scott's representation of history became the major topic of the ongoing critical discussion described by Shaw with clarity and precision. The first group of selected essays includes Scott's critical reception: what he meant to his own age, why his reputation declined, and what he might mean to our own time. The second group deals with Scott's representation of history, while the third provides analyses of Scott's major novels.

ZACK BOWEN
University of Miami

Publisher's Note

♦

Producing a volume that contains both newly commissioned and reprinted material presents the publisher with the challenge of balancing the desire to achieve stylistic consistency with the need to preserve the integrity of works first published elsewhere. In the Critical Essays series, essays commissioned especially for a particular volume are edited to be consistent with G. K. Hall's house style; reprinted essays appear in the style in which they were first published, with only typographical errors corrected. Consequently, shifts in style from one essay to another are the result of our efforts to be faithful to each text as it was originally published.

Introduction

◆

HARRY E. SHAW

Sir Walter Scott's fame in his own day was astonishing. To his own considerable annoyance, he was regularly compared to Shakespeare. ("The blockheads talk of my being like Shakespeare—not fit to tie his brogues," he wrote in his journal.) His poems, and then his novels, were eagerly awaited best-sellers. His work influenced writers of literature and of history across Europe and North America—Balzac, Hugo, Ranke, Pushkin, Cooper, Prescott—and of course innumerable British writers as well, Macaulay, George Eliot, and a host of others. The story of his life, as enshrined in the magnificent (if sometimes unreliable) biography written by his son-in-law John Gibson Lockhart, became a staple of Victorian mythology.[1]

Lockhart paints the picture of a young boy, crippled by polio, lying beneath an ancient Border tower, imagining the past whose remnants surrounded him and reliving the exploits of his ancestors. As a young man, he steeped himself in his country's history, suffered rejection in love, neglected the legal career his father had staked out for him (ultimately attaining the respectable but hardly brilliant post of Clerk of the Court of Session), began writing poems, and became instantly famous. When the poetic vein ran dry (and Byron threatened to eclipse him), he turned, anonymously, to prose. The novels of the Author of Waverley won fame even greater than that produced by the poetry of Walter Scott—and fortune sufficient to finance the building of a baronial mansion in the Border country, an attempt to recreate the past, this time in stone, not in words. With the mansion complete and his fame at its zenith, financial disaster struck. Scott had been a silent partner in the publishing firm that produced his novels; the financial panic of 1826 shook the rickety system of credit throughout Great Britain, and he found himself, largely because of the imprudence of his partners, personally liable for a huge sum, there being no incorporation to limit liability in those days. The customary response would have been to declare bankruptcy, but Scott's sense of honor closed this easy path, which would defraud his creditors of much he owed them. Instead, he heroically undertook to pay the debt single-handed and wrote himself to death doing so. Scott died believing he had paid his debts in full. (In fact, the final payments came from the proceeds of Lockhart's biography and posthumous sales of his works.) The ethical grandeur of this tale, with its finely symmetrical plot, transformed the writer who had made the past live for his contemporaries, entertaining them with his genial humor, into a hero of principle, a Victorian exemplar.

The progress of Scott's subsequent reputation has been less shapely and less edifying. By the end of the nineteenth century, comparisons of his works with those of Shakespeare were no longer forthcoming, and the fable of Scott's life had shared the fate of other Victorian pieties. There came a time when Scott was known primarily as a writer of books appropriate for children, and then as a writer not even they were likely to read. His critical reputation followed a similar downward trajectory.[2] Twenty years ago, it was common to write Scott off as "not quite first-rate," despite the efforts of a few critics to redeem him.[3] Instead of detailing this general critical decline, however, and before describing signs of a recent reversal, I'd like to consider the history of Scott criticism in a different light by concentrating on two images, drawn from Lockhart's biography, of the Author of Waverley at work.

The first image is domestic. Scott as a young man sits at his desk in his first Border home, writing fluently and effortlessly. His favorite dog leaps in and out of the window; his children come and go, and he always has time to answer a question or tell them a story. Later in life, we find him in the book-studded, baronial library at Abbotsford, writing early in the morning before he emerges to entertain the guests gathered at his estate. Here, Scott is happily embedded in his favored milieu; he is the man who became the Laird of Abbotsford. This is, of course, one aspect of the Victorian picture of Scott we have already considered. Scott is here the ideal representative of a certain class at a certain historical moment—who incidentally happened to have the gift of literary genius, a genius that seems a simple, unself-conscious expression of his natural vitality.

Early critics of Scott seized upon the image of the Laird of Abbotsford, turning it in different directions according to their own priorities. In what was probably the most influential piece of writing on Scott produced in the nineteenth century, Carlyle expresses a mixed view of Scott's relationship to his Border milieu. On the one hand, he calls Scott's early life in the Borders "the ideal of a country life in our time." On the other, he declares that Scott's "Ambition" to become "a country gentleman, the founder of a race of Scotch lairds" corrupted him, causing him to "manufacture and not create" his novels "to make more money; and rear mass on mass for a dwelling to himself, till the pile toppled, sank crashing, and buried him in its ruins."[4] Scott, the healthiest of authors, succumbs to the infection of ambition. A mixture of attraction to a certain kind of externality of character, and suspicion of it, lies at the heart of Carlyle's ambivalent view of Scott. He praises Scott for revealing that "the bygone ages of the world were actually filled by living men, not by protocols, state-papers, controversies, and abstractions of men. Not abstractions were they, not diagrams and theorems; but men, in buff or other coats and breeches, with colour in their cheeks, with passions in their stomach, and the idioms, features, and vitalities of very men" (337). Yet in the same breath he complains that this depiction involves mere costuming. Scott's unforgivable literary sin is his insensitivity to the spiritual side of human beings: he has no lesson to teach; his depiction of individual characters ignores the struggles of the soul. By the same token, Border life offers pastoral possibilities—before his corruption, Scott possessed "a right healthy soul, rendering him little dependent on outward circumstances" (316)—but it also seems to disperse his inner life into a set of "merely" external relationships with the society around him and even with the stones and mortar of Abbotsford. Just such a web of social relationships characterizes what is known as "organic society"—the traditional society whose passing Scott's fiction depicts and in part mourns, and which so many other nineteenth-century authors, among them Carlyle, drew upon as a contrast to the mechanical, utilitarian society surrounding them. Carlyle's ambivalence about Scott as the Laird of Abbotsford, then, shadows an ambivalence Scott himself shared and vivified in his fiction. In Carlyle's handling, Scott's life becomes an allegory of the very historical process Scott himself portrayed; the mixed response to his "worldliness" mirrors Scott's own response to the inevitability of the coming of modernity.

Many Victorian writers shared Carlyle's mixture of attraction and suspicion with regard to the Laird of Abbotsford. Scott was immensely entertaining, but he lacked seriousness; he was externally healthy, but neglected the inner man; he was too easy and fluent a writer, avoiding earnest effort; he was too interested in making money. Even Leslie Stephen, who defends him against a number of these charges, seems uncomfortable with the picture of Scott embedded in the Abbotsford milieu, preferring to think of him outdoors, on a barren Border hillside. There were of course those who objected simply to his Tory politics. In love with the past, the reactionary Author of Waverley attempted to stop history and progress and undo not only the French Revolution but that triumphant, peaceful progressiveness we have since come to associate with the Whig interpretation of history. Mark Twain charged that Scott, not slavery, created the exaggerated feelings of caste and class that developed in the American South and thus helped bring on the Civil War. (How much of Twain's animus came from his belief that Scott's style had been a disastrous influence on Southern writers?) In the 1920s, the great Scottish poet and nationalist Hugh MacDiarmid blamed Scott's fiction for promoting a cringing acceptance of the amalgamation of Scottish and British cultures.

Scott is presented as decidedly the creature of his milieu in perhaps the most influential work of modern Scott criticism produced on Twain's side of the Atlantic, Alexander Welsh's *The Hero of the Waverley Novels*. For Welsh,

Scott's heroes enact the conservative philosophy of Edmund Burke. Full of an anxiety to obey the law and to refrain from the sort of action that might produce a future different from the past, these heroes find themselves rewarded at the end of the novels with the landed property that is the foundation of conservative society. The Author of Waverley is, with a vengeance, the Laird of Abbotsford, speaking for the other landed lords of British creation. Welsh's book is written with great verve and with a mastery of its sources. What is more, it gives a resonant meaning to the "passivity" of Scott's heroes, who had traditionally been passed over as likable but insignificant. It's worth adding that, unlike some of the other critics of Scott's ideology, Welsh allows the Waverley novels a limited critical power; as he puts it, they tell "an extraordinary tale of property and force."[5]

The Hero of the Waverley Novels produced a number of rejoinders, among them Francis Hart's *Scott's Novels: The Plotting of Historic Survival* (Charlottesville: University Press of Virginia, 1966), which claims that the Waverley heroes learn to survive with the "nightmare" Stephen Dedalus (in James Joyce's *Ulysses*, 1922) tells us history represents for the individual consciousness. Hart's vision of a fiction of survival recalls a response to Scott depicted in the fiction of Joyce's contemporary, Virginia Woolf. In *To the Lighthouse* (1927), Mr. Ramsay (based on Woolf's father, Leslie Stephen, whose essay on Scott I have just mentioned) turns to Scott as an author whose works evoke a common humanity transcending time (and the unpleasant aspects of his own experience). Hart seeks to pry Scott loose from the immediate historical and ideological context in which Welsh embeds him. What both critics share, however, is the assumption that Scott's novels are not, at the most important level, about their nominal subjects. *Waverley* is about property or historical survival, not about the Jacobite rising of 1745 or the culture that produced it.

This brings us to the second image of Scott. Though Lockhart delighted in portraying Scott as a Laird in the Borders, he first saw him at work in a very different setting. "Carousing" after dinner at the Edinburgh home of a friend, Lockhart noticed that his host, who was sitting by a window in the upstairs room they occupied, had an odd look about him. When he asked what the trouble was, the friend replied that he found himself mesmerized by looking down and seeing, at a window of the adjoining house, a hand writing line after line, page after page, of manuscript. Only the hand was visible. A member of the party suggested it must belong to "some stupid, dogged, engrossing clerk, probably," only to be answered, "No . . . I well know what hand it is—'tis Sir Walter Scott's" (254). This vignette could be used to place Scott in a milieu very different from the Borders but nonetheless important to him, the commercial setting of the city where books were mechanically reproduced. I wish, however, to draw upon its note of impersonal productivity for a different purpose. The steadily writing hand at the window may serve as a figure for Scott seen as a conduit for the faithful depiction of historical actuality. For one stream of readers and critics, Scott has seemed to be the clerk, not only of the Court of Session, but of history itself.

In a contemporary review of *Waverley* (the novel Lockhart later came to believe the hand at the window was completing), Francis Jeffrey suggests that the anonymous Author of Waverley's display of "genius" involved "copying from actual existences, rather than from the phantasms of his own imagination." Four years later, Thomas Love Peacock asserts that Scott "is the historian of a peculiar and minute class of our own countrymen who, within a few years, have completely passed away" and that in recording their peculiarities, he "offers materials to the philosopher."[6] Those who compared Scott to Shakespeare tended to see both authors as unconscious, "natural" artists who give a faithful picture of reality. The idea that Scott is the unconscious servant of history takes a more sharply political form in William Hazlitt, who excoriates Scott's "servile" Tory politics while praising what he takes to be the objective story that Scott's novels, wiser than his political prejudices, tell. Hazlitt lashes out at Scott's political purposes: "Does he really think of making us enamoured of the 'good old times' by the faithful and harrowing portraits he has drawn of them?" Yet he praises Scott as "the amanuensis of truth and history" who has "found out (oh, rare discovery) that facts are better than fiction . . . With reverence be it spoken, he is like the man who having to imitate the squeaking of a pig upon the stage, brought the animal under his coat with him."[7] Hazlitt here anticipates the side of Carlyle that praises Scott for having taught us that men and not dusty parchments inhabited the past.

By far the most powerful statement of the view that Scott is the "amanuensis of history and truth" comes from our own century, in the work of the Marxist critic Georg Lukács.[8] The spectacle of a Marxist critic championing the novels of the Tory Scott might seem strange, but even Marx's own collaborator Friederich Engels was willing to praise the Royalist Balzac on much the same grounds as Hazlitt praised Scott—as a novelist whose works tell the objective historical truth, despite the conscious political beliefs of their author. For Lukács, Scott's novels are historical on every level of their being. Their heroes are indeed "mediocre," but not (as Welsh would have it) so that their passivity will enact an ideology intent on guarding property and bringing historical process to a halt while that property is in the right hands. Lukács believes that Scott's heroes mirror in their "middle of the road" careers the path British history itself has traditionally taken. Indeed, Scott's characterization as a whole follows from his historical bent. Great men enter his novels only late in the action, after the activities of the real movers of history, ordinary men and women, have created a context in which their limited significance can be grasped: we see rulers and statesmen riding the crest of a wave, not propelling it along. By the same token, Scott's often-noted superficiality (perhaps better, "externality") of characterization flows from his vision of men and women as inextricably enmeshed in their historical moments. Scott's novels mark an epoch in the history of Western literature, which for Lukács is the story of how the workings of historical process become available for artistic representation. History finds a place in European realistic fiction through the emergence of Scott's historical novel, at a time when history itself became visible to the masses, as huge citizen armies clashed, and governments rose and fell during the French Revolution and its Napoleonic aftermath. All great art is realistic; but as society moves toward ever-greater complexity, the reality it seeks to master becomes increasingly complex. The eighteenth-century novel had begun to achieve a successful representation of the intricacies of class society. Then with Scott, the historical novel, branching from the realist mainstream, moved such representation into the past, where it could more easily incorporate the historical determinants of social being. Finally, with Balzac, who self-consciously aspired to write the history of his own time, the insights thus gained re-entered the realist mainstream, enabling novels to depict what Lukács, following Hegel, calls "the present as history." Lukács, then, goes considerably beyond Carlyle's assessment of the significance of the Waverley novels for our consciousness of history. For Carlyle, Scott served to remind us that the past was peopled by living human beings. For Lukács, this is the tip of an iceberg: Scott's fiction made available to the novel the power to represent the very workings of historical process itself. It did not simply make figures in the past humanly vivid; through the creation of historically "typical" characters, it showed how human actions are conditioned by their historical moments and interweave to produce past, present, and future.

One might have expected that the appearance in English of *The Historical Novel* would have inaugurated a new era in Waverley studies in the English-speaking world, and there are references in subsequent criticism to its pervasive influence—especially in the pages of those who oppose a historicist view of Scott and find in the supposed hegemony of a Lukácsian school a convenient object of attack. In fact, the criticism of Lukács has had only a modest effect on recent writings about Scott. Few Scott critics have felt the need to engage Lukács's theoretical framework in any depth. One reason is that a historicist account of Scott had already been made available to readers of English in David Daiches's seminal essays, especially his 1948 introduction to a paperback edition of *The Heart of Midlothian* and his celebrated essay, "Scott's Achievement as a Novelist," published in 1951.[9] Daiches differs from Lukács in ways that made his version of Scott as historian more attractive to many readers even after Lukács's analysis was translated. He lays heavy stress on the timeless insights into man and society Scott affords, and he is richly aware of the Scottishness of Scott's works. The latter is an area where Lukács is notoriously weak, though at least one gaffe should not be laid to his score: where in the German version of *The Historical Novel* one of Scott's characters is described, accurately, as the "crown prince" (of Scotland), the English version (based on the German) reads "the prince of Wales."

Lukács's most celebrated error of fact involves a spectacular misdating of the action of Scott's *Rob Roy:* he assumes that *Rob Roy*'s action occurs after the action of *Waverley,* on the grounds that the clan life in *Rob Roy* seems in a greater state of disintegration. Alas for this "economic" argument, *Rob Roy* is actually set thirty years earlier than *Waverley.* This error has led a traditional critic to conclude that Lukács is a fraud, given to flights of theoretical fancy but short on matters of fact; a deconstructive critic has concluded it proves that the faithful historical representation Lukács so admires is something Scott has little interest in providing—indeed something that simply can't be provided by anyone.[10] In fact, the situation is less damning and more complex than either critic would have it. Lukács's search for larger historical patterns here leads him astray, but it also reveals an aspect of the two novels that apparently escapes those who gloat over his error. For the simple fact is that the clan in *Rob Roy* is indeed depicted as being in greater decline than the ones in *Waverley.*[11] One reason is that *Rob Roy* focuses on the Clan MacGregor, which (as Scott himself explains in the notes he added to the novels for the collected edition published at the end of his life) had been outlawed by the Scottish government as early as the seventeenth century, and harried and suppressed ever since. The strength of Lukács's historical vision can make his errors more fertile than the accuracy of lesser critics.

Another, more general factor inhibited Lukács's influence on Scott studies. One might have supposed that radical critics would admit Scott as a subject of serious study after Lukács's blessing; instead, Lukács himself became a prime object of influential attack within a few years of the publication in English of *The Historical Novel.* Louis Althusser's most celebrated works were made available in English between 1969 and 1971, soon after they appeared in French. Althusser sought to discredit the entire critical and ideological program of Lukács. Critics who followed his lead denigrated Lukács for espousing a "simple reflection theory," in which literature simply replicated social and historical reality, instead of being itself a dynamic component of that reality. In fact, Lukács's "reflection theory" was anything but simple; what really offended about it was its assumption that there exists a stable, objective historical reality, and that this reality can in principle be faithfully represented in works of art. To be sure, the passive aura of the "reflection" metaphor (which Lukács consistently employs) encourages such misreadings, and sometimes weakens Lukács's own analyses. The deceptively simple surface of Scott's novels can produce a similar effect. Hazlitt, we remember, finds himself calling Scott not a historical seer, but the amanuensis of history. The eminent contemporary Marxist critic, Fredric Jameson, has sought to rehabilitate "the flawed yet monumental achievements in this area [narrative analysis] of the greatest Marxist philosopher of modern times, Georg Lukács." But though this rehabilitation focuses in part on Balzac, it does not mention Scott. In the satirical "Ballad of English Literature" (1986) by Terry Eagleton, another leading contemporary Marxist critic, Scott does not join the slim pantheon of (ironically) approved writers—"Milton, Blake and Shelley / Will smash the ruling class yet"—but instead marches with the unredeemed: "Sam Johnson was a Tory / And Walter Scott a dope."[12]

The neglect of Scott by radical critics is part of a larger neglect, fueled by the rise of postmodern assumptions about literature and indeed about history itself. When the possibility of referring to anything in the real world, past or present, seems fraught and the independent reality of a "real world" itself becomes doubtful, Lukács's claims for Scott's mode of representation are bound to seem quaint. The rising prestige of the notion that the historian fashions history as a reflection of his own ideology, instead of recording it, has also had its effect. Hayden White's theory that all narrative historians "emplot" their works according to one of four literary tropes struck a congenial chord in the breasts of many literary critics, with the radically fictive nature of historical writing becoming a common point of departure.[13] Such a vision of historical representation is consonant with the familiar epistemological assumption that we are, all of us and all of the time, producers of our world, since we are caught in the individual consciousness with no way to get out.

Lukács's stress on Scott as a radically historical novelist was followed by a careful study of history in the major novels by David Brown. For Brown, the depiction of history includes the depiction of historical mentalities; in an arresting reading, he suggests that the sense of inchoate, inescapable doom pervading *The Bride of Lammermoor* expresses the state of mind of the doomed aristocracy represented by the novel's hero. An attempt to come to grips with Lukács is also a major concern of my own book, *The Forms of Historical Fiction*. My purpose in that book was to preserve Lukács's insight that historical representation is what matters most about the Waverley novels, but at the same time to take their formal properties and differences into account in a way Lukács could hardly attempt, given the scope of his project as a whole—and also his assumptions about aesthetics and ideology. Along the way, I tried to strengthen the case for the essential historicity of Scott's fiction (and of some other historical novels as well) by distinguishing between different ways in which history is employed in the fiction of the nineteenth century. Scott may sometimes use history to explore his present-day concerns by projecting them onto the past. He may also draw upon exciting or exotic historical settings simply to energize his novels. Yet his central concern, I argue, is to function as "the amanuensis of history," especially by conveying a rich and vivid sense of what should be included in a significant response to the past.[14]

Most recent discussions of Scott have followed the path that leads to his present. Their assessment of his ideological valence has, however, been quite varied. Marilyn Butler, whose work on Austen marked an important and widely influential step in placing novelists in their ideological contexts, takes an expansive view of Scott. In a brief comparison of his work with Austen's, Butler stresses Scott's humanity, his ability to relinquish the past, the sense of an ultimate human equality that balances his clear commitment to the maintenance of the social hierarchy. For Butler, it is Austen who is the rigidly conservative figure other critics see in Scott; Scott, by contrast, is in large measure a child of the Enlightenment, full of rebelliousness against external oppression, a rebelliousness that tempers and is tempered by his love for the past. All in all, he was the novelist who "preached the right lesson for Europe in the years of restoration and reconstruction after 1815. In preaching it he meant to help the gentry to survive, but to do so by wisdom and accommodation and by accepting the irreversibility of history."[15] Butler's view of form in the Waverley novels differs instructively from her view of form in Austen. With Austen, the emphasis falls on a central, overarching "fable" that dominates the meaning of her novels and is created by the workings of their plots. With Scott, plots and protagonists recede; Butler spends much of her time on minor characters and poignant episodes, and she stresses his formal variety and inventiveness. Would greater attention to Scott's plots and protagonists have produced a more conservative Scott? Is Butler right in finding the heart of the matter elsewhere in his novels? Gary Kelly, who has written extensively and authoritatively on the fiction of the turn of the nineteenth century, insists on the centrality of Scott's own contemporary concerns to his fiction, and he describes Scott's romance plots as giving the protagonist the values of the middle class and the social standing of the gentry. But, perhaps because he refuses to reduce the novels to plot and protagonist—for him, Scott is above all a novelist of description—he discovers multiple tensions in the ideology of the novels.[16]

Other critics of Scott's ideology have tended to focus on protagonist and plot. They find in his multitudinous and multifarious novels central, repetitive motifs and situations. Typically, these patterns employ actions set in the past to enact a political attitude toward the present. Graham McMaster's *Scott and Society* gives a clear statement of its underlying critical assumptions. For McMaster, Scott (following an "impulse to mythologize") returns throughout his novels to a limited number of recurrent "patterns, metaphors and symbols" that express his "need to keep the social relationships of his own day under his imaginative control."[17] In McMaster's eyes, following these patterns throughout Scott's career reveals a growing doubt about the results of historical progress: "it is only through symbol that Scott could do justice to his ever-deepening sense of wrong and loss" (224). Such a vision is metaphorical in at least two senses. In the first place, it looks to individual metaphors as the locus of literary meaning: "Whenever metaphor replaces metonymy as the principal mode of [a Scott] novel, this is the place to try to find its real significance" (142), McMaster suggests. Beyond that, it assumes that Scott's representation of history must itself be acting as a metaphor for something else, must imply an overarching symbolic pattern. Large symbolic patterns often

evoke the archetypal.[18] Perhaps because of Scott's immersion in his own culture—as well as the political cast of so much recent criticism—in recent Scott
criticism symbolic patterns are usually taken to refer to Scott's own historical
moment.

One means of producing a Scott centered in his own present has been to
insist that he writes "romances," not (realist) novels—a step which, again,
centers his novels firmly on their romantic (that is, love-interest) plots.
Throughout *The Hero of the Waverley Novels,* Welsh speaks of Scott's
"romances." (In a more recent essay, he states that Scott is "a great political
novelist as well as an historical novelist."[19]) In *Fiction Against History: Scott as
Story-Teller,* James Kerr suggests that Scott's full complexity can be grasped
only if we recognize that, simultaneously and contradictorily, he wished to
portray history objectively but also to shape its story to his desires by writing
not novels but romances. However Scott's impulses are balanced, the scale for
Kerr tips decidedly (if unobtrusively) in favor of romance. Kerr finds Scott's
wish to tell the truth about history naive. In part, this is because Kerr's study
draws heavily on an Althusserian framework, in which "history enters the
novel, but only in retextualized form, only as ideology." As a result, the (realist) novel becomes the junior partner in what Scott actually accomplished:
Scott employs "the transforming power of romance" as "a way of reshaping
the past, of mastering history."[20] The romance of protagonist and plot allows
Scott to shape history into forms that smooth over the social contradictions
surrounding him. Nicola Watson takes a dour view of the success of the
Waverley plot in "freezing the slippages of revolution." Where certain of
Scott's predecessors had used "the sentimental plot of passion" to give expression to rebellious energy, Scott in *Waverley* "reconstrues revolution within the
structures of national romance."[21] Some would suggest that Scott's plots and
protagonists are too slight and conventional to bear such interpretative
weight, and that other relationships between plot and meaning might more
appropriately be imagined.

Viewing Scott as a romancer can yield divergent assessments of his ideological significance. For Daniel Cottom, the notion that Scott might have
something useful to tell us about the past never arises; Scott (like Richardson
and Austen) is "preoccupied" with the problem of "finding an aesthetic solution to the conflicting values environing [his] artistic creations." As it hap-
pens, Scott's solution is both reprehensible and unpleasant. On the one hand,
the romance plots of the novels invite us to experience vicariously the ritual
abasement of their protagonists, who take masochistic delight in bowing to
aristocratic power, with which they covertly identify. At the same time, since
the novels place the heyday of aristocratic power safely in the past, they invite
us to taste the delights of "nostalgia, the middle-class passion: the superior
form of condescension."[22] The final effect of Scott's romance is to reinforce our
acceptance of the status quo. Romance, however, can also be viewed as rebellious and oppositional, as feminist studies of popular culture have made evi-

dent. Diane Elam discovers in Scott a "postmodernist" novelist and historian, whose works rebuke the certainties assumed by "modernist" writers. ("Modernism" here refers, not to the art of the early twentieth century, but to the "modernity" that begins with the Enlightenment.) Scott becomes a Derridean avant-la-lettre. Since Elam takes romance to be liberating, the Waverley novels, far from being complicit in maintaining an oppressive status quo, promote emancipation from the "representational framework of political judgment," leading us to rethink the politics of realism itself. Realism is naive and oppressive; what we require is not a politics more adequate to the realities around us, but an unsettling of our notion of the political itself. Such an unsettling, according to Elam, will by its very nature align itself with the best self of feminism. Romance in Scott's postmodern mode opens our repressive modernist frames of reference to "the play of desires which, emanating as they do from the excluded (women, lost tribes), are *a priori* irrepresentable."[23]

More closely and variously responsive to Scott's texts than Cottom, and much better informed about Scott than Elam, Judith Wilt gives an intriguing reading of Scott's fiction as an attempt to fashion a place of retreat from the history around him. Like other readers of Scott as romancer, Wilt discovers behind the novels' plots a single, overarching "fable." In Wilt's view, the keystone of Scott's fictional corpus is *Ivanhoe*, not one of the Scottish novels; the medieval novels as a whole are crucial because they extend his interest in historical rebellion to a subject that is nothing less than the fate of "Christendom," ever attempting to purge itself of the guilt of having usurped divine authority and replaced it with human, enlightened, political authority. Scott's central myth thus turns out to be religious, a version of the myth of the Holy Grail, of the search for a hidden source of spiritual power always just out of reach, from which one can nonetheless draw sustenance. Scott's novels enact "the profoundest experience of the citizens of the kingdom of Belief," which is "the experience of that kingdom's hidden proximity after its tangible loss."[24] In his novels, Scott retreats to the forest of Sherwood, keeping alive there the old, sometimes lawless vitality even as civilized society grows increasingly regimented and venal. Making plausible the notion that a religious meaning lies at the heart of Scott's novels is a remarkable achievement. (Scott's only overtly religious writings are two bland sermons he turned out with speedy facility. An anxious aspirant to clerical orders doubted his ability to write sermons; Sir Walter demonstrated that nothing was easier.) Quite aside from its thesis, which in my own view reflects a living current in Scott's works, Wilt's book is full of valuable insights, particularly into the ways in which the Waverley novels experiment with mixed gender roles but in the end, as a part of their story of the coming of modernity, redraw the boundaries firmly, though with a recognition of the psychic costs.

Recent criticism on Scott's novels has included some excellent scholarly work. A large-scale critical edition has begun to appear from the University of Edinburgh Press. Carefully edited and copiously annotated paperback versions of the most commonly taught novels are now available. We now have two expert studies of Scott's use of language, and especially of Scots vernacular.[25] There have been numerous accounts of Scott's influence at home and abroad, including two noteworthy studies of American fiction that take Scott into account.[26] Scott's place in literary history—a place that remains invisible to many otherwise well-informed critics of nineteenth-century literature and of the novel—has also received notable attention. Jane Millgate illuminates Scott's own literary career, focusing on the novels before *Ivanhoe* and drawing on his poetry as well. In an important reinterpretation of nineteenth-century British fiction, George Levine places Scott in the realist tradition, newly defined as the quest for a reality beyond the words that are the novelist's medium. Ian Duncan sees Scott as the creator of a version of romance tradition drawn heavily upon by Dickens and others. His book is of considerable theoretical interest. In a wide-ranging, expert study, Fiona Robertson places the Gothic at the heart of Scott's achievement.[27] Finally, Ina Ferris turns to Scott's role in the history of novel-reading. Her important contribution to both novel and gender studies takes a fine-grained look at the reception of Scott's work, demonstrating the important part he played in the sexual politics surrounding the writing and reading of novels in the early nineteenth century. Ferris's book is an impressive addition to the significant feminist work that is beginning to appear on Scott.[28]

The essays here gathered were selected with a number of aims in mind. Some exemplify the trends and achievements in Scott criticism I have been describing; others break new ground. Throughout, I have refrained from reproducing parts of books, or essays that later gave rise to books. As a result, the crucial work of Luckács (not to mention that of some of his significant opponents) does not find a place here.

The first group of essays focuses on Scott's reception, exploring what he meant to his own age, why his reputation has declined, and what he might mean to ours. Walter Bagehot's Victorian essay-review is typical of its age in focusing on Scott's characterization and on his vision of life—and also for deploring, as Carlyle had done, Scott's neglect of intellectual and religious strife within the individual. Bagehot is perhaps best known for his classic volume *The English Constitution* (1867). His mastery of the institutions, formal and informal, of Victorian society makes him keenly alive to the nature of Scott's historical vision: "As in the imagination of Shakespeare, so in that of Scott, the principal form and object were the structure—that is a hard word—the undulation and diversified composition of human society; the picture of this stood in the centre, and every thing else was accessory and secondary to it." The comparison to Shakespeare suggests that in 1858, Scott's works had lost little of their luster—as does the fact that Bagehot's essay was occasioned by the appearance of no fewer than six editions of the Waverley novels. John Henry Raleigh's "What Scott Meant to the Victorians" explores the question of why Scott appealed to readers like Bagehot, and why his appeal faded as the century progressed.[29] Raleigh paints a broad canvas, discussing art and architecture and drawing on journals and memoirs as well as on critical writings. Like Bagehot, he provides a discriminating sense of the nature of Scott's fictional achievement. Richard Waswo rounds out this section by challenging the critical ideology that excludes Scott. Scott's focus on the social, he argues, provides an important corrective to the obsession with individual interiority characteristic of modernist novels and the criticism they so heavily influenced. Scott reminds us of the possibility of efficacious group action at a time when we badly need to take charge of a historical process gone out of control.[30]

The second section explores Scott's representation of history, reflecting the belief that this aspect of Scott, far from being exhausted or outmoded, has a contribution to make not only to our understanding of the Waverley novels but to current literary criticism, which may not have become quite so historical as it would like to think. In a pathbreaking study published in the 1950s, Duncan Forbes charts the influence on Scott of the remarkable group of eighteenth-century Scottish writers who helped make Edinburgh "the Athens of the North." Critics today may feel that Forbes's stress on Scott's debt to the "philosophical historians" of the Edinburgh Renaissance is occasionally excessive: it is hard to agree, for instance, that "Scott was no jealous guardian of the individuality and uniqueness, of anything peculiar to Scotland, in either the old Border or the Highland way of life," though it is certainly true that, influenced by philosophical history, Scott believed that all societies progress through a limited number of broadly similar historical stages. Yet by placing Scott in the context of the first stirrings of the disciplines we now know as anthropology and sociology, Forbes left an indelible mark on Scott studies, shedding crucial light on the nature and the seriousness of his vision of history. After this early essay, Forbes among his other endeavors continued to make notable contributions to Scottish studies, including a book on David Hume's "philosophical politics," a deftly introduced edition of the first two volumes of Hume's *History of England* (1754–1762), and an edition of Adam Ferguson's classic example of "philosophical history," *An Essay on the History of Civil Society* (1767), again with a brilliant introduction. Forbes's death occurred shortly after he had given permission for his essay to appear in these pages; I am grateful for the opportunity to acknowledge his seminal work.

The other essays in this section focus on specifically literary matters. Quite different in scope and approach, they all assess Scott's representation of history. These three essays have little interest in Scott's plots or his "fables"; they concentrate instead on what we might call the "texture" of his works. Ina Ferris explores Scott's allegiance not to plot (which she identifies with the closed spatial design favored by E. M. Forster and his successors) but to "story." Story leads in many directions, not in one; it is the perfect medium for capturing the heterogeneity of history. Story throws the focus on the margins—on marginal characters and traditions. It allows breathing space for the local and regional, thereby allowing Scott to resist the assimilation of Scottish culture to English. Scott's narrative technique involves, not the one-way imposition of pattern and meaning by the author, but an act of cultural "transmission" that "places narrator and reader alongside rather than inside the world it seeks to represent, creating a gap which allows entry into but not fusion with the fictional world." My own essay sees Scott in a similar light. It focuses on the depiction of speech and thought in Scott—an aspect of novelistic representation fraught with perils and opportunities for the historical novelist, who must convey the saliency of different historical mind-sets without lapsing into exoticism or incomprehensibility. Though an odd revision in the manuscript of *The Heart of Midlothian* (1818) shows vividly how negligent Scott can be about individual minds, he is more careful when he depicts the mentality of a culture. In representing the mind of the past, Scott's narrator enlists us in a shared project of historical imagining that respects difference without mystifying it.

Rohan Maitzen's essay returns to the "philosophical" note sounded by Forbes, though here the philosophers are not eighteenth-century figures, but twentieth-century theorists of narrativity as a distinct mode of historical knowledge. Maitzen is prepared to grant that both historians and novelists are in an important sense makers of the history they represent, but she does not conclude that their works simply reflect the ideologies of their own day. Nor does Scott seek to produce examples of what some are pleased to call "photographic" realism. Instead, he creates characters and situations that reveal the "conditions of historical possibility" of an age, the social and historical framework that informs it. (Here we return to Bagehot's stress on Scott's interest in historical "structure" and the logic of events.) Sometimes, in fact, the conditions of historical possibility may best be revealed by depicting "events" that never happened. In *Redgauntlet* (1824), Scott is able to capture the mentality of the last stages of Jacobitism, and the objective historical reasons why their cause was doomed, by depicting a Jacobite uprising that never in fact occurred. Such a vision of Scott's historical representation has affinities with Lukács's notion of "typicality"; it is far removed from the idea that if Scott makes historical "mistakes," it only goes to show that history cannot really be represented at all.

A final group of essays provide analyses of Scott's major novels (with an essay on the not-yet-canonical *The Talisman* [1825] taking the place of one on *Ivanhoe* [1819]). In their variety, they reflect the basic tendencies in Scott criticism I have traced and suggest fertile areas of investigation. I have already mentioned the canonical status of David Daiches's writings on Scott. Included here is perhaps the richest of the lot, his essay on *Redgauntlet*. Daiches gives a broad and flexible view of the achievement of this remarkable novel, and particularly of its Scottishness. He praises Scott as a writer who, for all his love of his nation's past, views that past with critical intelligence. Scott's brilliant anatomy of the uses and abuses of Scots law in *Redgauntlet,* for instance, makes the larger point that "the realistic and critical mind is always necessary if national feeling and national institutions are to be properly guided." Clearly enough, Daiches believes that Scott himself possessed such a mind.

Daiches's essay was written in the 1950s. Carol Anderson's recent discussion of *The Heart of Midlothian* is if anything more firmly focused on the ways in which Scott speaks to modern Scots—especially those who share neither his class affiliation nor his gender. Her view of Scott is mixed. Scott may put a lower-class Scottish woman at the center of his novel, and he may make her Scots vernacular speech prominent throughout, but isn't there condescension here, and aren't other less-conforming women in the novel severely disciplined? The "realistic and critical mind" Daiches praises threatens to become the mind of the gentry, mired in prejudices of gender and class. Yet Anderson also hears other, more estimable voices in a novel in which Scott seems to her to be "writing against himself." The uneasiness Scott generates in a critic like Anderson suggests the continuing importance of the cultural issues his works raise.

Anderson discusses Scott's linguistic practices and their ideological implications on a number of levels, including the use of the vernacular and the choice of names for characters. Peter D. Garside's essay on *Old Mortality* (1816) shares an interest in the political implications of language. Garside shows how the various idiolects the characters speak in this novel initiate a search for a language of moderation and feeling to supplant the rhetorics of murderous, self-destructive fanaticism. For Garside, the hopes and fears this search reflects have everything to do with Scott's own situation at a historical moment in which fear of the lower orders and of "ideologues" like those thought to be responsible for the French Revolution was strong in men of his class. Yet Garside balances the class-based, exclusionary impulses of *Old Mortality* with its truly humane aspects, its honest faith in the importance of local ties and affections and in the efficacy of altruism. This essay is a judicious and well-informed example of the critical school that seeks to place Scott in his own contemporary milieu, a subject on which Garside is expert. With Marilyn Orr's essay on *Waverley* (1814), we return to Scott's commerce with history. Orr is interested in the way in which *Waverley,* as well as other Scott novels, enriches the reader's sense of how one comes to have a place in history, and knowledge of that place. *Waverley* provides, both for the reader and for the novel's protagonist, an education in the relationship between personal and public time. Orr's interest in the novel as a transaction between narrator and reader helps her elucidate the lesson about history the novel teaches. In other essays, her probing accounts of Scott's use of narrative personae shed further light on the narrative transactions in which the Waverley novels engage their readers.

The two remaining essays record fruitful encounters between what we have come to know as "theory" and the novels of Scott. With Bruce

Beiderwell's essay, the encounter is indirect. Beiderwell doesn't march under the colors of any theoretical school as he provides a perceptive account of the sources and significance of the hollowness that pervades *The Bride of Lammermoor* (1819). Yet his focus cannot but recall the importance of themes of absence and lack in contemporary critical theory.[31] The historicizing trend in recent critical practice is evident here, too, as Beiderwell provides a specific social and historical dimension, relevant to our own history and our current concerns, to the novel's powerful affective charge. The most recent essay in this collection confronts contemporary critical concerns in a more direct manner, dealing with questions of canonicity, race, imperialism, and "the Other." Caroline McCracken-Flesher is firmly in the camp of those who see Scott as writing ultimately about his own time and nation, not about the historical epochs that seem to provide his subjects. She nonetheless gives him credit for the "critical" powers admired by Daiches. For McCracken-Flesher, however, Scott's critique is filled with rebelliousness, not mellow understanding: *The Talisman* provides a model for the Scots (and perhaps not only the Scots) to employ in dealing with the cultural hegemony of their imperial masters, the English. In this account, as in the essays by Ferris and Shaw, Scott provides an imaginative texture in which the representation of cultural difference and heterogeneity find a central place. So that, even as McCracken-Flesher places Scott in his own milieu, he emerges as an author whose works illuminate the rigors of historical understanding.

Notes

1.   The full version of Lockhart's biography runs to many volumes (seven in the first edition) and is replete with Scott's letters. Lockhart produced a one-volume edition, reprinted in Everyman's Library as J. G. Lockhart, *The Life of Sir Walter Scott* (London: Dent, 1969); hereafter cited in the text. The standard modern biography is Edgar Johnson, *Sir Walter Scott: The Great Unknown* (New York: Macmillan, 1970); this corrects many factual errors in Lockhart. A more radical revision of the story Lockhart tells is John Sutherland, *The Life of Walter Scott: A Critical Biography* (Oxford: Blackwell, 1995), itself as much a product of our age as Lockhart's biography was of his.

2.   For an excellent study of Scott's reputation through the 1930s, see James T. Hillhouse, *The Waverley Novels and Their Critics* (Minneapolis: University of Minnesota Press, 1936). A good selection of nineteenth-century reviews, essays, and other commentary is contained in *Scott: The Critical Heritage*, ed. John O. Hayden (New York: Barnes and Noble, 1970). Recent work on Scott is listed in Jill Rubenstein's invaluable *Sir Walter Scott: An Annotated Bibliography of Scholarship and Criticism 1975–1990* (Aberdeen: Association for Scottish Literary Studies, 1994). I am indebted to Ms. Rubenstein for sharing her expertise with me.

3.   For useful introductions to Scott's works written during this period, see Robert C. Gordon, *Under Which King? A Study of the Scottish Waverley Novels* (Edinburgh: Oliver and Boyd, 1969); A. O. J. Cockshut, *The Achievement of Walter Scott* (London: Collins, 1969); and Thomas Crawford, *Scott* (1965; revised edition, Edinburgh: Scottish Academic Press, 1982).

4. Thomas Carlyle, review of *Memoirs of the Life of Sir Walter Scott, Baronet,* vols. 1–6, in *London and Westminster Review* 6 (1838):333; hereafter cited in the text.

5. Alexander Welsh, *The Hero of the Waverley Novels, with New Essays on Scott* (Princeton: Princeton University Press, 1992), 177; this book originally appeared in 1963 as *The Hero of the Waverley Novels.*

6. Francis Jeffrey, *Edinburgh Review* 24 (1814): 208. Peacock's comments appear in "An Essay on Fashionable Literature," written in 1818 but not published during his lifetime; extracts appear in *Scott: The Critical Heritage,* 144–45. The quotation here appears on 145.

7. William Hazlitt, "Sir Walter Scott," in *The Spirit of the Age,* vol. 11 of *The Complete Works of William Hazlitt,* ed. P. P. Howe (London: Dent, 1932): 65, 63, 62.

8. Georg Lukács, *The Historical Novel,* trans. from the German by Hannah and Stanley Mitchell (London: Merlin, 1962). Russian version, 1937; German translation, 1955.

9. David Daiches, "Scott's Achievement as a Novelist," first appeared in *Nineteenth-Century Fiction* 6 (1951): 81–95; 153–73. It was reprinted in his *Literary Essays* (Edinburgh: Oliver and Boyd, 1956; reprinted 1968); in *Scott's Mind and Art,* ed. A. Norman Jeffares (Edinburgh: Oliver and Boyd, 1969); and in *Walter Scott: Modern Judgements,* ed. D. D. Devlin (London: Macmillan, 1969).

10. Cockshut, 159n2; Elam (cited below, n. 23), 59–60.

11. To my knowledge, the only published account that finds insight behind Lukács's mistake is Elaine Jordan, "The Management of Scott's Novels," in *Europe and its Others, Volume Two,* Proceedings of the Essex Conference on the Sociology of Literature, July 1984 (Colchester: University of Essex, 1985), 160n25. Jordan argues that "the 'feel' of *Rob Roy* is later [than that of *Waverley*]—the Stewart cause more remote, hopeless and marginal, the flourishing of the Glasgow merchant much truer of the end of the century than of its first fifty years." Jordan is suspicious of the ideologies of both Lukács and Scott.

12. Fredric Jameson, *The Political Unconscious: Narrative as a Socially Symbolic Act* (Ithaca: Cornell University Press, 1981), 13; Terry Eagleton, *Against the Grain: Essays 1975–1985* (London: Verso, 1986), 185.

13. Hayden White, *Tropics of Discourse: Essays in Cultural Criticism* (Baltimore: Johns Hopkins University Press, 1978).

14. David Brown, *Walter Scott and the Historical Imagination* (London: Routledge and Kegan Paul, 1979); Harry E. Shaw, *The Forms of Historical Fiction: Sir Walter Scott and His Successors* (Ithaca: Cornell University Press, 1983).

15. Marilyn Butler, *Romantics, Rebels and Reactionaries: English Literature and Its Background 1760–1830* (Oxford: Oxford University Press, 1981), 111.

16. Gary Kelly, *English Fiction of the Romantic Period, 1789–1830* (London: Longman, 1989).

17. Graham McMaster, *Scott and Society* (Cambridge: Cambridge University Press, 1981), 6; hereafter cited in the text.

18. Northrop Frye writes briefly on Scott and archetypes in *The Secular Scripture: A Study of the Structure of Romance* (Cambridge, Mass.: Harvard University Press, 1976).

19. Welsh, *The Hero of the Waverley Novels, with New Essays on Scott,* 240.

20. James Kerr, *Fiction Against History: Scott as Story-Teller* (Cambridge: Cambridge University Press, 1989), 2, 17, 9; hereafter cited in the text. Althusser comes to Kerr by way of the early work of Terry Eagleton, whose version of Althusserian poetics was in turn influenced by Pierre Macherey, author of *A Theory of Literary Production,* trans. Geoffrey Wall (London: Routledge and Kegan Paul, 1978); originally published as *Pour une théorie de la production litteraire* (Paris: Libraire François Maspero, 1966).

21. Nicola J. Watson, *Revolution and the Form of the British Novel, 1790–1825: Intercepted Letters, Interrupted Seductions* (Oxford: Clarendon, 1994), 133, 135.

22. Daniel Cottom, *The Civilized Imagination: A Study of Ann Radcliffe, Jane Austen, and Sir Walter Scott* (Cambridge: Cambridge University Press, 1985), 31, 147.

23. Diane Elam, *Romancing the Postmodern* (London: Routledge, 1992), 78.

24. Judith Wilt, *Secret Leaves: The Novels of Walter Scott* (Chicago: University of Chicago Press, 1985), 184.

25. Graham Tulloch, *The Language of Sir Walter Scott: A Study of his Scottish and Period Language* (London: Deutsch, 1980); Emma Letley, *From Galt to Douglas Brown: Nineteenth-Century Fiction and Scots Language* (Edinburgh: Scottish Academic Press, 1988).

26. George Dekker, *The American Historical Romance* (Cambridge: Cambridge University Press, 1987); Susan Manning, *The Puritan-Provincial Vision: Scottish and American Literature in the Nineteenth Century* (Cambridge: Cambridge University Press, 1990).

27. Jane Millgate, *Walter Scott: The Making of the Novelist* (Toronto: University of Toronto Press, 1984); George Levine, *The Realistic Imagination: English Fiction from Frankenstein to Lady Chatterley* (Chicago: University of Chicago Press, 1981); Ian Duncan, *Modern Romance and Transformations of the Novel: The Gothic, Scott, Dickens* (Cambridge: Cambridge University Press, 1992); Fiona Robertson, *Legitimate Histories: Scott, Gothic, and the Authorities of Fiction* (Oxford: Clarendon, 1994). Levine makes Scott part of a major study of nineteenth-century culture in *Darwin and the Novelists: Patterns of Science in Victorian Fiction* (Cambridge, Mass.: Harvard University Press, 1988).

28. Ina Ferris, *The Achievement of Literary Authority: Gender, History, and the Waverley Novels* (Ithaca: Cornell University Press, 1991). Books already cited that treat Scott in a feminist context include Wilt, Millgate, and Elam. A pioneering essay was Susan Morgan, "Old Heroes and a New Heroine in the Waverley Novels," *ELH* 50 (1983): 559–85. For a feminist reading of Scott's poetry, see Nancy Moore Goslee, *Scott the Rhymer* (Lexington: University Press of Kentucky, 1988).

29. Readers interested in Scott's influence on nineteenth-century novelists will want to supplement Raleigh's essay with Judith Wilt, "Steamboat Surfacing: Scott and the English Novelists," *Nineteenth-Century Fiction* 35 (1981): 459–86. Other valuable essays on Scott by Raleigh include "*Waverley* as History," *Novel* 4 (Fall 1970): 14–29; and "*Waverley* and *The Fair Maid of Perth*," in *Some British Romantics,* ed. James V. Logan et al. (Columbus: Ohio State University Press, 1966), 233–66.

30. Waswo explores Scott's depiction of human beings in history on a more theoretical plane in an important and influential essay, "Story as Historiography in the Waverley Novels," *ELH* 47 (1980): 304–330.

31. The same can be said of Beiderwell's book *Power and Punishment in Scott's Novels* (Athens: University of Georgia Press, 1992), which is, as Alexander Welsh puts it, "a book that engages Foucault's work without being Foucauldian" (Welsh, xv). The collection from which this essay and Carol Anderson's essay are taken, *Scott in Carnival,* is highly recommended; it is available from the Association for Scottish Literary Studies (Department of English, University of Aberdeen, Aberdeen AB9 2UB, Scotland), as is information about the Society and its publications, including *The Scott Newsletter.*

SCOTT AND HIS READERS

◆

The Waverley Novels

Walter Bagehot

[A review of the following editions of the Waverley Novels:]

Library Edition. Illustrated by upwards of Two Hundred Engravings on Steel, after Drawings by Turner, Landseer, Wilkie, Stanfield, Roberts, &c., including Portraits of the Historical Personages described in the Novels. 25 vols. demy 8vo.

Abbotsford Edition. With One Hundred and Twenty Engravings on Steel, and nearly Two Thousand on Wood. 12 vols. superroyal 8vo.

Author's favourite Edition. 48 post foolscap 8vo vols.

Cabinet Edition. 25 vols. foolscap 8vo.

Railway Edition. Now publishing, and to be completed in 25 portable volumes, large type.

People's Edition. 5 large volumes royal 8vo.

It is not commonly on the generation which was contemporary with the production of great works of art that they exercise their most magical influence. Nor is it on the distant people whom we call posterity. Contemporaries bring to new books formed minds and stiffened creeds; posterity, if it regard them at all, looks at them as old subjects, worn-out topics, and hears a disputation on their merits with languid impartiality, like aged judges in a court of appeal. Even standard authors exercise but slender influence on the susceptible minds of a rising generation; they are become "papa's books"; the walls of the library are adorned with their regular volumes; but no hand touches them. Their fame is itself half an obstacle to their popularity; a delicate fancy shrinks from employing so great a celebrity as the companion of an idle hour. The generation which is really most influenced by a work of genius is commonly that which is still young when the first controversy respecting its merits arises; with the eagerness of youth they read and re-read; their vanity is not unwilling to adjudicate: in the process their imagination is formed; the creations of the author range themselves in the memory; they become part of the substance of the very mind. The works of Sir Walter Scott can hardly be said to have gone through this exact process: Their immediate popularity was unbounded. No one—a few most captious critics apart—ever questioned their peculiar power. Still they are subject to a transition, which is in principle the same. At the time

From the *National Review* 6 (1858): 444–72.

of their publication mature contemporaries read them with delight. Superficial the reading of grown men in some sort must ever be; it is only once in a lifetime that we can know the passionate reading of youth; men soon lose its eager learning power. But from peculiarities in their structure, which we shall try to indicate, the novels of Scott suffered less than almost any book of equal excellence from this inevitable superficiality of perusal. Their plain, and, so to say, cheerful merits, suit the occupied man of genial middle life. Their appreciation was to an unusual degree coincident with their popularity. The next generation, hearing the praises of their fathers in their earliest reading time, seized with avidity on the volumes; and there is much in very many of them which is admirably fitted for the delight of boyhood. A third generation has now risen into at least the commencement of literary life, which is quite removed from the unbounded enthusiasm with which the Scotch novels were originally received, and does not always share the still more eager partiality of those who, in the opening of their minds, first received the tradition of their excellence. New books have arisen to compete with these; new interests distract us from them. The time, therefore, is not perhaps unfavourable for a slight criticism of these celebrated fictions; and their continual republication without any criticism for many years seems almost to demand it.

There are two kinds of fiction which, though in common literature they may run very much into one another, are yet in reality distinguishable and separate. One of these, which we may call the *ubiquitous,* aims at describing the whole of human life in all its spheres, in all its aspects, with all its varied interests, aims, and objects. It searches through the whole life of man; his practical pursuits, his speculative attempts, his romantic youth, and his domestic age. It gives an entire feature of all these; or if there be any lineaments which it forbears to depict, they are only such as the inevitable repression of a regulated society excludes from the admitted province of literary art. Of this kind are the novels of Cervantes and Le Sage, and, to a certain extent, of Smollett or Fielding. In our own time, Mr. Dickens is an author whom nature intended to write to a certain extent with this aim. He should have given us *not* disjointed novels, with a vague attempt at a romantic plot, but sketches of diversified scenes, and the obvious life of varied mankind. The literary fates, however, if such beings there are, allotted otherwise. By a very terrible example of the way in which in this world great interests are postponed to little ones, the genius of authors is habitually sacrificed to the tastes of readers. In this age, the great readers of fiction are young people. The "addiction" of these is to romance; and accordingly a kind of novel has become so familiar to us as almost to engross the name, which deals solely with the passion of love; and if it uses other parts of human life for the occasions of its art, it does so only cursorily and occasionally, and with a view of throwing into a stronger or more delicate light those sentimental parts of earthly affairs which are the special objects of delineation. All prolonged delineation of other parts of human life is considered "dry," stupid, and distracts the mind of the youthful generation from the "fantasies" which peculiarly charm it. Mr. Olmsted has a story of some deputation of the Indians, at which the American orator harangued the barbarian audience about the "great spirit," and "the land of their fathers," in the style of Mr. Cooper's novels; during a moment's pause in the great stream, an old Indian asked the deputation, "Why does your chief speak thus to us? we did not wish great instruction or fine words; we desire brandy and tobacco." No critic in a time of competition will speak uncourteously of any reader of either sex; but it is indisputable that the old kind of novel, full of "great instruction" and varied pictures, does not afford to some young gentlemen and some young ladies either the peculiar stimulus or the peculiar solace which they desire.

The Waverley Novels were published at a time when the causes that thus limit the sphere of fiction were coming into operation, but when they had not yet become so omnipotent as they are now. Accordingly these novels every where bear marks of a state of transition. They are not devoted with any thing like the present exclusiveness to the sentimental part of human life. They describe great events, singular characters, strange accidents, strange states of society; they dwell with a peculiar interest—and as if for their own sake—on antiquarian details relating to a past society. Singular customs, social practices, even political institutions which existed once in Scotland, and even elsewhere, during the middle ages, are explained with a careful minuteness. At the same time the sentimental element assumes a great deal of prominence. The book is in fact, as well as in theory, a narrative of the feelings and fortunes of the hero and heroine. An attempt more or less successful has been made to insert an interesting love-story in each novel. Sir Walter was quite aware that the best delineation of the oddest characters, or the most quaint societies, or the strangest incidents, would not in general satisfy his readers. He has invariably attempted an account of youthful, sometimes of decidedly juvenile, feelings and actions. The difference between Sir Walter's novels and the specially romantic fictions of the present day is, that in the former the love-story is always, or nearly always, connected with some great event, or the fortunes of some great historical character, or the peculiar movements and incidents of some strange state of society; and that the author did not suppose or expect that his readers would be so absorbed in the sentimental aspect of human life as to be unable or unwilling to be interested in, or to attend to, any other. There is always a *locus in quo,* if the expression may be pardoned, in the Waverley Novels. The hero and heroine walk among the trees of the forest according to rule, but we are expected to take an interest in the forest as well as in them.

No novel, therefore, of Sir Walter Scott's can be considered to come exactly within the class which we have called the ubiquitous. None of them in any material degree attempts to deal with human affairs in all their spheres—to delineate as a whole the life of man. The canvas has a large background, in some cases too large either for artistic effect or the common reader's interest;

but there are always real boundaries—Sir Walter had no *thesis* to maintain. Scarcely any writer will set himself to delineate the whole of human life, unless he has a doctrine concerning human life to put forth and inculcate. The effort is *doctrinaire*. Scott's imagination was strictly conservative. He could understand (with a few exceptions) any considerable movement of human life and action, and could always describe with easy freshness every thing which he did understand; but he was not obliged by stress of fanaticism to maintain a dogma concerning them, or to show their peculiar relation to the general sphere of life. He described vigorously and boldly the peculiar scene and society which in every novel he had selected as the theatre of romantic action. Partly from their fidelity to nature, and partly from a consistency in the artist's mode of representation, these pictures group themselves from the several novels in the imagination, and an habitual reader comes to think of and understand what is meant by "Scott's world;" but the writer had no such distinct object before him. No one novel was designed to be a delineation of the world as Scott viewed it. We have vivid and fragmentary histories; it is for the slow critic of after-times to piece together their teaching.

From this intermediate position of the Waverley Novels, or at any rate in exact accordance with its requirements, is the special characteristic for which they are most remarkable. We may call this in a brief phrase their *romantic sense;* and perhaps we cannot better illustrate it than by a quotation from the novel to which the series owes its most usual name. It occurs in the description of the court-ball which Charles Edward is described as giving at Holyrood House the night before his march southward on his strange adventure. The striking interest of the scene before him, and the peculiar position of his own sentimental career, are described as influencing the mind of the hero. "Under the influence of these mixed sensations, and cheered at times by a smile of intelligence and approbation from the Prince as he passed the group, Waverley exerted his powers of fancy, animation and eloquence, and attracted the general admiration of the company. The conversation gradually assumed the line best qualified for the display of his talents and acquisitions. The gaiety of the evening was exalted in character, rather than checked, by the approaching dangers of the morrow. All nerves were strung for the future, and prepared to enjoy the present. This mood is highly favourable for the exercise of the powers of imagination, for poetry, and for that eloquence which is allied to poetry." Neither 'eloquence' nor 'poetry' are the exact words with which it would be appropriate to describe the fresh style of the Waverley Novels; but the imagination of their author was stimulated by a fancied mixture of sentiment and fact very much as he describes Waverley's to have been by a real experience of the two at once. The second volume of Waverley is one of the most striking illustrations of this peculiarity. The character of Charles Edward, his adventurous undertaking, his ancestral rights, the mixed selfishness and enthusiasm of the Highland chiefs, the fidelity of their hereditary followers, their striking and strange array, the

contrast with the Baron of Bradwardine and the Lowland gentry; the collision of the motley and half-appointed host with the formed and finished
English society, its passage by the Cumberland mountains and the blue lake
of Ullswater,—are unceasingly and without effort present to the mind of the
writer, and incite with their historical interest the susceptibility of his imagination. But at the same time the mental struggle, or rather transition, in the
mind of Waverley,—for his mind was of the faint order which scarcely struggles,—is never for an instant lost sight of. In the very midst of the inroad
and the conflict, the acquiescent placidity with which the hero exchanges the
service of the imperious for the appreciation of the 'nice' heroine, is kept
before us, and the imagination of Scott wandered without effort from the
great scene of martial affairs to the natural but rather unheroic sentiments of
a young gentleman not very difficult to please. There is no trace of effort in
the transition, as is so common in the inferior works of later copyists. Many
historical novelists, especially those who with care and pains have 'read up'
their detail, are often evidently in a strait how to pass from their history to
their sentiment. The fancy of Sir Walter could not help connecting the two.
If he had given us the English side of the race to Derby,[1] he would have
described the Bank of England paying in sixpences, and also the loves of the
cashier.

It is not unremarkable in connection with this the special characteristic
of the 'Scotch novels,' that their author began his literary life by collecting the
old ballads of his native country. Ballad poetry is, in comparison at least with
many other kinds of poetry, a sensible thing. It describes not only romantic
events, but historical ones, incidents in which there is a form and body and
consistence,—events which have a result. Such a poem as "Chevy Chace" we
need not explain has its prosaic side. The latest historian of Greece[2] has
nowhere been more successful than in his attempt to derive from Homer, the
greatest of ballad poets, a thorough and consistent account of the political
working of the Homeric state of society. The early natural imagination of
men seizes firmly on all which interests the minds and hearts of natural men.
We find in its delineations the council as well as the marriage; the harsh conflict as well as the deep love-affair. Scott's own poetry is essentially a mod-
ernised edition of the traditional poems which his early youth was occupied in
collecting. The *Lady of the Lake* is a sort of *boudoir* ballad, yet it contains its
element of common sense and broad delineation. The exact position of Low-
lander and Highlander would not be more aptly described in a set treatise
than in the well-known lines:

> "Saxon, from yonder mountain high
> I marked thee send delighted eye
> Far to the south and east, where lay,
> Extended in succession gay,
> Deep waving fields and pastures green,

> With gentle slopes and hills between:
> These fertile plains, that softened vale,
> Were once the birthright of the Gael.
> The stranger came with iron hand,
> And from our fathers rent the land.
> Where dwell we now! See rudely swell
> Crag over crag, and fell o'er fell.
> Ask we the savage hill we tread
> For fattened steer or household bread;
> Ask we for flocks those shingles dry,—
> And well the mountain might reply,
> To you, as to your sires of yore,
> Belong the target and claymore;
> I give you shelter in my breast,
> Your own good blades must win the rest.
> Pent in this fortress of the North,
> Think'st thou we will not sally forth
> To spoil the spoiler as we may,
> And from the robber rend the prey?
> Ay, by my soul! While on you plain
> The Saxon rears one shock of grain;
> While of ten thousand herds there strays
> But one along yon river's maze;
> The Gael, of plain and river heir,
> Shall with strong hand redeem his share."

We need not search the same poem for specimens of the romantic element, for the whole poem is full of them. The incident in which Ellen discovers who Fitz-James really is, is perhaps excessively romantic. At any rate the lines,—

> "To him each lady's look was lent;
> On him each courteous eye was bent;
> Midst furs and silks and jewels sheen,
> He stood in simple Lincoln green,
> The centre of the glittering ring,
> And Snowdoun's knight is Scotland's king,"—

may be cited as very sufficient example of the sort of sentimental incident which is separable from extreme feeling. When Scott, according to his own half-jesting but half-serious expression, was 'beaten out of poetry' by Byron, he began to express in more pliable prose the same combination which his verse had been used to convey. As might have been expected, the sense became in the novels more free, vigorous, and flowing, because it is less cramped by the vehicle in which it is conveyed. The range of character which can be adequately delineated in narrative verse is much narrower than that which can be described in the combination of narrative with dramatic prose;

and perhaps even the sentiment of the novels is manlier and freer; a delicate unreality hovers over the *Lady of the Lake.*

The sensible element, if we may so express it, of the Waverley Novels appears in various forms. One of the most striking is in the delineation of great political events and influential political institutions. We are not by any means about to contend that Scott is to be taken as an infallible or an impartial authority for the parts of history which he delineates. On the contrary, we believe all the world now agrees that there are many deductions to be made from, many exceptions to be taken to, the accuracy of his delineations. Still, whatever period or incident we take, we shall always find in the error a great, in one or two cases perhaps an extreme, mixture of the mental element which we term common sense. The strongest *un*sensible feeling in Scott was perhaps his Jacobitism, which crept out even in small incidents and recurring prejudice throughout the whole of his active career, and was, so to say, the emotional aspect of his habitual Toryism. Yet no one can have given a more sensible delineation, we might say a more statesmanlike analysis, of the various causes which led to the momentary success, and to the speedy ruin, of the enterprise of Charles Edward. Mr. Lockhart says, that notwithstanding Scott's imaginative readiness to exalt Scotland at the expense of England, no man would have been more willing to join in emphatic opposition to an anti-English party, if any such had presented itself with a practical object. Similarly his Jacobitism, though not without moments of real influence, passed away when his mind was directed to broad masses of fact and general conclusions of political reasoning. A similar observation may be made as to Scott's Toryism; although it is certain that there was an enthusiastic, and in the malicious sense, poetical element in Scott's Toryism, yet it quite as indisputably partook largely of two other elements, which are in common repute prosaic. He shared abundantly in the love of administration and organisation, common to all men of great active powers. He liked to contemplate method at work and order in action. Every body hates to hear that the Duke of Wellington asked "how the king's government was to be carried on." No amount of warning wisdom will bear so fearful a repetition. Still he *did* say it, and Scott had a sympathising foresight of the oracle before it was spoken. One element of his conservatism is his sympathy with the administrative arrangement, which is confused by the objections of a Whiggish opposition, and is liable to be altogether destroyed by uprisings of the populace. His biographer, while pointing out the strong contrast between Scott and the argumentative and parliamentary statesmen of his age, avows his opinion that in other times, and with sufficient opportunities, Scott's ability in managing men would have enabled him to "play the part of Cecil or of Gondomar."[3] We may see how much an insensible enthusiasm for such abilities breaks out, not only in the description of hereditary monarchs, where the sentiment might be ascribed to a different origin, but also in the delineation of upstart rulers, who could have no hereditary sanctity in the eyes of any Tory. Roland Græme, in the *Abbot,* is well

described as losing in the presence of the Regent Murray the natural imperti-
nence of his disposition. "He might have braved with indifference the presence of an earl merely distinguished by his belt and coronet; but he felt over-
awed in that of the soldier and statesman, the wielder of a nation's power, and
the leader of her armies." It is easy to perceive that the author shares the feeling of his hero by the evident pleasure with which he dwells on the regent's
demeanour: "He then turned slowly round toward Roland Græme, and the
marks of gaiety, real or assumed, disappeared from his countenance as completely as the passing bubbles leave the dark mirror of a still profound lake
into which the traveller has cast a stone; in the course of a minute his noble
features had assumed their natural expression of melancholy gravity," &c. In
real life Scott used to say that he never remembered feeling abashed in any
one's presence except the Duke of Wellington's. Like that of the hero of his
novel, his imagination was very susceptible to the influence of great achievement, and prolonged success in wide-spreading affairs.

The view which Scott seems to have taken of democracy indicates
exactly the same sort of application of a plain sense to the visible parts of the
subject. His imagination was singularly penetrated with the strange varieties
and motley composition of human life. The extraordinary multitude and
striking contrast of the characters in his novels show this at once. And even
more strikingly is the same habit of mind indicated by a tendency never to
omit an opportunity of describing those varied crowds and assemblages
which concentrate for a moment into a unity the scattered and unlike varieties of mankind. Thus, but a page or two before the passage which we
alluded to in the *Abbot,* we find the following: "It was indeed no common
sight to Roland, the vestibule of a palace, traversed by its various groups,—
some radiant with gaiety—some pensive, and apparently weighed down by
affairs concerning the state, or concerning themselves. Here the hoary statesman, with his cautious yet commanding look, his furred cloak and sable pan-
toufles; there the soldier in buff and steel, his long sword jarring against the
pavement, and his whiskered upper lip and frowning brow looking an habitual defiance of danger, which perhaps was not always made good; there again
passed my lord's serving-man, high of heart and bloody of hand, humble to
his master and his master's equals, insolent to all others. To these might be
added, the poor suitor, with his anxious look and depressed mien—the officer,
full of his brief authority, elbowing his betters, and possibly his benefactors,
out of the road—the proud priest, who sought a better benefice—the proud
baron, who sought a grant of church lands—the robber chief, who came to
solicit a pardon for the injuries he had inflicted on his neighbours—the plun-
dered franklin, who came to seek vengeance for that which he had himself
received. Besides there was the mustering and disposition of guards and soldiers—the despatching of messengers, and the receiving them—the tram-
pling and neighing of horses without the gate—the flashing of arms, and
rustling of plumes, and jingling of spurs within it. In short, it was that gay

and splendid confusion, in which the eye of youth sees all that is brave and brilliant, and that of experience much that is doubtful, deceitful, false, and hollow—hopes that will never be gratified—promises which will never be fulfilled—pride in the disguise of humility—and insolence in that of frank and generous bounty." As in the imagination of Shakespeare, so in that of Scott, the principal form and object were the structure—that is a hard word—the undulation and diversified composition of human society; the picture of this stood in the centre, and every thing else was accessory and secondary to it. The old "rows of books," in which Scott so peculiarly delighted, were made to contribute their element to this varied imagination of humanity. From old family histories, odd memoirs, old law-trials, his fancy elicited new traits to add to the motley assemblage. His objection to democracy—an objection of which we can only appreciate the emphatic force, when we remember that his youth was contemporary with the first French Revolution, and the controversy as to the uniform and stereotyped rights of man—was, that it would sweep away this entire picture, level prince and peasant in a common *égalité*,—substitute a scientific rigidity for the irregular and picturesque growth of centuries,—replace an abounding and genial life by a symmetrical but lifeless mechanism. All the descriptions of society in the novels,—whether of feudal society, of modern Scotch society, or of English society,—are largely coloured by this feeling. It peeps out every where, and liberal critics have endeavoured to show that it was a narrow Toryism; but in reality it is a subtle compound of the natural instinct of the artist with the plain sagacity of the man of the world.

It would be tedious to show how clearly the same sagacity appears in his delineation of the various great events and movements in society which are described in the Scotch novels. There is scarcely one of them which does not bear it on its surface. Objections may, as we shall show, be urged to the delineation which Scott has given of the Puritan resistance and rebellions, yet scarcely any one will say there is not a worldly sense in it. On the contrary, the very objection is, that it is too worldly, and far too exclusively sensible.

The same thoroughly well-grounded sagacity and comprehensive appreciation of human life is shown in the treatment of what we may call *anomalous* characters. In general, monstrosity is no topic for art. Every one has known in real life characters which if, apart from much experience, he had found described in books, he would have thought unnatural and impossible. Scott, however, abounds in such characters. Meg Merrilies, Edie Ochiltree, Radcliffe, are more or less of that description. That of Meg Merrilies especially is as distorted and eccentric as any thing can be. Her appearance is described as making Mannering "start;" and well it might: "She was full six feet high, wore a man's greatcoat over the rest of her dress, had in her hand a goodly sloethorn cudgel, and in all points of equipment except the petticoats seemed rather masculine than feminine. Her dark elf-locks shot out like the snakes of the gorgon between an old-fashioned bonnet called a bongrace, heightening the singular effect of her strong and weather-beaten features, which they partly shadowed, while her eye had a wild roll that indicated something of insanity." Her career in the tale corresponds with the strangeness of her exterior. "Harlot, thief, witch, and gipsy," as she describes herself, the hero is preserved by her virtues; half-crazed as she is described to be, he owes his safety on more than one occasion to her skill in stratagem, and ability in managing those with whom she is connected, and who are most likely to be familiar with her weakness and to detect her craft. Yet on hardly any occasion is the natural reader conscious of this strangeness. Something is of course attributable to the skill of the artist; for no other power of mind could produce the effect, unless it were aided by the unconscious tact of detailed expression. But the fundamental explanation of this remarkable success is the distinctness with which Scott saw how such a character as Meg Merrilies arose and was produced out of the peculiar circumstances of gipsy life in the localities in which he has placed his scene. He has exhibited this to his readers not by lengthy or elaborate description, but by chosen incidents, short comments, and touches of which he scarcely foresaw the effect. This is the only way in which the fundamental objection to making eccentricity the subject of artistic treatment can be obviated. Monstrosity ceases to be such when we discern the laws of nature which evolve it: when a real science explains its phenomena, we find that it is in strict accordance with what we call the natural type, but that some rare adjunct or uncommon casualty has interfered and distorted a nature which is really the same, into a phenomenon which is altogether different. Just so with eccentricity in human character; it becomes a topic of literary art only when its identity with the ordinary principles of human nature is exhibited in the midst of, and, as it were, by means of, the superficial unlikeness. Such a skill, however, requires an easy careless familiarity with usual human life and common human conduct. A writer must have a sympathy with health before he can show us how, and where, and to what extent, that which is unhealthy deviates from it; and it is this consistent acquaintance with regular life which makes the irregular characters of Scott so happy a contrast to the uneasy distortions of less sagacious novelists.

A good deal of the same criticism may be applied to the delineation which Scott has given us of the *poor*. In truth, poverty is an anomaly to rich people. It is very difficult to make out why people who want dinner do not ring the bell. One half of the world, according to the saying, do not know how the other half lives. Accordingly, nothing is so rare in fiction as a good delineation of the poor. Though perpetually with us in reality, we rarely meet them in our reading. The requirements of the case present an unusual difficulty to artistic delineation. A good deal of the character of the poor is an unfit topic for continuous art, and yet we wish to have in our books a lifelike exhibition of the whole of that character. Mean manners and mean vices are unfit for prolonged delineation; the everyday pressure of narrow necessities is too petty a pain and too anxious a reality to be dwelt upon. We can bear the mere description of the *Parish Register*—

> "But this poor farce has neither truth nor art
> To please the fancy or to touch the heart.
> Dark but not awful, dismal but yet mean,
> With anxious bustle moves the cumbrous scene;
> Presents no objects tender or profound,
> But spreads its cold unmeaning gloom around;"—[4]

but who could bear to have a long narrative of fortunes "dismal but yet mean," with characters "dark but not awful," and no objects "tender or profound." Mr. Dickens has in various parts of his writings been led by a sort of pre-Raphaelite *cultus* of reality into an error of this species. His poor people have taken to their poverty very thoroughly; they are poor talkers and poor livers, and in all ways poor people to read about. A whole array of writers have fallen into an opposite mistake. Wishing to preserve their delineations clear from the defects of meanness and vulgarity, they have attributed to the poor a fancied happiness and Arcadian simplicity. The conventional shepherd of ancient times was scarcely displeasing: that which is by every thing except express avowal removed from the sphere of reality does not annoy us by its deviations from reality; but the fictitious poor of sentimental novelists are brought almost into contact with real life, half claim to be copies of what actually exists at our very doors, are introduced in close proximity to characters moving in a higher rank, over whom no such ideal charm is diffused, and who are painted with as much truth as the writer's ability enables him to give. Accordingly, the contrast is evident and displeasing: the harsh outlines of poverty will not bear the artificial rose-tint; they are seen through it, like high cheek-bones through the delicate colours of artificial youth; we turn away with some disgust from the false elegance and undeceiving art; we prefer the rough poor of nature to the petted poor of the refining describer. Scott has most felicitously avoided both these errors. His poor people are never coarse and never vulgar; their lineaments have the rude traits which a life of conflict will inevitably leave on the minds and manners of those who are to lead it; their notions have the narrowness which is inseparable from a contracted experience; their knowledge is not more extended than their restricted means of attaining it would render possible. Almost alone among novelists Scott has given a thorough, minute, life-like description of poor persons, which is at the same time genial and pleasing. The reason seems to be, that the firm sagacity of his genius comprehended the industrial aspect of poor people's life thoroughly and comprehensively, his experience brought it before him easily and naturally, and his artist's mind and genial disposition enabled him to dwell on those features which would be most pleasing to the world in general. In fact, his own mind of itself and by its own nature dwelt on those very peculiarities. He could not remove his firm and instructed genius into the domain of Arcadian unreality, but he was equally unable to dwell principally, peculiarly, or consecutively, on those petty, vulgar, mean details in which such a writer as Crabbe lives and breathes. Hazlitt said that Crabbe described a poor man's cottage like a man who came to distrain for rent; he catalogued every trivial piece of furniture, defects and cracks and all. Scott describes it as a cheerful but most sensible landlord would describe a cottage on his property: he has a pleasure in it. No detail, or few details, in the life of the inmates escape his experienced and interested eye; but he dwells on those which do not displease him. He sympathises with their rough industry and plain joys and sorrows. He does not fatigue himself or excite their wondering smile by theoretical plans of impossible relief. He makes the best of the life which is given, and by a sanguine sympathy makes it still better. A hard life many characters in Scott seem to lead; but he appreciates, and makes his reader appreciate, the full value of natural feelings, plain thoughts, and applied sagacity.

His ideas of political economy are equally characteristic of his strong sense and genial mind. He was always sneering at Adam Smith, and telling many legends of that philosopher's absence of mind and inaptitude for the ordinary conduct of life. A contact with the Edinburgh logicians had, doubtless, not augmented his faith in the formal deductions of abstract economy; nevertheless, with the facts before him, he could give a very plain and satisfactory exposition of the genial consequences of old abuses, the distinct necessity for stern reform, and the delicate humanity requisite for introducing that reform temperately and with feeling:

"Even so the Laird of Ellangowan ruthlessly commenced his magisterial reform, at the expense of various established and superannuated pickers and stealers, who had been his neighbours for half a century. He wrought his miracles like a second Duke Humphrey; and by the influence of the beadle's rod, caused the lame to walk, the blind to see, and the palsied to labour. He detected poachers, black-fishers, orchard-breakers, and pigeon-shooters; had the applause of the bench for his reward, and the public credit of an active magistrate.

All this good had its rateable proportion of evil. Even an admitted nuisance, of ancient standing, should not be abated without some caution. The zeal of our worthy friend now involved in great distress sundry personages whose idle and mendicant habits his own *lachesse* had contributed to foster, until these habits had become irreclaimable, or whose real incapacity for exertion rendered them fit objects, in their own phrase, for the charity of all well-disposed Christians. 'The long-remembered beggar,' who for twenty years had made his regular rounds within the neighbourhood, received rather as an humble friend than as an object of charity, was sent to the neighbouring workhouse. The decrepit dame, who travelled round the parish upon a hand-barrow, circulating from house to house like a bad shilling, which every one is in haste to pass to his neighbour; she, who used to call for her bearers as loud, or louder, than a traveller demands post-horses, even she shared the same disastrous fate. The 'daft Jock,' who, half knave, half idiot, had been the sport of each succeeding race of village children for a good part of a century, was remitted to the county bridewell, where, secluded from free air and sunshine, the only advantages he was capable of enjoying, he pined and died in the course of six months. The old sailor, who had so long rejoiced the smoky rafters of every kitchen in the country, by singing *Captain Ward and Bold Admiral Benbow,* was banished from the country for no better reason, than that he was supposed to speak with a strong Irish accent. Even the annual rounds of the pedlar were abolished by the Justice, in his hasty zeal for the administration of rural police.

These things did not pass without notice and censure. We are not made of wood or stone, and the things which connect themselves with our hearts and habits cannot, like bark or lichen, be rent away without our missing them. The farmer's dame lacked her usual share of intelligence, perhaps also the self-applause which she had felt while distributing the *awmous* (alms), in shape of a *gowpen* (handful) of oatmeal to the medicant who brought the news. The cottage felt inconvenience from interruption of the petty trade carried on by the itinerant dealers. The children lacked their supply of sugar-plums and toys; the young women wanted pins, ribbons, combs, and ballads; and the old could no longer barter their eggs for salt, snuff, and tobacco. All these circumstances brought the busy Laird of Ellangowan into discredit, which was the more general on account of his former popularity. Even his lineage was brought up in judgment against him. They thought 'naething of what the like of Greenside, or Burnville, or Viewforth, might do, that were strangers in the country; but Ellangowan! that had been a name amang them since the mirk Monanday, and lang before—*him* to be grinding the puir at that rate!—They ca'd his grandfather the Wicked Laird; but, though he was whiles fractious aneuch, when he got into roving company, and had ta'en the drap drink, he would have scorned to gang on at this gate. Na, na, the muckle chumlay in the Auld Place reeked like a killogie in his time, and there were as mony puir folk riving at the banes in the court and about the door, as there were gentles in the ha'. And the leddy, on ilka Christmas night as it came round, gae twelve siller pennies to ilka puir body about, in honour of the twelve apostles like. They were fond to ca' it papistrie; but I think our great folk might take a lesson frae the papists whiles. They gie another sort o' help to puir folk than just dinging down a saxpence in the brod on the Sabbath, and kilting, and scourging, and drumming them a' the sax days o' the week besides.' "

Many other indications of the same healthy and natural sense, which gives so much of their characteristic charm to the Scotch novels, might be pointed out, if it were necessary to weary our readers by dwelling longer on a point we have already laboured so much; one more, however, demands notice because of its importance, and perhaps also because, from its somewhat less obvious character, it might escape otherwise without notice. There has been frequent controversy as to the penal code, if we may so call it, of fiction; that is, as to the apportionment of reward and punishment respectively to the good and evil personages therein delineated; and the practice of authors has been as various as the legislation of critics. One school abandons all thought on the matter, and declares that in the real life we see around us good people often fail, and wicked people continually prosper; and would deduce the precept, that it is unwise in an art which should hold the "mirror up to nature," not to copy the uncertain and irregular distribution of its sanctions. Another school, with an exactness which savours at times of pedantry, apportions the success and the failure, the pain and the pleasure, of fictitious life to the moral qualities of those who are living in it—does not think at all, or but little, of every other quality in those characters, and does not at all care whether the penalty and reward are evolved in natural sequence from the circumstances and characters of the tale, or are owing to some monstrous accident far removed from all relation of cause or consequence to those facts and people. Both these classes of writers produce works which jar on the natural sense of common readers, and are at issue with the analytic criticism of the best critics. One school leaves an impression of an uncared-for world, in which there is no right and no wrong; the other, of a sort of Governesses' Institution of a world, where all praise and all blame, all good and all pain, are made to turn on special graces and petty offences, pesteringly spoken of and teasingly watched for. The manner of Scott is thoroughly different; you can scarcely lay down any novel of his without a strong feeling that the world in which the fiction has been laid, and in which your imagination has been moving, is one subject to *laws* of retribution which, though not apparent on a superficial glance, are yet in steady and consistent operation, and will be quite sure to work their due effect, if time is only given to them. Sagacious men know that this is in its best aspect the condition of life. Certain of the ungodly may, notwithstanding the Psalmist, flourish even through life like a green bay-tree; for providence, in external appearance (far differently from the real truth of things, as we may one day see it), works by a scheme of averages. Most people who ought to succeed, do succeed; most people who do fail, ought to fail. But there is no exact adjustment of "mark" to merit; the competitive examination system appears to have an origin more recent than the creation of the world;—"on the whole," "speaking generally," "looking at life as a whole," are the words in which we must describe the providential adjustment of visible good and evil to visible goodness and badness. And when we look more closely, we see that these general results are the consequences of certain principles which work half unseen, and which are effectual in the main, though thwarted here and there. It is this comprehensive though inexact distribution of good and evil, which is suited to the novelist, and it is exactly this which Scott instinctively adopted. Taking a firm and genial view of the common facts of life,—seeing it as an experienced observer and tried man of action,—he could not help giving the representation of it which is insensibly borne in on the minds of such persons. He delineates it as a world moving according to laws which are always producing their effect, never *have* produced it; sometimes fall short a little; are always nearly successful. Good sense produces its effect, as well as good intention; ability is valuable as well as virtue. It is this peculiarity which gives to his works, more than any thing else, the life-likeness which distinguishes them; the average of the copy is struck on the same scale as that of reality; an unexplained, uncommented-on adjustment works in the one, just as a hidden imperceptible principle of apportionment operates in the other.

The romantic susceptibility of Scott's imagination is as obvious in his novels as his matter-of-fact sagacity. We can find much of it in the place in which we should naturally look first for it,—his treatment of his heroines. We are no indiscriminate admirers of these young ladies, and shall shortly try to show how much they are inferior as imaginative creations to similar creations of the very highest artists. But the mode in which the writer speaks of them every where indicates an imagination continually under the illusion which we term romance. A gentle tone of manly admiration pervades the whole delineation of their words and actions. If we look carefully at the narratives of some remarkable female novelists—it would be invidious to give the instances by name—we shall be struck at once with the absence of this; they do not half like their heroines. It would be satirical to say that they were jealous of them; but it is certain that they analyse the mode in which their charms produce their effects, and the minutiæ of their operation, much in the same way in which a slightly jealous lady examines the claims of the heroines of society. The same writers have invented the atrocious species of *plain* heroines. Possibly none of the frauds which are now so much the topic of common remark are so irritating as that to which the purchaser of a novel is a victim on finding that he has only to peruse a narrative of the conduct and sentiments of an ugly lady. "Two-and-sixpence to know the heart which has high cheek-bones!" Was there ever such an imposition? Scott would have recoiled from such conception. Even Jeanie Deans, though no heroine, like Flora Macivor, is described as "comely," and capable of looking almost pretty when required, and she has a compensating set-off in her sister, who is beautiful as well as unwise. Speaking generally, as is the necessity of criticism, Scott makes his heroines, at least by profession, attractive, and dwells on their attractiveness, though not with the wild ecstasy of insane youth, yet with the tempered and mellow admiration common to genial men of this world. Perhaps at times we are rather displeased at his explicitness, and disposed to hang back and carp at the admirable qualities displayed to us. But this is only a stronger evidence of the peculiarity which we speak of,—of the unconscious sentiments inseparable from Scott's imagination.

The same romantic tinge undeniably shows itself in Scott's pictures of the past. Many exceptions have been taken to the detail of mediæval life as it is described to us in *Ivanhoe;* but one merit will always remain to it, and will be enough to secure to it immense popularity. It describes the middle ages as we should have wished them to have been. We do not mean that the delineation satisfies those accomplished admirers of the old church system who fancy that they have found among the prelates and barons of the fourteenth century a close approximation to the theocracy which they would recommend for our adoption.[5] On the contrary, the theological merits of the middle ages are not prominent in Scott's delineation. "Dogma" was not in his way: a cheerful man of the world is not anxious for a precise definition of peculiar doctrines. The charm of *Ivanhoe* is addressed to a simpler sort of imagination,—to that kind of boyish fancy which idolises mediæval society as the "fighting time." Every boy has heard of tournaments, and has a firm persuasion that in an age of tournaments life was thoroughly well understood. A martial society, where men fought hand to hand on good horses with large lances, in peace for pleasure, and in war for business, seems the very ideal of perfection to a bold and simply fanciful boy. *Ivanhoe* spreads before him the full landscape of such a realm, with Richard Cœur-de-Lion, a black horse, and the passage of arms at Ashby. Of course he admires it, and thinks there was never such a writer, and will never more be such a world. And a mature critic will share his admiration, at least to the extent of admitting that nowhere else have the elements of a martial romance been so gorgeously accumulated without becoming oppressive; their fanciful charm been so powerfully delineated, and yet so constantly relieved by touches of vigorous sagacity. One single fact shows how great the romantic illusion is. The pressure of painful necessity is scarcely so great in this novel as in novels of the same writer in which the scene is laid in modern times. Much may be said in favour of the mediæval system as contradistinguished from existing society; much has been said. But no one can maintain that general comfort was as much diffused as it is now. A certain ease pervades the structure of later society. Our houses may not last so long, are not so picturesque, will leave no such ruins behind them; but they are warmed with hot water, have no draughts, and contain sofas instead of rushes. A slight daily unconscious luxury is hardly ever wanting to the dwellers in civilisation; like the gentle air of a genial climate, it is a perpetual minute enjoyment. The absence of this marks a rude barbaric time. We may avail ourselves of rough pleasures, stirring amusements, exciting actions, strange rumours; but life is hard and harsh. The cold air of the keen North may brace and invigorate, but it cannot soothe us. All sensible people know that the middle ages must have been very uncomfortable; there was a difficulty about "good food;"—almost insuperable obstacles to the cultivation of nice detail and small enjoyment. No one knew the abstract facts on which this conclusion rests better than Scott; but his delineation gives no general idea of the result. A thoughtless reader rises with the impression that the middle ages had the same elements of happiness which we have at present, and that they had fighting besides. We do not assert that this tenet is explicitly taught; on the contrary, many facts are explained, and many customs elucidated from which a discriminating and deducing reader would infer the meanness of poverty and the harshness of barbarism. But these less imposing traits escape the rapid, and still more the boyish reader. His general impression is one of romance; and though, when roused, Scott was quite able to take a distinct view of the opposing facts, he liked his own mind to rest for the most part in the same pleasing illusion.

The same sort of historical romance is shown likewise in Scott's picture of remarkable historical characters. His Richard I. is the traditional Richard, with traits heightened and ennobled in perfect conformity to the spirit of tradition. Some illustration of the same quality might be drawn from his delineations of the Puritan rebellions and the Cavalier enthusiasm. We might show that he ever dwells on the traits and incidents most attractive to a genial and spirited imagination. But the most remarkable instance of the power which romantic illusion exercised over him is his delineation of Mary Queen of Scots. He refused at one time of his life to write a biography of that princess "because his opinion was contrary to his feeling." He evidently considered her guilt to be clearly established, and thought, with a distinguished lawyer, that he should "direct a jury to find her guilty;" but his fancy, like that of most of his countrymen, took a peculiar and special interest in the beautiful lady who, at any rate, had suffered so much and so fatally at the hands of a queen of England. He could not bring himself to dwell with nice accuracy on the evidence which substantiates her criminality, or on the still clearer indications of that unsound and over-crafty judgment, which was the fatal inheritance of the Stuart family, and which, in spite of advantages that scarcely any other family in the world has enjoyed, has made their name an historical by-word for misfortune. The picture in the *Abbot,* one of the best historical pictures which Scott has given us, is principally the picture of the queen as the fond tradition of his countrymen exhibited her. Her entire innocence, it is true, is never alleged: but the enthusiasm of her followers is dwelt on with approving sympathy; their confidence is set forth at large; her influence over them is skilfully delineated; the fascination of charms chastened by misfortune is delicately indicated. We see a complete picture of the beautiful queen, of the suffering and sorrowful but yet not insensible woman. Scott could not, however, as a close study will show us, quite conceal the unfavourable nature of his fundamental opinion. In one remarkable passage the struggle of the judgment is even conspicuous, and in others the sagacity of the practised lawyer,—the thread of the attorney, as he used to call it,—in his nature, qualifies and modifies the sentiment hereditary in his countrymen, and congenial to himself.

This romantic imagination is a habit or power (as we may choose to call it) of mind which is almost essential to the highest success in the historical novel. The aim, at any rate the effect, of this class of works seems to be to deepen and confirm the received view of historical personages. A great and acute writer may from an accurate study of original documents discover that those impressions are erroneous, and by a process of elaborate argument substitute others which he deems more accurate. But this can only be effected by writing a regular history. The essence of the achievement is the proof. If Mr. Froude[6] had put forward his view of Henry the Eighth's character in a professed novel, he would have been laughed at. It is only by a rigid adherence to attested facts and authentic documents, that a view so original could obtain even a hearing. We start back with a little anger from a representation which is avowedly imaginative, and which contradicts our impressions. We do not like to have our opinions disturbed by reasoning; but it is impertinent to attempt to disturb them by fancies. A writer of the historical novel is bound by the popular conception of his subject; and commonly it will be found that this popular impression is to some extent a romantic one. An element of exaggeration clings to the popular judgment: great vices are made greater, great virtues greater also; interesting incidents are made more interesting, softer legends more soft. The novelist who disregards this tendency will do so at the peril of his popularity. His business is to make attraction more attractive, and not to impair the pleasant pictures of ready-made romance by an attempt at grim reality.

We may therefore sum up the indications of this characteristic excellence of Scott's novels by saying, that more than any novelist he has given us fresh pictures of practical human society, with its cares and troubles, its excitements and its pleasures; that he has delineated more distinctly than any one else the framework in which this society inheres, and by the boundaries of which it is shaped and limited; that he has made more clear the way in which strange and eccentric characters grow out of that ordinary and usual system of life; that he has extended his view over several periods of society, and given an animated description of the external appearance of each, and a firm representation of its social institutions; that he has shown very graphically what we may call the worldly laws of moral government; and that over all these he has spread the glow of sentiment natural to a manly mind, and an atmosphere of generosity congenial to a cheerful one. It is from the collective effect of these causes, and from the union of sense and sentiment which is the principle of them all, that Scott derives the peculiar healthiness which distinguishes him. There are no such books as his for the sick-room, or for freshening the painful intervals of a morbid mind. Mere sense is dull, mere sentiment unsubstantial; a sensation of genial healthiness is only given by what combines the solidity of the one and the brightening charm of the other.

Some guide to Scott's defects, or to the limitations of his genius, if we would employ a less ungenial and perhaps more correct expression, is to be discovered, as usual, from the consideration of his characteristic excellence. As it is his merit to give bold and animated pictures of this world, it is his defect to give but insufficient representations of qualities which this world does not exceedingly prize,—of such as do not thrust themselves very forward in it— of such as are in some sense above it. We may illustrate this in several ways.

One of the parts of human nature which are systematically omitted in Scott, is the searching and abstract intellect. This did not lie in his way. No man had a stronger sagacity, better adapted for the guidance of common men, and the conduct of common transactions. Few could hope to form a more correct opinion on things and subjects which were brought before him in actual life; no man had a more useful intellect. But on the other hand, as will be generally observed to be the case, no one was less inclined to that probing and seeking and anxious inquiry into things in general which is the necessity of some minds, and a sort of intellectual famine in their nature. He had no call to investigate the theory of the universe, and he would not have been able to comprehend those who did. Such a mind as Shelley's would have been entirely removed from his comprehension. He had no call to mix "awful talk and asking looks" with his love of the visible scene. He could not have addressed the universe:

> "I have watched
> Thy shadow, and the darkness of thy steps;
> And my heart ever gazes on the depth
> Of thy deep mysteries. I have made my bed
> In charnels or in coffins, where black death
> Keeps records of the trophies won from thee,
> Hoping to still these obstinate questionings
> Of thee and thine, by forcing some lone ghost,
> Thy messenger, to render up the tale
> Of what we are."[7]

Such thoughts would have been to him "thinking without an object," "abstracted speculations," "cobwebs of the unintelligible brain." Above all minds his had the Baconian propensity to work upon "stuff." At first sight, it would not seem that this was a defect likely to be very hurtful to the works of a novelist. The labours of the searching and introspective intellect, however needful, absorbing, and in some degree delicious, to the seeker himself, are not in general very delightful to those who are not seeking. Genial men in middle life are commonly intolerant of that philosophising which their prototype in old times classed side by side with the lisping of youth. The theological novel, which was a few years ago so popular, and which is likely to have a recurring influence in times when men's belief is unsettled, and persons who cannot or will not read large treatises have thoughts in their minds and inquiries in their hearts, suggests to those who are accustomed to it the absence elsewhere of what is necessarily one of its most distinctive and prominent subjects. The desire to attain a belief, which has become one of the most familiar sentiments of heroes and heroines, would have seemed utterly incongruous to the plain sagacity of Scott, and also to his old-fashioned art. Creeds are *data* in his novels: people have different creeds, but each keeps his own. Some persons will think that this is not altogether amiss; nor do we particularly wish to take up the defence of the dogmatic novel. Nevertheless, it will strike those who are accustomed to the youthful generation of a cultivated time, that the passion of intellectual inquiry is one of the strongest impulses in many of them, and one of those which give the predominant colouring to the conversation and exterior mind of many more. And a novelist will not exercise the most potent influence over those subject to that passion if he entirely omit the delineation of it. Scott's works have only one merit in this relation: they are an excellent rest to those who have felt this passion, and have had something too much of it.

The same indisposition to the abstract exercises of the intellect shows itself in the reflective portions of Scott's novels, and perhaps contributes to their popularity with that immense majority of the world who strongly share in that same indisposition: it prevents, however, their having the most powerful intellectual influence on those who have at any time of their lives voluntarily submitted themselves to this acute and refining discipline. The reflections of a practised thinker have a peculiar charm, like the last touches of the accomplished artist. The cunning exactitude of the professional hand leaves a trace in the very language. A nice discrimination of thought makes men solicitous of the most apt expressions to diffuse their thoughts. Both words and meaning gain a metallic brilliancy, like the glittering precision of the pure Attic air. Scott's is a healthy and genial world of reflection, but it wants the charm of delicate exactitude.

The same limitation of Scott's genius shows itself in a very different portion of art—in his delineation of his heroines. The same blunt sagacity of imagination, which fitted him to excel in the rough description of obvious life, rather unfitted him for delineating the less substantial essence of the female character. The nice *minutiæ* of society, by means of which female novelists have been so successful in delineating their own sex, were rather too small for his robust and powerful mind. Perhaps, too, a certain unworldliness of *imagination* is necessary to enable men to comprehend or delineate that essence: unworldliness of *life* is no doubt not requisite; rather, perhaps, worldliness is necessary to the acquisition of a sufficient experience. But an absorption in the practical world does not seem favourable to a comprehension of any thing which does not precisely belong to it. Its interests are too engrossing; its excitements too keen; it modifies the fancy, and in the change unfits it for every thing else. Something, too, in Scott's character and history made it more difficult for him to give a representation of women than of men. Goethe used to say, that his idea of woman was not drawn from his experience, but that it came to him before experience, and that he explained his experience by a reference to it. And though this is a German, and not very happy, form of expression, yet it appears to indicate a very important distinction. Some efforts of the imagination are made so early in life, just as it were at the dawn of the conscious faculties, that we are never able to fancy ourselves as destitute of them. They are part of the mental constitution with which, so to speak, we awoke to existence. These are always far more firm, vivid, and definite, than any other images of our fancy, and we apply them, half unconsciously, to any facts and sentiments and actions which may occur to us later in life, whether arising from within or thrust upon us from the outward world. Goethe doubtless meant that the idea of the female character was to him one of these first elements of imagination; not a thing puzzled out, or which he remembered having conceived, but a part of the primitive conceptions which, being coeval with his memory, seemed inseparable from his consciousness. The descriptions of women likely to be given by this sort of imagination will probably be the best descriptions. A mind which would arrive at this idea of the female character by this process, and so early, would be one obviously of more than usual susceptibility. The early imagination does not commonly take this direction; it thinks most of horses and lances, tournaments and knights; only a mind with an unusual and instinctive tendency to this kind of thought, would be borne thither so early or so effectually. And even independently of this probable peculiarity of the individual, the primitive imagination in general is likely to be the most accurate which men can form; not, of course, of the external manifestations and detailed manners, but of the inner sentiment and characteristic feeling of women. The early imagination conceives what it does conceive very justly; fresh from the facts, stirred by the new aspect of things, undimmed by the daily passage of constantly forgotten images, not misled by the irregular analogies of a dislocated life,— the early mind sees what it does see with a spirit and an intentness never given to it again. A mind like Goethe's, of very strong imagination, aroused at the earliest age,—not of course by passions, but by an unusual strength in that undefined longing which is the prelude to our passions,—will form the best idea of the inmost female nature which masculine nature can form. The trace is evident in the characters of women formed by Goethe's imagination or Shakespeare's, and those formed by such an imagination as that of Scott. The latter seems so external. We have traits, features, manners; we know the heroine as she appeared in the street; in some degree we know how she talked, but we never know how she felt—least of all what she was: we always feel there is a world behind, unanalysed, unrepresented, which we cannot attain to. Such a character as Margaret in *Faust* is known to us to the very soul; so is Imogen; so is Ophelia. Edith Bellenden, Flora Macivor, Miss Wardour, are young ladies who, we are told, were good-looking, and well-dressed (according to the old fashion) and sensible; but we feel we know but very little of them, and they do not haunt our imaginations. The failure of Scott in this line of art is more conspicuous, because he had not in any remarkable degree the later experience of female detail, with which some minds have endeavoured to supply the want of the early essential imagination, and which Goethe possessed in addition to it. It was rather late, according to his biographer, before Scott set up for "a squire of dames;" he was a "lame young man, very enthusiastic about ballad poetry;" he was deeply in love with a young lady, supposed to be imaginatively represented by Flora Macivor, but he was unsuccessful. It would be over-ingenious to argue, from his failing in a single love-affair, that he had no peculiar interest in young ladies in general; but the whole description of his youth shows that young ladies exercised over him a rather more divided influence than is usual. Other pursuits intervened, much more than is common with persons of the imaginative temperament, and he never led the life of flirtation from which Goethe believed that he derived so much instruction. Scott's heroines, therefore, are, not unnaturally, faulty, since from a want of the very peculiar instinctive imagination he could not give us the essence of women, and from the habits of his life he could not delineate to us their detailed life with the appreciative accuracy of habitual experience. Jeanie Deans is probably the best of his heroines, and she is so because she is the least of a heroine. The plain matter-of-fact element in the peasant-girl's life and circumstances suited a robust imagination. There is little in the part of her character that is very finely described which is characteristically feminine. She is not a masculine, but she is an epicene heroine. Her love-affair with Butler, a single remarkable scene excepted, is rather commonplace than otherwise.

A similar criticism might be applied to Scott's heroes. Every one feels how commonplace they are—Waverley excepted, whose very vacillation gives him a sort of character. They have little personality. They are all of the same type;—excellent young men—rather strong—able to ride and climb and jump. They are always said to be sensible, and bear out the character by being not unwilling sometimes to talk platitudes. But we know nothing of their inner life. They are said to be in love; but we have no special account of their individual sentiments. People show their character in their love more than in any thing else. These young gentlemen all love in the same way—in the vague commonplace way of this world. We have no sketch or dramatic expression of the life within. Their souls are quite unknown to us. If there is an exception, it is Edgar Ravenswood. But if we look closely, we may observe that the notion which we obtain of his character, unusually broad as it is, is not a notion of him in his capacity of hero, but in his capacity of distressed peer. His proud poverty gives a distinctness which otherwise his lineaments would not have. We think little of his love; we think much of his narrow circumstances and compressed haughtiness.

The same exterior delineation of character shows itself in its treatment of men's religious nature. A novelist is scarcely, in the notion of ordinary readers, bound to deal with this at all; if he does, it will be one of his great difficulties to indicate it graphically, yet without dwelling on it. Men who purchase a novel do not wish a stone or a sermon. All lengthened reflections must be omitted; the whole armory of pulpit eloquence. But no delineation of human nature can be considered complete which omits to deal with man in relation to the questions which occupy him as man, with his convictions as to the theory of the universe and his own destiny; the human heart throbs on few subjects with a passion so intense, so peculiar, and so typical. From an artistic view, it is a blunder to omit an element which is so characteristic of human life, which contributes so much to its animation, and which is so picturesque. A reader of a more simple mind, little apt to indulge in such criticism, feels "a want of depth," as he would speak, in delineations from which so large an element of his own most passionate and deepest nature is omitted. It can hardly be said that there is an omission of the religious nature in Scott. But at the same time there is no adequate delineation of it. If we refer to the facts of his life, and the view of his character which we collect from thence, we shall find that his religion was of a qualified and double sort. He was a genial man of the world, and had the easy faith in the kindly *Dieu des bons gens*[8] which is natural to such a person; and he had also a half-poetic principle of superstition in his nature, inclining him to believe in ghosts, legends, fairies, and elfs, which did not affect his daily life, or possibly his superficial belief, but was nevertheless very constantly present to his fancy, and affected, as is the constitution of human nature, by that frequency, the indefined, half-expressed, inexpressible feelings which are at the root of that belief. Superstition was a kind of Jacobitism in his religion; as a sort of absurd reliance on the hereditary principle modified insensibly his leanings in the practical world, so a belief in the existence of unevidenced, and often absurd, supernatural beings, qualifies his commonest speculations on the higher world. Both these elements may be thought to enter into the highest religion; there is a principle of cheerfulness which will justify in its measure a genial enjoyment, and also a principle of fear which those who think only of that enjoyment will deem superstition, and which will really become superstition in the over-anxious and credulous acceptor of it. But in a true religion these two elements will be combined. The character of God images itself very imperfectly in any human soul; but in the highest it images itself as a whole; it leaves an abiding impression which will justify anxiety and allow of happiness. The highest aim of the religious novelist would be to show how this operates in human character; to exhibit in their curious modification our religious love, and also our religious fear. In the novels of Scott the two elements appear in a state of separation, as they did in his own mind. We have the superstition of the peasantry in the *Antiquary,* in *Guy Mannering,* every where almost; we have likewise a pervading tone of genial easy reflection characteristic of the man of the world who produced, and agreeable to the people of the world who read, these works. But we have no picture of the two in combination. We are scarcely led to think on the subject at all, so much do other subjects distract our interest; but if we do think, we are puzzled at the contrast. We do not know which is true, the uneasy belief of superstition, or the easy satisfaction of the world; we waver between the two, and have no suggestion even hinted to us of the possibility of a reconciliation. The character of the Puritans certainly did not in general embody such a reconciliation, but it might have been made by a sympathising artist the vehicle for a delineation of a struggle after it. The two elements of love and fear ranked side by side in their minds with an intensity which is rare even in minds that feel only one of them. The delineation of Scott is amusing, but superficial. He caught the ludicrous traits which tempt the mirthful imagination, but no other side of the character pleased him. The man of the world was displeased with their obstinate interfering zeal; their intensity of faith was an opposition force in the old Scotch polity, of which he liked to fancy the harmonious working. They were superstitious enough; but nobody likes other people's superstitions. Scott's were of a wholly different kind. He made no difficulty as to the observance of Christmas-day, and would have eaten potatoes without the faintest scruple, although their name does not occur in Scripture. Doubtless also his residence in the land of Puritanism did not incline him to give any thing except a satirical representation of that belief. You must not expect from a Dissenter a faithful appreciation of the creed from which he dissents. You cannot be impartial on the religion of the place in which you live; you may believe it, or you may dislike it; it crosses your path in too many forms for you to be able to look at it with equanimity. Scott had rather a rigid form of Puritanism forced upon him in his infancy; it is asking too much to expect him to be partial to it. The aspect of religion which Scott delineates best is that which appears in griefs, especially in the grief of strong characters. His strong *natural* nature felt the power of death. He has given us many pictures of rude and simple men subdued, if only for a moment, into devotion by its presence.

On the whole, and speaking roughly, these defects in the delineation which Scott has given us of human life are but two. He omits to give us a delineation of the soul. We have mind, manners, animation, but it is the stir of this world. We miss the consecrating power; and we miss it not only in its own peculiar sphere, which, from the difficulty of introducing the deepest elements into a novel, would have been scarcely matter for a harsh criticism, but in the place in which a novelist might most be expected to delineate it. There are perhaps such things as the love-affairs of immortal beings, but no one would learn it from Scott. His heroes and heroines are well dressed for this world, but not for another; there is nothing even in their love which is suitable for immortality. As has been noticed, Scott also omits any delineation of the abstract unworldly intellect. This too might not have been so severe a reproach, considering its undramatic, unanimated nature, if it had stood alone; but taken in connection with the omission which we have just spoken of, it is most important. As the union of sense and romance makes the world of Scott so characteristically agreeable,—a fascinating picture of this world in the light in which we like best to dwell in it, so the deficiency in the attenuated, striving intellect, as well as in the supernatural soul, gives to the "world" of Scott the cumbrousness and temporality, in short, the materialism, which is characteristic of the world.

We have dwelt so much on what we think are the characteristic features of Scott's imaginative representations, that we have left ourselves no room to criticise the two most natural points of criticism in a novelist—plot and style. This is not, however, so important in Scott's case as it would commonly be. He used to say, "It was of no use having a plot; you could not keep to it." He modified and changed his thread of story from day to day,—sometimes even from bookselling reasons, and on the suggestion of others. An elaborate work of narrative art could not be produced in this way, every one will concede; the highest imagination, able to look far over the work, is necessary for that task. But the plots produced, so to say, by the pen of the writer as he passes over the events are likely to have a freshness and a suitableness to those events, which is not possessed by the inferior writers who make up a mechanical plot before they commence. The procedure of the highest genius doubtless is scarcely a procedure: the view of the whole story comes at once upon its imagination like the delicate end and the distinct beginning of some long vista. But all minds do not possess the highest mode of conception; and among lower modes, it is doubtless better to possess the vigorous fancy which creates each separate scene in succession as it goes, than the pedantic intellect which designs every thing long before it is wanted. There is a play in unconscious creation which no voluntary elaboration and preconceived fitting of distinct ideas can ever hope to produce. If the whole cannot be created by one bounding effort, it is better that each part should be created separately and in detail.

The style of Scott would deserve the highest praise if M. Thiers could establish his theory of narrative language. He maintains that an historian's language approaches perfection in proportion as it aptly communicates what is meant to be narrated without drawing any attention to itself. Scott's style fulfils this condition. Nobody rises from his works without a most vivid idea of what is related, and no one is able to quote a single phrase in which it has been narrated. We are inclined, however, to differ from the great French historian, and to oppose to him a theory derived from a very different writer. Coleridge used to maintain that all good poetry was untranslatable into words of the same language without injury to the sense: the meaning was, in his view, to be so inseparably intertwined even with the shades of the language, that the change of a single expression would make a difference in the accompanying feeling, if not in the bare signification: consequently, all good poetry must be remembered exactly,—to change a word is to modify the essence. Rigidly this theory can only be applied to a few kinds of poetry, or special passages in which the imagination is exerting itself to the utmost, and collecting from the whole range of associated language the very expressions which it requires. The highest excitation of feeling is necessary to this peculiar felicity of choice. In calmer moments the mind has either a less choice, or less acuteness of selective power. Accordingly, in prose it would be absurd to expect any such nicety. Still, on great occasions in imaginative fiction, there should be passages in which the words seem to cleave to the matter. The excitement is as great as in poetry. The words should become part of the sense. They should attract our attention, as this is necessary to impress them on the memory; but they should not in so doing distract attention from the meaning conveyed. On the contrary, it is their inseparability from their meaning which gives them their charm and their power. In truth, Scott's language, like his sense, was such as became a bold sagacious man of the world. He used the first sufficient words which came uppermost, and seems hardly to have been sensible, even in the works of others, of that exquisite accuracy and inexplicable appropriateness of which we have been speaking.

To analyse in detail the faults and merits of even a few of the greatest of the Waverley Novels would be impossible in the space at our command on the present occasion. We have only attempted a general account of a few main characteristics. Every critic must, however, regret to have to leave topics so tempting to remark as many of Scott's stories, and a yet greater number of his characters.

Notes

1. The "race for Derby" was the invasion of England by Jacobite forces during the rebellion of 1745–46; the Jacobites penetrated England as far as Derby, but then returned to Scotland, faced with the approach of a much larger English army. Their leader, Charles Edward Stuart, was attempting to restore his father, James ("Jacobus" in Latin; hence "Jacobite"), to the British throne; the invasion was swift (a "race") largely because the army was small [ed. note].

2. George Grote (1794–1871) published his *History of Greece* from 1846–56 [ed. note].

3. Robert Cecil (1563–1612) was Secretary of State for England 1596–1608, holding other important positions as well; Diego Sarmien de Acuña, Count of Gondomar (1567?–1626) was Spanish Ambassador to England 1613–18, 1620–22; both were adroit statesmen and diplomats [ed. note].

4. George Crabbe, "The Parish Register" (1807) 3.272–73, 278–81 [ed. note].

5. Bagehot is referring to the "high church" wing of the Church of England, who (influenced by the Oxford Movement and more generally by Victorian medievalism, which Scott's works helped to inspire) favored a return to the rituals and doctrines of the Middle Ages [ed. note].

6. James Anthony Froude (1818–94) wrote a *History of England* (1856–70), which praised Henry VIII [ed. note].

7. Percy Bysshe Shelley, "Alastor; or, The Spirit of Solitude" (1816), 20–29 [ed. note].

8. Bagehot wishes here to suggest that Scott was a worldly man with little interest in religious doctrines or spiritual struggles. "Le Dieu des bonnes gens" (1817), a song by the popular French poet Pierre-Jean de Béranger (1780–1857), rejects the fulminations of priests and has as its refrain: "Le verre en main, gaiement je me confie/Au Dieu des bonnes gens" ("With my wineglass in my hand, I put my faith in the God of good folk") [ed. note].

What Scott Meant to the Victorians

JOHN HENRY RALEIGH

Will our posterity understand at least why he was once a luminary of the first magnitude, or wonder at their ancestors' hallucination about a mere will-o'-the-wisp?

—Leslie Stephen, "Sir Walter Scott" (1871)

In the nineteenth century Scott was ubiquitous; in the twentieth he virtually disappears. Never before or since in Western culture has a writer been such a power in his own day and so negligible to posterity. All writers' reputations, including that of Shakespeare (with whom Scott was often compared favorably in his own day), undergo vicissitudes, but none can equal the meteoric rise and fall of Scott. In the analogy of the meteor, as it is commonly used, the stress is on the first part of the metaphor—the preternatural blaze of light in the sky. But Scott, more than any other writer, acted out the full, complete, and finished image. Now, in the limbo of forgotten writers, he still circles, an inert, lightless, mass—poetry, novels, editions, criticism, letters, histories, a life of Napoleon, mostly unread and unsung. He has even been dealt the cruelest blow of all, in that, although Scotsmen, professional and amateur, continue to revere his memory and, presumably, read his novels, he and his works have been dismissed and stigmatized as an anathema by the most vociferous and voluble of the modern Scottish nationalists, Hugh MacDiarmid. MacDiarmid, whose real name is Christopher Murray Grieve, only grudgingly allows Scott one accomplishment in Scottish history—his issuing of the Swiftian "Letters of Malachi Malagrowther." Subsequent to 1825–26, the year of Scott's financial disaster, the English government concluded that the general financial decline had in part been due to the freedom with which private banks could issue currency. Accordingly, a law was proposed that private banks, both in England and in Scotland, should no longer have this privilege. As the measure would have worked considerable hardship on Scottish bankers, besides increasing English control over Scotland, there was an outburst of hostility in Scotland. Scott's letters were the single most influential

From *Victorian Studies* 7 (1963): 7–34. Reprinted by permission of the Trustees of Indiana University.

protest, and the proposed measure was dropped. But MacDiarmid goes on to say that Scott was a "Tory of Tories, and a national liability rather than an asset in most respects."[1] In his autobiography, MacDiarmid singles out Scott (along with Burns for different reasons) as one of the real villains of Scottish history. Scott was Anglophile, bourgeois, a user of the English language (only the language of Dunbar is worthy of Scots), and a sentimentalizer of his race: "Scott's novels are the great source of the paralyzing ideology of defeatism in Scotland."[2] His only value, MacDiarmid argues, lay in his objective treatment of parts of Scottish history and in the fact that with the character of Redgauntlet he revealed his own suppressed longings in the direction of passionate Scottish nationalism; but he always remained a member of the "unionist clique" which had reduced Scotland to its present state.

Such was not the view, however, in the early nineteenth century, when Scott was not only the leading representative of his race and the great writer of his day but also what can only be described as an international force. If no other "great" writer ever disappeared so completely, no other writer before or after exerted such a profound influence upon the life of his times. Wherever one looks in the life and the letters of the nineteenth century, not only in England but in the Western world as a whole, one finds the impress of "the Wizard of the North." Then one begins to have an inkling of what a towering figure he was a century ago. He seemed in fact a wizard, and, as is often forgotten, he had not one career but two, first as a poet and then as a novelist. Keats remarked in a letter written in 1818 that in "our Time" there have been three literary kings: Scott, Byron, and the "Scotch novels."[3] The poet was the first figure to disappear and probably deservedly so. Wordsworth in his solemn and succinct way summed it up by saying that Scott's poetry could not possibly last since it never addressed itself to the "immortal" part of man.[4] The poems, then, caused only a few ripples, but the novels set up tidal waves.

It is impossible in the compass of an article to give full documentation and generalization to what Scott as a man, novelist, and historian-thinker meant in the nineteenth century—to the Scots, the English, the Irish, the Americans (both North and South), the French, the Germans, the Italians, the Spanish, and the Russians. I shall confine myself here to a discussion of what he meant to nineteenth-century England, to the Victorians, and then only in his capacities as novelist and historian-thinker, leaving aside the man and the poet. Furthermore, I shall not point out his specific legacies to individual novelists, which are manifold, but will attempt only to give some sense of what the Waverley novels, as novels and as history, meant to the Victorian reader. There is a further limitation in that I shall by-pass—taking it for granted that the reader is familiar with them—the more celebrated Victorian pronouncements on Scott: Carlyle's and Lewes' deflations, Newman's and Ruskin's extravagant encominums. Rather, I shall concentrate upon some lesser-known and, in my opinion, more meaningful analyses, especially those by Walter Bagehot, Leslie Stephen, and Nassau Senior. Nor shall I be much concerned with the immediate reception of the novels.[5]

Victorian criticism, not only of Scott but of most other matters, was half-way between—and a mixture of—Dr. Johnson and Coleridge; it was on the one hand judicious, concerned with analyzing and weighing faults and virtues, wrongs and rights, while on the other it was, under the influence of Coleridge, concerned with meaning. As for the judicious criticism of Scott, there was, and is, nothing new under the sun. Scott himself, and most of his readers, were fully aware of all his faults: the vapid hero and heroine, the often sloppy or bookish prose, the difficulty in getting a novel started, the careless improvisation of the plot, the repetitiousness, the historical mistakes and anachronisms, the evident haste of the whole operation. Almost everyone agreed that his early work was superior to his later and that his Scottish novels were more authentic than his medieval ones. Andrew Lang remarked that by the 1880's any tyro could get things going better than Scott. And after Scott's death George Eliot made the novel serious, James made it an art, and Joyce and others have made it a raid on the Absolute. To go from Joyce or James to Scott is like going from *King Lear* and *Hamlet* to *Faustus* and *The Jew of Malta.*

But the meaning of the Waverley novels to the Victorians is quite another matter. All his defects on his head, Scott was an original and powerful cultural and intellectual force. Like Wordsworth, to whom he was allied in many ways, he had put together a new combination and, like Wordsworth, he was a mover and shaker: the world would never be seen in quite the same way after the Waverley novels had been absorbed. Scott did not cause the American Civil War, as Mark Twain claimed; nevertheless, almost every steam-boat that pulled in to Hannibal bore the name of a Scott heroine. To have been alive and literate in the nineteenth century was to have been affected in some way by the Waverley novels.

The obvious appeals of the Waverley novels can easily be enumerated: their originality, their humor, the earthiness and quaintness of the Scottish dialogue, the individuality of the characters, the melodrama, the sentiment, the good spirits, the "sound" morality, the conventional love story and happy ending, the nature descriptions, the historical accounts, the thrilling battles, the intriguing mystery of the author—the splendid profusion of it all as the early Waverleys poured forth. Scott had put together a whole new amalgam of literary elements, unique in England and in Europe. Coleridge had foreseen much of this when he described to an unknown correspondent, in December 1811, the elements that had gone into Scott's poetry:

> But no insect was ever more like in the color of it's skin & juices to the Leaf it fed on, than Scott's Muse is to Scott himself—Habitually conversant with the antiquities of his country, & of all Europe during the ruder periods of Society, living as it were, in whatever is found in them imposing either to the Fancy or

interesting to the Feelings, passionately fond of natural Scenery, abundant in local Anecdote, and besides learned in

> All the Antique Scrolls of Faery Land,
> And all the thrilling Tales of Chivalry
> Processions, Tournaments, Spells, Chivalry.[6]

I wish to do two things in this essay: first, to point out the less readily apparent reasons why Scott should have appealed to the Victorians, and second, with the gift of hindsight, such as it is, and even at the cost of indulging in a little amateur sociological analysis, to speculate about the possible appeals that Scott had to nineteenth-century people, appeals of which they were probably not fully aware.

One of the least understandable appeals of Scott's novels is what was thought to be their great realism, of which, in the context of the conventional novel of the day (Austen, of course, excepted), they were prize examples. In 1853 Delacroix read Lermontov and Pushkin for the first time, and they brought back to his mind the initial response to Scott: "There is an extraordinary feeling of reality about them, the quality that took everybody by surprise in Sir Walter Scott's novels when they first appeared."[7] But in his own lifetime, and in consequence of his theories about the "advance" of art, Delacroix, who had once admired Scott and in fact had gone to England in the 1820's to study him and Byron and Hunt, came to admire him less and less as he grew older. By the 1850's he was complaining about the long-windedness and the over-abundance of detail in Scott's and Cooper's novels.

It is often forgotten that one of Scott's impulses in writing *Waverley* was the same one that initially set off Cervantes, Fielding, and Jane Austen—that is, to laugh off the stage the currently fashionable romances in the name of realism. Thus in the first chapter of *Waverley*, Scott announced what the novel could have been but was not, and ticked off the current fashions. He could have called it "Waverley: a Tale of Other Days," with a castle, an aged butler, owls shrieking, and so on; or "Waverley: A Romance from the German," with an evil Abbot, a tyrannous Duke, Rosicrucians, and so on; or "Waverley: A Sentimental Tale," with a heroine with "auburn hair"; or "Waverley: A Tale of the Times," concerned with the latest doings in the world of Fashion. His own object, he said, was to describe men rather than manners; to show those possessions common to men in all stages of society; to show the violence of "our ancestors"; and to take his leaves from "the great book of Nature." In the fifth chapter he paused to apologize to those readers "who take up novels merely for amusement," for going into so much detail about "old-fashioned politics," that is, Whig and Tory, Hanoverians and Jacobites, but his story would be unintelligible without this knowledge. His hero, however pallid he turns out to be, comes not out of the world of fiction and romance but is rooted in history itself by belonging to a historic family that had hereditarily fought for idealistic, and often losing, causes. The first Scottish village encountered in *Waverley* is a miserable cluster of mud huts, around which play children in a "primitive" state of nakedness. Their features were "rough," although Scott adds, like a good Scotsman, "remarkably intelligent." As it turns out, Rosa Bradwardine is the heroine with the "auburn hair," metaphorically speaking, but she is counterbalanced by Flora MacIvor, the strong woman and dedicated Jacobite. The whole Highland part had a ring of authenticity. Even Wordsworth, who was not lavish of praise, especially not for Scott, thought this aspect of *Waverley* completely convincing. Moreover, the romantic and conventional plot of the hero and the two young ladies of his affections did not hang in the air but was embedded in, and dominated by, authentic history, by what had actually happened—the Jacobite uprising of 1745—and that not too long ago. (The original subtitle had been " 'Tis fifty years since.") All the subsidiary Scottish characters were convincing and spoke a colorful, bizarre, funny, and seemingly realistic speech. Throughout his career Scott was always aware of the physicality of his characters, heroes and heroines excepted. The men tend to be burly and the women shapely, and one is always made aware, either by description or by action, of this great physical vitality. Finally, it was a world where people would fight at an instant and die for a cause. At the same time Scott's realism was not eighteenth-century realism with its descriptions of sexual peccadillos and its scatological references. There was none of the odor of "the bad century" in Scott's world, nothing that could not be read to the whole family.

A second original characteristic of the world of the Waverley novels was a great enlargement of the genre itself, temporally, spatially, and sociologically. Scott moved things back into the past but not into a past that was finished or irrelevant to contemporary concerns. Even the later medieval novels usually possessed a contemporary relevance. Similarly, great spatial panoramas began to appear in English fiction: the snow-covered mountains of northern Scotland in *A Legend of Montrose;* in *Old Mortality,* a castle tower commanding two immense panoramas: one wasted and dreary, the other cultivated and beautiful; then through the trees of the cultivated one comes a troop of soldiers, half-seen, half-hidden, winding their way to the castle; in *Rob Roy,* a huge lake in the northern Highlands. Finally, what had been predominantly a middle-class affair, the novel, Scott enlarged upwards to include nobility and royalty and downwards to include farmers, peasants, barbarians, and all the gradations of society, although, it should be said, the middle class always remained the real balance wheel and the center of gravity for all other classes.

At the same time, and over in the other direction, the Waverley novels were great compendiums of fact and information. Like a history book they had footnotes, and not only for historical facts but for general information as well. What did Glasgow Cathedral look like at the time of Rob Roy? How was a Highland hut built and what did the Highlanders use for fuel? Scott's novels were full of *things:* swords, armour, clothing, books, and so on. In *Rob*

Roy before a dinner: "huge, smoking dishes, loaded with substantial fare, . . . cups, flagons, bottles, yea, barrels of liquor."

As no novels before, they pointed to and were allied with contemporary art and architecture. Historically, Scottish art had largely manifested itself in portraits, but after the advent of the Waverley novels pictures from Scottish history and legend became as popular as those based upon domestic and social incidents. Similarly, in the genre of landscape painting Scott fired the imaginations of his own and the next generation. William Allan, who had been helped by Scott's purchases of his work, was specifically influenced by Scott to turn to pictures of historical romance. David Wilkie too devoted himself, like Scott, to memorializing what was passing away.[8] Twice in his career, in 1818 and again in 1831, Turner himself was engaged to do illustrations for Scott's work. In 1831, Robert Cadell, Scott's publisher, suggested that Turner's pencil was needed to secure the success of an edition of Scott's collected poems. Without Turner, they could expect 3,000 subscribers, with him 8,000. In 1831 Turner visited Scotland, annoyed a lot of people, and made his sketches, twelve of which, as drawings, were exhibited in London in 1832.[9] Scott's appeal, then, was eminently pictorial, and his work and that of contemporary painters seemed to go hand in hand. J. G. Lockhart, early in his biography, referred to Pitt's quoting some lines of Scott's poetry and remarking: "This is the sort of thing which I might have expected in painting, but would never have fancied capable of being given in poetry."[10] Moreover, Scott's frequent references to Wilkie in the Waverley novels and his attempts to rival painting—he was in fact a frustrated painter himself—in his natural descriptions, with the resulting inference that prose and painting were analogous, were taken up later by Henry James and Proust and a whole generation of Western writers who conceived of writing, at least in part, in terms of painting.

In architecture Scott had a similar effect. Henry Russell-Hitchcock says that Scottish Baronial architecture was always "evocative" of Scott's novels and that associated with the Baronial style was a whole iconography of literary and patriotic figures: Scott's characters, kilts, tartans, Wilkie's Highland peasants, and Edwin Landseer's animals. And of course the two most famous Scottish Baronial homes were first, Abbotsford and, second, Balmoral. The rage for this architecture became so strong in Scotland that by the 1850's even the warehouses in Edinburgh were turreted.[11] Moreover, the same style finally permeated the architecture of the entire island. "The Scottish Baronial, combining the feudally romantic picturesqueness of the Castellated with the muddled Mannerist detail of the Jacobethan, was an almost perfect Early Victorian stylism" (Hitchcock, p. 284).

Other appeals of Scott are less readily obvious, but they were nevertheless real to the Victorians. Nassau Senior, who reviewed each of the Waverley novels as it appeared and later published abstracts of his reviews, is a case in point.[12] He had first read *Waverley* (author then anonymous) at a watering place. He was feeling dull and disgusted with the usual novel fare at his disposal, one item of which was *Waverley*. But any port in a storm: "So we opened it, at hazard, in the second volume, and instantly found ourselves, with as much surprise as Waverley himself, and with about the same effect, in the centre of the Chevalier's court" (p. 17).

Three years later Senior wrote that the Waverley series had grown to "a line of three and twenty volumes" (p. 8). This phenomenon was enough to alarm German diligence, and in English it constituted "the most striking literary phenomena of the age" (p. 1). Historically, said Senior, imaginative prose had been allied either to comedy and had given accurate and pleasing pictures of human nature, or to tragic romance, taking place in a remote Gothic past and falsifying human nature. Scott abolished this dichotomy and put together a completely original mixture of the two previously antithetical sides. He made the great familiar, and he made the past believable; his agents were the mighty of the earth, his subject the happiness of states. He managed to treat lofty subjects with a minuteness of detail, something that only Homer, Euripides, and Shakespeare had been able to do before. The legal background and trappings that Scott attached to so many of his novels gave them a great plausibility. For it was law that controlled and regulated the greater part of human actions. Scott's other subject, war, was ostensibly an interruption of the working of the law; yet, Senior goes on to say, in time of war, "the forms of law are never in more constant use. Men who would not rob or murder, will sequestrate and condemn" (p. 6). Dealing with battles, princes, lost causes, and so on, the Waverley novels were in the lofty regions of romance, yet, for the first time in fiction, these subjects were treated with telling and realistic detail, with the everyday facts of life always apparent: "we feel convinced that though the details presented to us never existed, yet they must resemble what really happened; and that while the leading persons and events are as remote from those of ordinary life as the inventions of Scuderi, the picture of human nature is as faithful as could have been given by Fielding or Le Sage" (p. 8). Added to this unique combination of romance and realism were other amalgams, principally the mingling of mirth and pathos in the mood and the alternation of the narrative and the dramatic in the mode. At times these admixtures were objectionable, but by and large it was all so admirably managed that it pleased both the reader who was partial to a particular mode and the one whose taste was universal. Senior was by no means uncritical of Scott, and he reiterated all the familiar criticisms: the often sloppy prose, the confused plots, the historical mistakes, the involved and tedious beginnings, the constant recreation, in book after book, of the same cast of characters.

Yet there was no Waverley novel without some merit, and in his best efforts there was always the joy of watching what the unknown author could or would do with a particularly demanding or difficult scene. Of the prison scene in *The Heart of Midlothian* (which he considered the most perfect, *Waverley* perhaps excepted, of the Waverley novels), Senior said, "we trembled for the author when we found he really meant to exhibit it" (p. 22). But Scott pulled it off perfectly. The trial itself was "striking" in its execution. On the other hand, the other famous scene in the novel, Jeannie's pleading with the Queen for her sister's life, Senior thought was not brought off to perfection because Jeannie's speeches were too rhetorical. In short, Senior, and other Victorian readers of Scott, were like spectators at a sport, watching everything with a practiced eye, or like gourmets savoring the choice bits of the feast.[13] Lockhart quotes a letter to Scott in 1818 in which his correspondent analyses *The Heart of Midlothian:* Scott had done what so many have tried to do and failed, namely to make the perfectly good character (Jeannie) the most interesting; he had by this feat enlisted the affections of the reader on the side of virtue ten times more than had Richardson. Admitting that she [Lady Louisa Stuart] was tired of Edinburgh lawyers and that the ending of *The Heart of Midlothian* was "lame" and "huddled," the lady correspondent continued with her catalogue of praise for dramatic high-points: the prison and the trial scenes were great; the end of Madge Wildfire was suitably "pathetic"; the meeting at Muschat's Cairn, "tremendous"; the characters of Dumbiedikes and Rory Bean "delightful"; the portrait of Argyll, whom she had heard much about in her youth, "to the very life"; Queen Caroline, "exactly right."[14] Likewise, Scott's new narrative techniques gained the admiration of people like Senior, who thought that the device in *Ivanhoe* of recounting the storming of the castle through the eyes and sensibility of Rebecca (through, in other words, a point of view) immeasurably enhanced the total effect by putting together such disparities as an actual battle and the wonder, horror, and anxiety of the persecuted maiden. But the real cause of Scott's success and triumph, according to Senior, was his ability to unite the most irreconcilable forms and the most opposite materials. This was his real distinction and originality.

If Scott was unique in some ways, he was familiar in others, most importantly in the ways in which his concerns coincided with those of Wordsworth. Wordsworth and Scott were the two single most important literary influences on the Victorians, and they overlapped, and reinforced one another, in three major ways. First, and most obvious, is the turn from city to country for background. The real revolt against the modern city begins here, at the opening of the nineteenth century, and the work of Scott and Wordsworth is its chief literary embodiment. The second way is in Scott and Wordsworth's ability to describe landscapes so effectively that they add a new dimension, in the imagination of the observer, to the landscape itself. Humphry House, admitting the difficulty of putting the phenomenon into words, says that Wordsworth gave the English people new spectacles after which they never saw their landscape again in quite the same way.[15] Similarly, nineteenth-century literature is filled with references to Scott's evocative powers. In his autobiography John Stuart Mill said that Scott could describe a landscape better than Wordsworth although he adds, realistically, that any second-rate landscape itself would do better than both. But more literary sensibilities were more deeply affected. In 1881 Henry James visited Scotland; he drove through a Scottish twilight, forded a river, drove up dim avenues to a great lighted castle. A certain Lady A put her "handsome" head out of a clock tower window: "I was in a Waverley novel."[16] In 1889 Lord Coleridge, the Lord Chief Justice of England, visited a rural region where Scott had never been—as Coleridge knew. But Scott had heard or read about the region and then described it in a novel. Coleridge was impressed with "the extraordinary fidelity with which Walter Scott had caught the air and general feeling of the place."[17] Visiting New Forest in 1900, Leslie Stephen remarked, "By crossing the road I get to the first scene in 'Ivanhoe'—the best beginning of a novel ever written, I think."[18]

A third way in which Scott and Wordsworth coincided was in their pictures of common life. Scott himself said repeatedly that he agreed with the Preface to the *Lyrical Ballads,* especially with its notion that, among the lowly, human passions received more strong and direct expression. This aspect of Scott's work and its similarity to that of Wordsworth was clearly seen by Keats in a letter written in 1818. He had been contrasting Scott and Smollett, to Smollett's disfavor: "Scott endeavors to throw so interesting and romantic a colouring into common and low characters as to give them a touch of the Sublime" (*Letters,* I, 199–200).

There were two other general concerns of Scott which helped to endear him to the later nineteenth century. First, the faint stirrings of feminism could be seen in the Waverley novels. The unconventional, almost pre-Meredithian heroine, was one of Scott's trademarks. These heroines were famous in the early nineteenth century, especially Diana (known popularly as "Di") Vernon of *Rob Roy* (one of the Mississippi riverboats was named after her), with her independence, intelligence, bravery, unconventionality, and continual protests against the inferior position of women. Scott's independent heroines seem innocuous now, but in their own day they were original and striking. Harriet Martineau, of course, seized on this aspect of the Waverley novels and claimed that Scott was a great feminist in both a negative and a positive way. Negatively, in his conventional heroines like Rosa of *Waverley,* he showed how frivolous, passionless, and uninteresting are unemancipated women. Postively, in Flora MacIvor, Di Vernon, and Jeannie Deans, he showed what a woman could be, if free, or partially free.[19]

Finally, although Scott was not particularly didactic and although justice in his novels is not dealt out with the stern legalism of the Victorian novel proper, still the world of Waverley seemed to be under the aegis of the angels. Dean Stanley of Westminster venerated Scott all of his life. He called him "one of the great religious teachers of Scottish Christendom," and used to say "I am of the religion of Walter Scott."[20] Harriet Martineau claimed that Scott had "done more for the morals of our society" than all the divines and moral teachers of the century past and that his influence was "just beginning its course of a thousand years" (*Miscellanies,* I, 30). She thought Scott was inimitable and that unless new channels for fiction were found, it would expire with him.

Nor was Scott's morality a simple affair. Noting the tact and sympathy—despite his own moral disapproval—of Scott's handling of Mary Stuart, Senior said that at last she had fallen into the hands of an author who deserved her, and went on to say in a discussion of *The Abbot* that in contemporary literature the rule of poetical justice was much too severe and unequivocal (pp. 61–62). Likewise, according to Senior, the character of Effie Deans in *The Heart of Midlothian* was exactly right—not too bad, not too good—for her fictitious misfortune; her crime too was precisely right (p. 22).

But the most complex and accurate description of Scott's morality is in Walter Bagehot's essay "The Waverley Novels."[21] According to Bagehot, Scott occupied in matters of morality a realistic position between two oversimplifications. The common oversimplifications were either to be "realistic" and to say that since there is no relationship between merit and award in life, there ought to be none in art, or—the opposite tendency—to be rigidly "moralistic," weigh exactly good and evil, and deal out exact justice to all characters. But life, says Bagehot, is not like either of these extremes, nor was Scott. Bagehot's summation of and answer to this complicated problem of morality in life and art is worth quoting at length. Scott's fictional world

> is one subject to laws of retribution which, though not apparent at a superficial glance, are yet in steady and consistent operation, and will be quite sure to work their due effect, if time is only given to them. Sagacious men know that this is in its best aspect the condition of life. Certain of the ungodly may, notwithstanding the Psalmist, flourish even through life like the green bay tree; for providence (far differently from the real truth of things, as we may one day see it), works by a scheme of averages. Most people who ought to succeed, do succeed; most people who do fail, ought to fail. But there is no exact adjustment of "work" to merit; . . . "on the whole," "speaking generally," "looking at life as a whole," are the words in which we must describe the providential adjustment of visible good and evil to visible goodness and badness.
>
> It is this comprehensive though inexact distribution of good and evil, which is suited to the novelist, and it is exactly this which Scott instinctively adopted. (pp. 55–56)

In short, Scott's world was "real": "Good sense produces its effect, as well as good intuition; ability is valuable as well as virtue" (p. 56).

There are still other, more general ways of accounting for the Victorian love of the Waverley novels. Scotland was no longer the hereditary enemy and could be safely enjoyed as quaint and colorful. At the same time Scotland herself was, so to speak, conquering England—intellectually in the eighteenth century because of "the Athenian Age" in Edinburgh, and actually in the nineteenth century through Scott himself, Gladstone, the Mills, Carlyle,

Ruskin, and all the other Scottish authors, intellectuals, and politicians who lived in England or visited there frequently and played a major role in Victorian culture and public life. The reaction against the French Revolution advanced Scott in many ways, the most important being the renewal of atavistic interest, in England and elsewhere, in the concrete complexities of history and race and culture. The Waverley novels were a monumental demonstration of the complexities, contradictions, and ironies of human (in this case Scottish) character and history. Fear of revolution was one of the great concerns of Victorian England, and here in the Scottish novels was a panorama of plots, uprisings, civil strife—but always put down in the name of the English crown. At the same time the underdog, the loser, in the Waverley novels was always colorful, sympathetic, inordinately brave, and, as such, was a literary symbol for all the underdogs in England, on the Continent, and in America. Thus, strangely, the Waverley novels became symptomatic in some minds of the aspirations for human freedom that were agitating the Western world in the nineteenth century. In Edinburgh itself on 1 April 1863, at a banquet for Lord Palmerston, George Douglas, the Eighth Duke of Argyll, made an impassioned speech for the cause of the American North against the American South in the Civil War. The speech was specifically aimed at Gladstone, whose complex sympathies at this time still lay with the South. All freedom, said Argyll, was earned with human blood. "Who are we, that we should speak of civil war as in no cases possible or permissible?" He conjured up the number of gory heads that had been nailed to public places in Edinburgh. And then he invoked one of Scott's martyrologists: "Do we not rather turn back to these pages of history with the loving chisel of Old Mortality, to refresh in our minds the recollection of their immortal names?" The speech was a great success—Gladstone himself called it strikingly eloquent—and Argyll received congratulatory letters from Whittier, Motley, and Henry Ward Beecher.[22]

Finally, in an even more general way the Victorians were longing for a national epic and got, for vicarious enjoyment anyway, a Scottish one. In the early nineteenth century the Western past was beginning to disappear at an ever-accelerating pace. Scott's novels constituted a vast memorial to part of that past.

It should be said also that the Victorian reaction to Scott was not invariably as clear cut or as serious as has been described above.[23] The Victorians certainly used novels as a kind of soporific or drug, the way mystery stories and television are used today, without any concern for quality. Burne-Jones, for example, read *The Antiquary* twenty-seven times and urged others to do the same.[24] Furthermore, many of the Victorians had a penchant for positively bad novels, to be enjoyed for their very ineptitude.[25] And the humor of Scott's obsession with the past was not overlooked either. On 11 September 1822, Sir Robert Peel wrote to Scott and, among other things, expressed his regret that the two were so far apart geographically. He wished Scott could visit him at Lulworth: "I can promise you a castle, two abbeys, besides a Roman camp and tumuli without end."[26]

Beside Scott the novelist, there was also Scott the historian-thinker. As an historian Scott and his work are best examined in three distinct but over-lapping ways. First there is the factual and fictional historian who actually reconstructed the past in all its concrete variety. Second there is the conscious thinker, Hazlitt's wrong-headed reactionary, who knew all about the past and cared nothing for the future. Third, and most profoundly, there is the creator of the Waverley world with its various implicit comments on the nature of the past and the present and the relationship between them. At this level Scott himself was doubtless not conscious of the final implications for other men's minds of his own work. At this level too he is not just a simple reactionary either but a rather complex phenomenon, meaning different things to differ-ent people.

What immediately delighted his contemporaries was the concrete recon-struction of the past in all its multiplicity and color. Scott had been storing up historical lore for more than forty years. *Waverley* and those novels that fol-lowed so rapidly were like a dam bursting, as through these novels the past spilled out into the present. The Scottish reaction, of course, was nationalistic delight, and for the Scot these novels are full of nuances that the non-Scot could not perceive. W. P. Ker, for example, in discussing *Rob Roy,* makes some-thing of the fact that it takes place in west Scotland. Though Scott was not a west Scotland man himself, he had caught all the distinctiveness of this type in the characters of Andrew Fairservice and Bailie Jarvie.[27]

But for the English, and Europeans and Americans generally, the inter-est lay in the fact that Scott had cut back under dynasties, dates, kings, and the abstractions of contemporary historians to present the flesh and blood of the past at all levels of society. If Macaulay did not approve of Scott the man, he immediately saw the value of the method of the Waverley novels for the historian. Macaulay's histories themselves would not have been what they were—he tried to make them as "interesting" as novels—had it not been for the Waverley novels. As H. J. C. Grierson says, Carlyle's *French Revolution* would not have been composed so vividly and dramatically were it not for the Waverleys. This side of Scott's work was summed up in Carlyle's famous statement: "He understood what history meant; this was his chief intellectual merit."[28] All this statement meant was that Scott, showing a past peopled by genuine human beings, made that past come alive again, a commonplace idea now but not so in the early nineteenth century. Actually, however, Scott's appeal was more complex than Carlyle's statement would indicate.

Senior pointed out that the early nineteenth century was precisely the time in human history when the "veil of high life" was being rent or torn away, when all men first began to feel themselves competent to scrutinize and judge kings and statesmen, considering them not demigods but men. The Waverley novels seemed to illustrate this fact. Furthermore, Scott's picture of history was dynamic rather than static, and his recreated past was peopled not only by concrete individuals but by historical forces as well: Anglo-Saxon vs. Norman; Scottish vs. English; Royalist vs. Puritan; Presbyterian vs. Catholic; the Past vs. the Present. Scott invariably chose for his novelistic background a crucial or seminal moment in history, a time when civilization itself was taking an irreversible direction. As Senior said about *Quentin Durward* (which had had the success in Paris that *Waverley* had had in Edinburgh): "Perhaps at no time did the future state of Europe depend more on the conduct of two individuals than when the crown of France and the coronet of Burgundy descended on Louis XI and Charles the Bold" (p. 145). Since then France has been a mainspring of European politics and Flanders merely an arena of combat.

But if history was complex and dynamic, it was also monolithic, resting on a vast communal experience that overstepped national boundaries. As Senior said, the fact that Scott was so popular in European countries with people whose historical memories were non-English and non-Scottish demonstrated that the novels were based on a "deep knowledge of the human character, and of the general feelings recognized by all" (p. 144). History was monolithic too in that, despite its complexity and ironies, it was all of a piece. According to Senior, once more, the Waverley novels showed how essential was national tranquility for individual happiness and what vice and misery follow civil strife. For always in Scott's world the public and the private intermingled, as they do in life itself.

Still, history was also process, change, and metamorphosis, and Scott showed this side of the matter as well. The feeling that nineteenth-century people had, that human nature itself had become softened and subtilized, more civilized and sophisticated than it had been in the past seems naïve enough now, after what has happened in the twentieth century. But this is the wisdom of hindsight. There was no real reason for anybody living in the nineteenth century, especially in England, to think otherwise. Thus George Eliot, in a letter to Alexander Main of 3 August 1871, expressed her annoyance at how people misunderstood *Romola* because they had not the historic empathy to see that Italian Renaissance man was a cruder person than modern man and therefore enjoyed very crude practical jokes which would offend moderns. She then invoked Scott: "I suppose that our beloved Walter Scott's imagination was under the influence of a like historical need when he represented the chase of the false herald in 'Quentin Durward' as a joke which made Louis XI and Charles of Burgundy laugh even to tears, and turned their new political amity into a genuine fellowship of buffoonery."[29]

It should be pointed out that Scott the historian did not go scot-free, even in his own day. Mistakes and anachronisms were always being pointed out. If it were a contest between accuracy and color, Scott would sacrifice accuracy immediately and happily. In *Old Mortality* he has a British regiment playing kettle drums as it marches through the wilds of Scotland at night. He was informed, of course, that regimental music was never played at night, but in subsequent editions he left the incident in for "the picturesque effect." Scott's Waterloo as an historian proper came when young John Stuart Mill dismembered his biography of Napoleon for the *Westminster Review* in 1828. In preparing to write Napoleon's life Scott ambitiously collected a lot of books and documents, but the actual research was hasty, sketchy, and superficial, as he was the first to admit. In his *Journal* for 22 December 1825, he said: "Superficial it must be"; but better be superficial than dull.[30] Scott prefaced his life of Napoleon with a sketch of the history and nature of the French Revolution, from his hostile point of view: "The feudal system of France, like that of the rest of Europe, had, in its original composition, all the germs of national freedom,"[31] because everyone knew his place. Nature, said Scott, had always avoided equality: to try to erect a society along these lines was a "gross and ridiculous contradiction of the necessary progress of society" (*Napoleon*, I, 69).

Mill had been reviewing regularly for the *Westminster Review,* but he rightly regarded his demolition of Scott as his masterpiece. He spoke of it in the *Autobiography* as a labor of love, for he was defending the Revolution against the "Tory" misrepresentations of Scott (throughout the review Mill calls him "sir Walter Scott"). His critique of Scott was twofold: the research was superficial and the outlook was provincial. "It is for sir Walter Scott to assert: *our* part must be to *prove*."[32] Burying Scott under a mountain of original sources, Mill said that Scott's point of view was the simple one "that whatever is English is best," and best for the whole world (p. 257). This parochialism made it impossible for Scott to understand that "mighty power, of which, but for the French Revolution, mankind perhaps would never have known the surpassing strength—that force which . . . converts a whole people into heroes . . . binds an entire nation as one man" (p. 255). Scott, the haphazard reader, and Scott, the simple Tory, were shown at their worst in this encounter. Scott's *Life of Napoleon* deservedly disappeared into limbo, but the Waverley novels did not.[33]

The picture of history in the Waverley novels is anything but simple-minded. On one level it constitutes a literary embodiment of Burke's principles. On 10 January 1831, Scott wrote to his friend Henry Francis Scott (no relative), an M. P., about the impending Reform Bill: "I am old enough to remember well a similar crisis. About 1792, when I was entering life, the admiration of the godlike system of the French Revolution was so rife, that only a few old-fashioned Jacobites and the like ventured to hint a preference for the land they lived in; or pretended to doubt that the new principles must be infused into our worn-out constitution. Burke appeared, and all the gibberish about the superior legislation of the French dissolved like an enchanted castle when the destined knight blows his horn before it."[34] Of course Burke did not dissolve all the claims for the principles of the French Revolution, as Mill attests. But Burke's position was not simple Toryism, and the link between the Scott of the Waverley novels and Burke now seems clear. And Burke was just one of several powerful voices in the late eighteenth and early nineteenth century—Dr. Johnson, Burke, and Scott were most commonly invoked—that spoke for the valid claims of the past. Mill himself was to recognize these claims in his later writings about Carlyle and Coleridge.

Even so decided a liberal as David Masson could see the validity of these claims. In his lecture on Scott at Edinburgh in 1859, Masson described what had happened to the nineteenth-century outlook and how this change had come about. The great dividing line in both life and literature was 1789. After that:

> Our philosophy begins to deepen itself, affected partly by the deeper social questions which the French Revolution had forced on the attention of mankind, partly by the quiet diffusion among us, through such interpreters as Coleridge, of ideas taken from the rising philosophy of Germany. Our historical literature also takes on a different hue, and begins to be characterized, on the one hand, by more of that spirit of political innovation and aspiration after progress which belonged to the revolutionary epoch, and on the other, by a kind of reactionary regard for that past which the revolution misrepresented and maligned.[35]

There follows an interest in "the permanent and invariable facts of life" (rather than in "the changing aspect of human manners") and a "deeper reverence for nature" (Masson, p. 177). Wordsworth and Scott, then, were the literary representatives of this mode of thought.

This is all obvious; but there was a third Scott, a member of no particular party, and certainly not a simple and narrow-minded Tory, who is revealed not explicitly but implicitly in the construction and content of the Waverley novels. Going on the assumption that the proof of the pudding is in the eating, and that the complexity of a cultural organism is known by the multiplicity of its effects, I would cite once more the Victorian reaction to Scott, in all its variousness, as proof positive that the single-minded or simple-minded Scott in his own day was an argument of political opponents and, in ours, is a literary cliché. This variousness of appeal can be underlined by citing the passionate and lifelong love of Scott by such widely divergent temperaments and outlooks as those of Gladstone, Newman, Stephen, and Ruskin. By the same token, Scott's influence was equally various. By her own admission, it was Scott who first unsettled George Eliot's orthodoxy and started her on the way to agnosticism. But, according to Newman and others, it was Scott who helped to prepare the way for the Catholic revival. With the Brontës, on the other hand, Scott pointed in the direction of the wildest kind of romanticism.

Specific Victorian critiques of the intellectual freight of the Waverley novels reveal an equally complex reaction, which, already apparent in Nassau Senior's estimate of Scott, can also be seen in the essays by Walter Bagehot and Leslie Stephen. Bagehot pointed out how impossible it was to classify Scott's works under the conventional rubrics; so far in history there had been two types of novels: the "ubiquitous," which is concerned with the life of man in its totality (of which *Don Quixote* would be an example), and, over at the other extreme and an invention of more modern times, the "love-story," wherein everything is concentrated on the fate of the hero and heroine. But Scott's work represents a transition in which the fate of the hero and heroine is attached to the life of man in the largest sense (pp. 38–40). Again Bagehot says that although Scott was a "romantic" and a "Tory," no one of any political persuasion could have given a more "statesman-like analysis, of the various causes which led to the momentary success, and to the speedy ruin, of the enterprise of Charles Edward," as described in *Waverley* (p. 45). Again, in the matter of the treatment of the poor in fiction, Bagehot said that novelists in general treated the poor in two opposed ways—either they catalogued their dreariness or made them into Arcadians. Scott did neither: "Almost alone among novelists Scott has given us a thorough, minute, life-like description of poor persons, which is at the same time pleasing and genial" (pp. 50–52). Bagehot should have added that Scott was describing a non-urban, non-industrialized poor.

This same instinctive sense to seize on a kind of *via media* between two unsatisfactory extremes was attributed by Leslie Stephen[36] to Scott's choice of the historical period in which he placed the Scottish novels like *Waverley* and *Redgauntlet*. In theory a novelist could treat any subject from the most contemporaneous to the most antique. But Stephen argued that either extreme was unsatisfactory. The present could only be viewed in a harsh, confusing glare, while the remote past was lost in darkness; and he admitted that most of Scott's medieval novels were false. The ideal time was the remembered past, where things could still be seen but not in a harsh light—"the twilight of history," as Stephen called it (p. 219). And he said that all of Scott's best work could have been called, "Tales of a Grandfather." Everything that Scott was depicting was fast disappearing in his own day; he was thus keeping alive what was in fact dead, and his works are then a "vivification of history" (p. 220).

But, as Stephen went on to say, Scott was not only an antiquarian, for his "best service" was "not so much in showing the past as it was when it was present; but in showing us the past as it is really still present." His chief innovation was "his clear perception that the characters whom he loved so well and described so vividly were the products of a long historical evolution" (pp. 220–21). Fielding's lawyers imply nothing about lawyers in the seventeenth century or the sixteenth century, but "Scott can describe no character without assigning to it its place in the social organism which has been growing up since the earliest dawn of history" (p. 221). Scott was thus the first imaginative observer who saw how the national type of character is "the product of past history, and embodies all the great social forces by which it has slowly shaped itself" (p. 224). Although Stephen does not say so (and although it may well have been entirely unconscious on his part), what he very possibly has in mind—and he is writing in 1871, twelve years after the first publication of Darwin—is an analogy to the conclusion of *On the Origin of Species,* which closes on the precise point about the biological world that Stephen here makes about Scott's fictional world. In this celebrated passage Darwin called up the picture of a river bank with its incredibly complex myriad of life, animal and vegetable, everything radically unique, and yet all interrelated and made mutually dependent by general laws working so slowly that they could only be seen in the contrast between the present and "the earliest dawn of history."

Writing in 1858, before Darwin, Bagehot, in similar fashion, anticipated *On the Origin of Species.* One of Darwin's assertions that caused the most anguish and debate was that in the biological world there were no special creations and no freaks, as odd as many individual species may appear. Nothing had happened in isolation, and everything was under the simultaneous pressure of environment, time, and general laws. By an almost exact analogy Bagehot made the same point about Scott's more bizarre characters. In *Guy Mannering* Scott introduced one of the most outlandish of his creations, Meg Merrilies—a kind of queen among the gypsies, six feet tall, with wild eyes and locks like the snakes of Gorgon, "Beelzebub's post-mistress," "a harlot, thief, witch, and gypsy." Bagehot's point was that in any other novel such a character would be a freak, melodramatic and unbelievable, but that in Scott's world she is explained by her context. Scott showed how she "happened" in the same way that Darwin was to show how things in general "happened" (pp. 49–50). And in the Waverley novels generally it was shown how strange and eccentric characters developed naturally out of social norms.

This side of the Waverley world both Bagehot and Stephen took as a legitimate protest against the ideas behind the French Revolution. Stephen said that the radicals thought that what Scott, Wordsworth, and others stood for was a muddle of "sentimentalities." The Whigs, in their turn, thought the revolution would never extend beyond the Reform Bill of 1832. But in Scott, Wordsworth, and Coleridge, "Conservatism had its justification, and . . . good farseeing men might well look with alarm at changes whose far-reaching consequences cannot be estimated" (p. 224). Burke had denounced the abstractions and prescriptions of the French Revolution: "What Scott did afterwards was precisely to show the concrete instances, most vividly depicted, of the value and interest of a natural body of traditions" (p. 222). Bagehot made the same point and said that this essential assumption colored all of Scott's panoramas, from feudal society to modern Scotland: "the uniform and stereotyped rights of man—. . . would sweep away this entire picture, level prince and peasant in a common *égalité*—substitute a scientific rigidity for the irregular and picturesque growth of centuries,—replace abounding and genial life by a symmetrical but lifeless mechanism" (p. 48). The protests against the "symmetrical but lifeless mechanism" which today grow louder and louder were first uttered, or more importantly, first dramatized by Scott a century and a half ago, as Bagehot and Stephen saw.

But if anything, Scott's whole picture of history is even more profound and more disturbing than Bagehot and Stephen realized. For if Scott saw what was being lost with the march of progress, he saw too the inevitability of that progress. Perhaps the deepest insight into the nature of Scott's concept of history was that of Coleridge. In a letter on the Waverley novels, amidst many telling criticisms, Coleridge had this to say:

> the essential wisdom and happiness of the subject consists in this,—that the contest between the loyalists and their opponents can never be *obsolete,* for it is the contest between the two great moving principles of social humanity; religious adherence to the past and the ancient, the desire and admiration of permanence, on the one hand; and the passion for increase of knowledge, for truth, as the offering of reason—in short, the mighty instincts of *progression* and *free agency,* on the other. In all subjects of deep and lasting interest, you will detect a struggle between the opposites, two polar forces, both of which are alike necessary to human well being, and necessary each to the continued existence of the other.[37]

For the first time in literature Scott had dramatized the basic processes of modern history. Not that he believed in First Causes or Ultimate Ends—he was a sceptic intellectually and a stoic morally—or in a Single Explanation for the ways of history; but he perceived what in fact did happen in modern times. It was a struggle between the past and the future. But Scott's outlook was more complicated than that attributed to him by Bagehot and Stephen and more pessimistic than that attributed to him by Coleridge.

For Scott saw not only the value of the disappearing past, he saw also the inevitability and necessity of progress away from it. This is why—to the continuing indignation of present day Scottish nationalists—he always acquiesced in the final defeat of the colorful lost causes that he wrote about. At the same time he never lost sight of the value of what was being swept away in the onrush of progress, or of what can be called "the reason of the unreasonable," or the logic of completely irrational traditions. In *Guy Mannering* a certain Mr. Bertram is made a justice, an office which he has long coveted. Hitherto an inert, good-natured man, he is galvanized by his new dignity and rigorously applies the letter of the law. He ruthlessly commenced his magisterial reform at the expense of various established and superannuated pickers and stealers who had been his neighbors for half a century (although he also pursued and imprisoned criminals, for which he earned the applause of the bench and public credit). But all this good, said Scott, had its "rateable" proportion of evil. Similarly, in the figure of Edie Ochiltree, the beggar in *The Antiquary,* Scott gives a defense of the ancient and at one time honorable office of begging, and above all of the beggar's social function in his community: their genealogist, their newsman, their master of revels, their doctor at a pinch, or their divine. As for the economic status of the beggar, Scott points out that some of the licensed beggars around the University of Edinburgh in older times were supporting sons who were students at that same institution.[38]

It should not be inferred from this that Scott would have liked justices to be inert or beggary to be revived. He knew, and no one knows this better than a Scotsman, that modernity, with its impulse to control and to rationalize, and to organize all phases of human activity, was an irresistible, irreversible, and in a deep sense, necessary process. He saw too, unlike Coleridge, that the contest between the past and the future was unequal and quickly becoming ever more unequal. Lord Cockburn's memoirs—and he was a contemporary of Scott—are in a sense one long lament over the ever-accelerating disappearance of historic sites and beautiful natural vistas in and around Edinburgh. Similarly, the bleak determinism, heavy and historical, that was to mark later nineteenth- and twentieth-century Western culture in general had its real inception in the Waverley novels.

Scott's novels are peculiarly feckless at their center, that is, in the mind or sensibility of the hero, who invariably undergoes in his own person Coleridge's struggle and always comes out on the side of modernity. But while this eventuality is shown to be necessary and just, it never seems very exciting or colorful, nor is there any attempt to make it so.[39] This is why finally the Waverley novels come out for neither side—although Scott himself is consciously on the side of the modern—but merely dramatize the process in all its irony, that is, that the dictates of the intelligence are inimical to the urges of the instincts but that eventually and despite some mighty kickbacks and counter-revolutions on the part of the instincts, rationalization will finally control all of human life. As such, the Waverley novels constitute the first, faint, sometimes inchoate picture of an historical process that has become more and more in evidence since Scott's own time. In the twentieth century an entire literature has grown up around this problem, variously called "the rise of conformism," the "bureaucratization of human life," "the disappearance of individuality," and so on. It is a strange literature because while it points out an evil, it is not only at a loss to suggest any remedy, it cannot help but say that the cause of the evil is in fact a good because it seems to be the historical destiny of man to control his life and his environment by the exercise of his reason, which means, of course, conscious control and organization of all phases of human activity. Thus the Waverley novels are really in the mode of modern authors like Hannah Arendt or Roderick Seidenberg. The concluding paragraph of Seidenberg's *Posthistoric Man* could well be the epigraph for the Waverley novels:

> In the course of his development man has been constrained from time to time to abandon his most cherished myths. Thus he has abandoned his animism; his Ptolemaic astronomy that assured his position in the center of the

universe; his faith in a hereafter that endowed him with eternal life; his belief
in the supreme and infinite worth of his person that assured him a position of
isolate dignity in an otherwise meaningless and impersonal world; and even
perhaps his faith in a God whose attributes, under the impact of man's ratio-
nalistic scrutiny, became ever more abstract until He vanished in the meta-
physical concept of the Whole. The shedding of these inestimable illusions
may be merely stages in his diminishing stature before he himself vanishes
from the scene—lost in the icy fixity of his final state in a posthistoric age.[40]

But this is perhaps too simple; certainly Scott had a different perspective on
the problem. In a letter to Maria Edgeworth on 4 February 1829, he offered a
more problematical picture of the contest between the things that were and
the things that were to come (the part of the letter quoted here was provoked
by the notorious Burke murderers, ruffians who killed people in order to
deliver the bodies to vivisectionists and anatomists—Burke himself was
finally hanged):

> The state of high civilization to which we have arrived, is perhaps scarcely
> a national blessing, since, while the *few* are improved to the highest point, the
> *many* are in proportion tantalized and degraded, and the same nations display
> at the same time the very highest and the very lowest state in which the
> human race can exist in point of intellect. *Here* is a doctor who is able to take
> down the whole clock-work of the human frame, and may find in time some
> way of repairing and putting it together again; and *there* is Burke with the
> body of his murdered country-woman on his back, and her blood on his hands,
> asking his price from the learned carcass-butcher. After all, the golden age was
> the period for general happiness, when the earth gave its stores without labour,
> and the people existed only in the numbers which it could easily subsist; but
> this was too good to last. As our numbers grew, our wants multiplied—and
> here we are, contending with increasing difficulties by the force of repeated
> inventions. Whether we shall at last eat each other, as of yore, or whether the
> earth will get a flap with a comet's tail first, who but the reverend Mr. Irving
> will venture to pronounce?—[*Life of Scott*, v, 236]

Scott was quite correct in his intuition that for the masses of Scotland
there was much brutality in store. By the mid-nineteenth century no other
European cities could match the mass degradation of Scotland's industrial
warrens. Frazier Hunt, an American, visited Glasgow in company with Sinclair Lewis and others in 1922. In his book *One American,* Hunt described his
own impressions of, and Lewis' reaction to, the city.

> It was a Saturday afternoon when we reached Glasgow. That night Red and I
> wandered off to the slums. I had seen Chicago's red-light district and New
> York's Bowery, and I had watched men have the D.T.'s on the streets of Bris-
> bane, Australia. I had seen opium dens in Shanghai and tequila and *aguardiente*
> bars in Mexico, but never had I seen anything to compare with this Scotch bor-

der town at the hour when the pubs closed for the week end. Men, women, and children were fighting in the dirty streets; gin-drinking charwomen were lying helpless in the gutters and alleys; a quarter of a great city was over-run with hundreds of poor, helpless, drunken wretches whose only sin was poverty, and who for a few hours were finding escape from their everlasting fears and their defeats by the only road they knew.

Finally Red stopped and raised his clenched fists to high heaven. Tears were streaming down his cheeks. "I can't stand it any more," he cried. "I can't stand it!"

All the way back to the hotel he cursed and raved. "God damn the society that will permit such poverty! God damn the religions that stand for such a putrid system! God damn 'em all!"[41]

Still the past cannot withstand the future, though the two must remain enemies and though generations must be trod down in their contest. A growl from the past, such as Leslie Stephen's concluding sentence to his essay on Scott, "Those to come must take care of themselves" (p. 229), is endurable only if one can assent to Santayana's dictum: "The necessity of rejecting and destroying some things that are beautiful is the deepest curse of existence."

Notes

1. C. M. Grieve, *Albyn* (London, 1927), p. 86.

2. MacDiarmid, *Lucky Poet* (London, 1943), p. 202.

3. *The Letters of John Keats,* ed. Hyder Rollins (Cambridge, 1958), II, 16.

4. *The Critical Opinions of William Wordsworth,* ed. Markham Peacock (Baltimore, 1950), p. 340.

5. See James Hillhouse, *The Waverley Novels and their Critics* (London, 1936).

6. *Letters of Samuel Taylor Coleridge,* ed. Earl Leslie Griggs (Oxford, 1959), III, 360–61.

7. *The Journal of Eugène Delacroix,* ed. Hubert Wellington (London, 1951), p. 205.

8. James L. Caw, *Scottish Painting* (Edinburgh, n.d.), pp. 94, 97, 108, 147–49, 477, and *passim.*

9. A. J. Finberg, *The Life of J. M. W. Turner* (Oxford, 1961), pp. 332–33, 334.

10. *Life of Sir Walter Scott* (London, 1900), I, 394.

11. Henry-Russell Hitchcock, *Early Victorian Architecture in Britain* (New Haven, 1954), pp. 245–48.

12. *Essays on Fiction* (London, 1864). Senior's reviews were originally published in the *Quarterly, Edinburgh, London,* and *North British* Reviews. In reviewing the earlier Waverleys Senior was unaware that Scott was the author. For example, in reviewing *Ivanhoe* he picked up a heraldic error and noted its coincidence with "a similar mistake in his great rival, Sir Walter Scott": "The Black Knight bears what Rebecca calls a 'bar and padlock painted blue,' or, as Ivanhoe corrects her, 'a fetterlock and shackle bolt azure' on a black shield; that is, azure upon sable. This, as colour upon colour, is false heraldry. Now on the shield of Sir Walter's Marmion, a falcon 'Soared sable in an azure field.' The same fault reversed. It is a curious addition to the coincidences of these two great writers, that, with all their minute learning on chivalrous points, they should both have been guilty of the same oversight" (pp. 52–53). In reviewing *The Fortunes of Nigel* Senior noted the archetypal Waverley situation—a virtuous and passive hero

who marries the heroine; a fierce, active hero who dies a violent death; and a fool or bore (Caleb in *Lammermoor* or Dalgetty in *Montrose*)—and said, "it is too obvious an imitation of Sir Walter Scott" (p. 101).

13.   The analogy to a feast is not fanciful: "Today [8 Oct. 1820] I perform alone upon a roast chicken, and mean to devour 'Kenilworth' with it. There are different opinions. Charles Greville told me last night that he did not stir out or go to bed till five in the morning the day he begun it"; see *Letters of Harriet Countess Granville, 1810–1845,* ed F. L. Gower (London, 1894), I, 186.

14.   *Life of Scott,* III, 209–11. These judicial and part by part assessments of Scott's novels occur frequently in Victorian letters, biographies, and memoirs. For example, in a letter to Lord Abercorn of 18 Jan. 1818, the Earl of Aberdeen discussed *Rob Roy,* which was good on five points (characters and scenes) but bad on five others (characters and plot); each work of the unknown author had its characteristic "excellence": see Lady Frances Balfour, *The Life of George Fourth Earl of Aberdeen* (London, 1922), I, 198–99. In Sydney Colvin's *Memories and Notes of Persons and Places* (New York, 1921), pp. 196–98, there is recounted a detailed and authoritative structural analysis of *The Bride of Lammermoor* that might give pause to a New Critic–given by Mr. Gladstone.

15.   "Wordsworth's Fame," in *All in Due Time* (London, 1955), p. 43.

16.   *The Notebooks of Henry James,* ed. F. O. Matthiessen and Kenneth Murdock (New York, 1947), p. 36.

17.   Ernest Hartley Coleridge, *Life and Correspondence of John Duke Lord Coleridge* (London, 1904), p. 359.

18.   Frederic Maitland, *Life and Letters of Leslie Stephen* (London, 1906), p. 458.

19.   Harriet Martineau, *Miscellanies* (Boston, 1836), I, 48–49.

20.   Rowland E. Prothero, *The Life and Correspondence of Dean Stanley* (London, 1893), p. 384.

21.   *The Works and Life of Walter Bagehot,* ed. Mrs. Russell Barrington (London, 1915), III, 37–72.

22.   Duke of Argyll, *Autobiography and Memories* (London, 1906), II, 196.

23.   Victorians seemed at times to like Scott even for his defects: Countess Granville wrote, "I delight in even the faults of the novels, 'Ivanhoe' excepted." (*Letters,* I, 181).

24.   G B-J [Lady Georgiana Macdonald Burne-Jones], *Memorials of Edward Burne-Jones* (London, 1904), II, 329.

25.   Macaulay and his sister once made the *Mysteries of Udolpho* the prize of a bet between them as to who could make the most puns in conversation over a certain period of time (Macaulay won with two-hundred bad puns in two hours); see G. O. Trevelyan, *The Life and Letters of Lord Macaulay* (New York, 1876), I, 170.

26.   *Sir Robert Peel,* ed. Charles S. Parker (London, 1899), I, 319.

27.   *Collected Essays* (London, 1925), I, 190.

28.   H. J. C. Grierson, "Scott and Carlyle," in *Essays and Studies* (London, 1928), XIII, 88, 90.

29.   *The George Eliot Letters,* ed. Gordon Haight (New Haven, 1954–55), V, 174–75.

30.   *The Journal of Sir Walter Scott,* ed. J. G. Tait (Edinburgh, 1950), p. 53.

31.   *The Life of Napoleon Buonaparte* (Exeter, 1836), I, 33.

32.   *The Westminster Review,* VIII (1828), 296.

33.   Scott as a conscious philosopher of history was old-style even in his own day when the great secular philosophies of history were beginning to arise. In his Introduction, originally written in 1887, to Scott's *The Tales of a Grandfather* (London, 1911), F. W. Farrar said Scott "would have said with the great Vico, that 'History is a civil theology of Divine Providence'; with Bolingbroke that it is 'Philosophy teaching by examples'; with Wilhelm von Humboldt, that "The History of the world is not intelligible apart from a government of the world"; and with Fichte, that 'Every step in advance in history is an inflowing of God'; 'God alone makes

history, but he does this by the agency of man' " (p. xv). Farrar notes that since *Tales of a Grand-father* was written there had been conceived at least fourteen French and thirteen German philosophies of history, all of them tending "to become more technical, more elaborate, more exhaustive and more scientific" (p. xix). Scott then represented the "power of bright narration." If Scott himself in *Tales of a Grandfather* points any historical moral, it is that good comes out of evil although, "We must not do evil even that good may come of it" (p. 47).

34. *Letters of Sir Walter Scott,* ed. H. J. C. Grierson (London, 1932), XI, 455.

35. *British Novelists and their Styles* (London, 1859), p. 176.

36. Leslie Stephen, "Sir Walter Scott," *Hours in a Library* (London, 1907), I, 186–229. The essay on Scott was originally published in 1871.

37. *Coleridge's Miscellaneous Criticism,* ed. T. M. Raysor (London, 1936), pp. 341–42.

38. Sir Lewis Namier makes somewhat the same point about the logic of irrational tra-ditions when discussing secret service pensions in the time of George III: "they show . . . the charitable character of that very humane institution, and the utter unimportance of the acqui-sitions which the Government made through it"; see *The Structure of Politics at the Accession of George III,* 2nd ed. (London, 1957), p. xii.

39. In his *History of Scotland* (Philadelphia, 1830), Scott concludes his account of the accession of James I by saying the disadvantages of the union of the crowns, which marked the beginning of the end for Scotland as an indigenous culture, were "finally incalculably overbal-anced by the subsequent benefits" (p. 427). But previous to this he quotes a long lament made by an old man to James before he left for London about Scotland becoming England's province. Some of the impossibilities involved in a Scotsman committing himself on either side of this momentous question of the Union can be glimpsed from a statement by MacDiarmid: "I believe that the Industrial Revolution would have spread to Scotland much less injuriously if England had suddenly disappeared about 1700" (*Albyn,* p. 29).

40. *Posthistoric Man* (Chapel Hill, N. C., 1950), pp. 337–38.

41. Quoted by Mark Schorer, *Sinclair Lewis* (New York, 1961), p. 331.

Scott and the Really Great Tradition

RICHARD WASWO

In the nineteenth century Scott was ubiquitous; in the twentieth he virtually disappears. Never before or since in Western culture has a writer been such a power in his own day and so negligible to posterity.[1] The scholar who made this observation about twenty years ago did not consider what I shall briefly attempt to sketch here—the reasons for so unprecedented a decline. It is instructive to take the meteoric descent of Scott's reputation as a novelist as the subject of just the kind of inquiry his novels teach us to make: as an episode in the history of cultural tastes that is inseparable from the history of social attitudes.

Among the small fraction of society that consists of us professional read-ers, one could observe that with the mild resurgence of serious critical interest in Scott's fiction on both sides of the Atlantic in the last twenty years, the nadir of his decline has perhaps been passed. Yet the presses are still not quite humming with Scott criticism; examples drawn from his fiction do not nor-mally (if ever) appear in the current flood of books and articles on narrative theory. The same very few Waverley novels continue to slide in and out of print (almost exclusively in the Everyman series)—a sure indication that no increased attention is being paid to Scott in university syllabi. There, he appears to maintain the brief or prefatory place he has long occupied in lec-tures on the nineteenth-century English novel: glanced at with varying degrees of condescension between Austen and Dickens, Scott is a kind of obstacle to be got over between the works that really matter. His importance is secure; but it has been relegated, by the academic sterilization of the adjec-tive to which he gave much vaster meaning, to the "historical". That is, one should be aware of him only because he was important once, not because he has anything to say to us now. Such assumptions appear even among the smaller fraction of readers who are Scott enthusiasts at least to the extent of

From *Scott and His Influence*, The Papers of the Aberdeen Scott Conference, 1982, ed. J. H. Alexander and David Hewitt (Aberdeen: Association for Scottish Literary Studies, 1983), 1–12. Reprinted by permission of the Association for Scottish Literary Studies and Richard Waswo.

attending conferences like this one. At the last one I attended, after a lively panel discussion that brought to bear on the novels meticulous historical investigation as well as techniques from theories of reader response, one gentleman in the audience arose to express mild astonishment that such heavy analytic artillery was being aimed at the fragile entertainments of Sir Walter Scott. 'After all', he said, 'Scott is a second-rate writer, not like James or Eliot or Lawrence.'

The gentleman's comparisons are crucial, and of course invidious. That Scott is not 'like' these later novelists is taken as sufficient evidence of his inferiority. The most immediate source for this justification of the continued negligence of Scott was identified by Northrop Frye:

> The prevailing conception of serious fiction is enshrined in the title of F.R. Leavis' book *The Great Tradition,* a study of George Eliot, Henry James, and Joseph Conrad which assumes that these writers are central in a hierarchy of realistic novelists extending roughly from Defoe to D. H. Lawrence. The assumption seems reasonable, yet when empires start building walls around themselves it is a sign that their power is declining, and the very appearance of such a title indicates a coming change of fashion on the part of both writers and readers.[2]

The change Frye detects is in the popularity of romance forms—murder mysteries, science fiction, Tolkien, and fantasy generally. Scott, however, has still not profited much from this trend, and is still excluded from the canonical hierarchy of the great so-called 'realists'. Leavis himself was nothing if not categorical about Scott: 'Out of Scott a bad tradition came.'[3] The enormous and still prevalent influence (especially in school and university curricula) of the empire that thrusts this 'bad' tradition outside its walls should encourage us to hasten their crumbling by undermining their foundations—that is, by finding their assumptions rather less 'reasonable' than Frye casually allows.

The terrain offers quite ample avenues for attack: we might ask what possible definition of 'realism' could encompass both *Robinson Crusoe* and *The Ambassadors;* we could point out the vagueness of Leavis's criteria of novelistic merit; we could logically object to the whole procedure that cannot describe differences without prescribing norms. But our interest in the canonized assumptions of 'serious' fiction less concerns what Leavis made of them than, in general, the attitudes towards human experience they involve, and in particular, the way in which these attitudes so thoroughly cast Scott into limbo. Leavis merely gave the assumptions crystallized form, having inherited them largely from the kinds of novelists he admitted to his exclusive empire.

The assumptions, however, are detectable much earlier—in criticisms of Scott's fiction made in his own day, which were at the time small voices amid the chorus of adulation for the Author of *Waverley.* Of these, the most subsequently quoted is that of Carlyle. Finding Scott not 'altogether deficient ... in the ... highest excellence, of drawing character', Carlyle nonetheless went on to draw the famous comparison with Shakespeare, who 'fashions his characters from the heart outwards; your Scott fashions them from the skin inwards, never getting near the heart of them!'[4] In the same vein, Stendhal found that Scott paid too much attention to costume and too little to 'the movements of the heart', and that whenever his characters were 'moved by passion' or by elevated sentiments, they express themselves unconvincingly and unnaturally. Writing in 1830, Stendhal also made one accurate prophecy: 'In a hundred and forty-six years time, Scott will be less esteemed than Corneille still is a hundred and forty-six years after his death.' But Stendhal's equally prophetic quantification of this process was mistaken: 'in ten years time, the reputation of the Scottish novelist will have declined by half'.[5]

Although Scott's decline took a bit longer than this, its primary terms are established: he fails to penetrate the "hearts" of his characters. What the contemporary and later choral consensus praised as the panoramic, usually 'Shakespearean', breadth of his novels here becomes their superficiality. Scott may be broad, but he is not deep. Once this sort of conviction gains ground, there is no need for argument—and indeed there was none. No full critical controversy was ever staged about Scott, no definitive demolishment was ever printed. He simply stopped being read, which is what makes his decline symptomatic of a general movement in culture and society at large. The *Zeitgeist* moved on and left him behind, a casualty to the kind of historical process to which he had drawn the attention of the whole century.

We may observe the *Zeitgeist* getting a push from the young Henry James, who evokes precisely the idea of progress in order to shut Scott up in two different kinds of past: that of the art and that of the reader. In both, the presumption of superficiality is implicit, while the tone is one of patronizing tribute. James presents Scott as 'the inventor of a new style' whose 'machinery' has worn out and been replaced by the cleverer 'contrivances' of subsequent artisans, like Dickens, Thackeray, and Eliot. Crediting Scott with the total absence of pretence and of any didactic intention, James praises the vast richness of his imagination and then proceeds to describe its products in such a way as to deprive them of any title to sustained attention. The passage must be savoured at length:

> [Scott's novels] are emphatically works of entertainment. As such let us cherish and preserve them ... There are few of us but can become sentimental over the uncounted hours they have cost us. There are moments of high-strung sympathy with the spirit which is abroad when we might find them rather dull—in parts; but they are capital books to have read ... Scott was a born story-teller: we can give him no higher praise ... we can liken him to nothing better than to a strong and kindly elder brother, who gathers his juvenile public about him at eventide, and pours out a stream of wondrous improvisation.

Who cannot remember an experience like this? On no occasion are the delights of fiction so intense. Fiction? These are the triumphs of fact. In the richness of his invention and memory, in the infinitude of his knowledge, in his improvidence for the future, in the skill with which he answers, or rather parries, sudden questions, in his low-voiced pathos and his resounding merriment, he is identical with the ideal fireside chronicler. And thoroughly to enjoy him, we must again become as credulous as children at twilight.[6]

The pleasure James claims to recall may be real, but it is distinctly subliterary; when we grow up, we put away childish things. To the 'spirit' now abroad, Scott has receded into the infancy of narrative art and the childhood of its consumers. James's images give concrete substance to Leavis's favorite oracular adjective: Scott is decidedly not 'adult'. This opinion makes James an even better prophet than Stendhal, since it forecasts Scott's actually diminished status in the earlier part of this century as a writer of classics for adolescents—'an author', said Georg Brandes about 1904, 'whom all grown-up people have read and no grown-up people read'.[7]

Even this reduced regard then became too much for E. M. Forster, who denied to Scott in *Aspects of the Novel* (1927) even the sub-literary skill that James had granted him: the ability to tell a story. The language and plotting that James had found merely old-fashioned and ponderous seemed to Forster intolerably digressive, clumsy, and incompetent. As such, both style and structure were appropriate vehicles for the superficiality that Forster decried in the usual terms: 'think how all Scott's laborious [scenery] . . . call[s] out for passion, passion and how it is never there!'[8]

Though the fastidious severity of Forster's estimate has since been modified (not by Leavis and his disciples), the march of the *Zeitgeist* that relegated Scott to the juvenile fireside and then sank him in virtual oblivion seems clear. The 'spirit' that can ignore Scott is one that, first and foremost, takes the depiction of 'character' to be the 'highest excellence' of the novelist's art; second, locates such 'character' in the interior motions of the human 'heart', i.e., its passions and sentiments; and third, demands that the art of dealing with such emotions be evident in a highly unified plot and a highly self-conscious style—by implication the opposite of easy, popular, and fluent. These are the assumed criteria that, gradually developing from the Romantic premise of the primacy of unmediated, individual feelings, came to define 'serious' fiction in the nineteenth century and to dominate its production, more or less, from Eliot through Forster and Lawrence.

Had these criteria been employed only to describe, they would be 'reasonable' enough; but their consciously normative use to denigrate Scott (and to cast suspicions on Dickens) makes them considerably less so. For there is no self-evident reason why a novel, or any narrative, cannot violate these criteria and still be a great work of art. Carlyle is not Moses, to lay down the depiction of 'character' as the first commandment of literary composition;

Aristotle had, equally dogmatically, given this honor to the 'fable' or plot. That 'character' in literature is to be expressed by direct authorial penetration into individual 'hearts' is also indefensible as a standard of judgment. So to regard and apply it would be to deny the literary greatness of all traditional stories that express character mainly through action, with help from speech, figurative language, and symbolic devices of all kinds. Homer, Chaucer, Cervantes, and Fielding could then join Scott in oblivion. The demand for a highly wrought, not easily accessible, style is liable to similar objections—since it excludes many traditional devices, like Homer's extended similes or Fielding's addresses to the 'classical reader', and approves only the kinds of 'style' that serve the purpose of interiorizing character as personal emotion.

My point is not only that such pretended norms of literary evaluation are themselves historical—the simple preferences of a particular time and place—though this fact suffices to invalidate their use to form an exclusive canon. My point is rather that such criteria are by no means merely 'literary', that they contain farther-reaching assumptions and implications about human experience and society. Those elements of the nineteenth-century *Zeitgeist* that exiled Scott from 'serious' fiction function, like all literary theories, 'to determine literature as evidence or expression in relation to ideology', as 'dubious excuses for accommodating literature to various notions of the contemporary real'.[9]

Implicit in the criticisms of Scott we have reviewed is the developing nineteenth-century notion of the 'real'. What this amounted to is best seen in a later statement by one of those critics whose whole artistic career exemplified that development. Henry James began, inspired by Balzac, by wishing to become the 'secretary' of American society (an ambition, we recall, that came to Balzac by way of Scott). Thus stimulated, James published *The American* in 1877. Thirty years later he sat down to write a preface to that novel and discovered, to his surprise, that it was not 'realistic' at all, but a romance. The preface mentions Scott and Balzac as 'men of the largest responding imagination before the human scene', and rejects the simple definitions of romance as exotic adventure or costume. James then arrives at his own formulation:

> The only *general* attribute of projected romance that I can see, the only one that fits all its cases, is the fact of the kind of experience with which it deals—experience liberated, so to speak; experience disengaged, disembroiled, disencumbered, exempt from the conditions that we usually know to attach to it and, if we wish so to put the matter, drag upon it, and operating in a medium which relieves it, in a particular interest, of the inconvenience of a *related,* a measurable state, a state subject to all our vulgar communities.[10]

This single sentence is not merely James's own discovery of the quintessentially Jamesian subject of his later novels that he had been writing about all along; it summarizes, in a pregnant and ornate nutshell, the direction in which the nineteenth-century novel was moving, and in which the modern novel continued to move, as it moved away from Scott. The move is made in the powerful name and vocabulary of freedom—experience literally cut loose from its 'earth' (in a subsequent metaphor) and 'uncontrolled by our general sense of "the way things happen"'.

From 'character' as consisting of strong personal feelings to experience freed from its worldly context: these are views of life as well as literature. They locate 'real' life in private emotions—the more private, the better. They assert in theory and present in the practice of novel-plotting an ideology of freedom that is predominantly negative: freedom *from* ('disengaged, disembroiled, disencumbered') constraints supposedly external to the self (the inconveniences of relatedness) rather than freedom *to* act in any purposeful way. So the self becomes an absolute in a vacuum: it soars above all the relations that would drag it down (family, race, religion, education, class, politics, work) into an empyrean of pure feeling. But what does it, what can it, do there? Very little, of course, except to seek a similar self to attach its feelings to. The only relations that count are the only ones that are possible: personal relations—of passion, friendship, or sentimental affinity—between selves that have achieved at least some degree of liberation. Hence the enormous privilege and structural centrality, in most Victorian and much modern fiction, of the individual consciousness and its personal, emotional relations. This privilege is most extreme, of course, in the later novels of James himself; but it is characteristic of even the classic works in the genre that have a wider and more circumstantial focus. In *Middlemarch,* for instance, or the early novels of Lawrence, where the characters are initially presented in detail as embedded and formed in a solid network of communal relations, the thrust of the plot is to get them out of it, to move them to a crisis of private feeling that will prompt their escape from some vulgar community into a more elegant emotional isolation where an ostensibly 'profounder' life is to be lived. This escape, even where it retains some social dimension (as in Dorothea's marriage to Ladislaw, or the career of Paul Morel), is often associated with, or achieved by means of, art. The supreme example is the flight of Stephen Dedalus past the nets that Ireland has set to trap his soul. Art and the self are thus presented as ideally and equally autonomous; what the literature of the period enacts is articulated in its aesthetic theories.[11]

The ideology of the freedom of the private self—its escape into art or connoisseurship or language—is the major response of nineteenth-century fiction to the social and political revolutions of nineteenth-century experience and to the major discoveries of its thought. The fiction says an everlasting and Romantic 'nay' to all the forms of determinism—social, historical, economic, biological—that produced the modern social sciences. And the very negativity of this freedom made its main beneficiary, the individual consciousness, its own prison. By rejecting all that "conditions" it, by insisting that its identity is not social, but uniquely personal, the human self freezes into immobility, locked in a blind alley or a garbage can. This logical conclusion of the ideology of negative freedom is reached in the plays and novels of Samuel Beckett, where all we have are individual selves and the (sometimes mutually incomprehensible) languages they speak; all else—the world—has disappeared. There is still one condition and one relation that cannot be avoided even here: that between the individual speaker and his language. But when the speaker conceives of speech itself as a condition, as imposed on him from elsewhere, full of relations from which he is now excluded, he is condemned to the perpetual futility of obsessive iteration and becomes, appropriately enough, *The Unnameable*. Identity, now absolutely unmoored from any context that could give it meaning, becomes non-identity. The private self, free from everything, must also disappear.

I am rehearsing all this in order to suggest that the ideology of negative freedom, the nineteenth-century development of the ideology of bourgeois individualism, which is as familiar to us as the air we breathe, is really quite peculiar. Postulating that the real profundity of human life lies within the individual sensibility not only isolates that sensibility to the point of extinction, it also deprives of any title to serious significance all of the necessary associations, encounters, and activities that make up the vast bulk of our daily lives. These become the banal, superficial, oppressive, grinding routine from which we are presented with models for escape or for transfiguration in the crucible of our private feelings. Virtually all we are, as members of families and communities, and all we must do, to earn a living, is somehow *not* us, is irrelevant or hostile to our 'selves.' This post-Romantic vision of life has tried to apply homeopathic medicine to the great malaise it felt: to overcome the fact of alienation by intensifying it into willed isolation. Thus to embrace the disease is a bizarre remedy, and it has brought no cure.

The ideology it produced, however, certainly accounts for the neglect of Sir Walter Scott, who is nothing if not the great celebrator of 'all our vulgar communities.' It is a capital irony that James, offering a definition of romance 'that fits all its cases,' should have described precisely the opposite of what Scott's romances perform. For the Waverley Novels exempt no experience from the usual conditions that attach to it. Their protagonists are constantly subject to the 'inconveniences' of their related states, which, indeed, are usually conflicting. Above all, of course, in his notoriously casual use of a sentimental plot as a peg on which to hang greater actions and in his conduct of those actions, Scott grants no privilege whatever to, and even suggests the inefficacy of, individual consciousness and will. Private emotions count for very little in his fiction—and this for posterity is his supreme defect, the presumed "superficiality" of his concerns. These concerns were well appreciated long ago by R. H. Hutton:

> The most striking feature of Scott's romances is that, for the most part, they are pivoted on public rather than mere private interests and passions. With but few exceptions . . . Scott's novels give us an imaginative view, not of mere individuals, but of individuals as they are affected by the public strifes and social divisions of the age.

But even Hutton was enough of a child of his age not to find these concerns entirely satisfactory. For he concludes that Scott could never touch the 'higher paradoxes of the spiritual life,' that, remaining 'within the well-defined forms of some one or other of the conditions of outward life and manners . . . was, no doubt, one of the secrets of his genius; but it was also its greatest limitation.'[12]

This limitation, however, is surely far less limited than the ideology that rejected Scott: the incredible limitation of the human self to its own emotional interior, finding profundity in its lack of relation to 'the conditions of outward life and manners'. Scott found profundity precisely in that relation, not merely in the effect on private individuals of public events, but in the very formation of personal character by a dense and antagonistic network of social associations. Identity in Scott is always social; it does not well up from the interior 'movements of the heart', but is imposed or bestowed, refused or withheld, by a social group. It is therefore highly fragile and precarious, requiring constant care for one's reputation. The discovery of identity for a Scott hero is a matter of finding out what group he belongs to, or, if that is impossible or unwelcome, of deciding which among various competing groups to belong to. Identity is never fixed; it may be modified or lost, but it is always a function of belonging. In this context, the external is not divorced from the internal but is a part of it. Here the delineation of 'outward' behavior, speech, and dress is not superficial at all: for our 'manners' declare what group we belong to and therefore who we are. They still do.

The central energy of Scott's fiction, however, while it includes problems of identity, is focused elsewhere: on the process of historical change. It is this concern, most threatening to, and hence most overlooked by, the ideology of negative freedom, that provides the most valuable corrective to it. In the Waverley Novels not only identity but reality is socially determined. I have elsewhere described how this conviction operates at every level in the romances to produce an historiography of social allegiance and interpretation: history becomes the believed fictions that social groups tell about each other and themselves.[13] But the crucial implication of Scott's historiography in respect to the decline of his reputation is that what is socially determined can be socially changed. Taking as the primary subject of his concern the great transition in the Western world from a feudal, aristocratic society based on principle and personal loyalty to a capitalist, bourgeois society based on expediency and the impersonal rule of law, Scott shows that the institutions human beings set up, they can pull down. They can of course do neither alone—not even if they are kings and queens. This is why Scott is the celebrator of our 'vulgar communities'—because it is only by collective action that history is made. The novels unfold a continuous pageant of social struggle between groups of people bound together, often precariously, by a common cause: to bring down a government, or defend it; to plant a new form of religion, or impose an old one. Just as personal identity in Scott is in the gift of a social group, so the duration of political and religious institutions depends on social assent and allegiance. The inexorably social ideology of Walter Scott supplies just that remedy for alienation that the ideology of the negatively free individual sensibility was created in order to avoid: the association of human beings in collective, political, and violent action. The remedy is impeccably logical: if we are dehumanized by our work, oppressed by the banal vacuity of our communities, we can indeed change these 'conditions'— not, of course, by retreating from them into our private selves, but only by association, by belonging to and acting with a group. It is no wonder that the rich prospects for collective, social action offered by the Waverley Novels should have been degraded into 'superficiality' by high Arnoldian 'culture', or that they should have been first pointed out in this century by a Marxist critic, Georg Lukács.[14] For by enacting the possibilities of human association in often violent social struggle, Scott's fiction was telling the culture of the late nineteenth century and most of the twentieth what it least wanted to hear.

As a result, it refused to hear what Scott was saying. The refusal extends into our own time as a deafness to Scott's subject manifested by contempt for his 'style'. David Craig, for example, offers as proof positive of 'Scott's Shortcomings as an Artist' the juxtaposition, without any argument at all, of passages from his work with those from novelists in the 'great' tradition (Conrad, Eliot, and so on).[15] The single comment he vouchsafes on one of the Scott passages clearly reveals the ideology latent in the refusal to apprehend it. The passage (too long to quote here) is the final two paragraphs from the sixth chapter of *The Heart of Mid-Lothian,* which describes the assault by the Porteous Mob on the gate of the Edinburgh tolbooth, its eventual destruction by fire, and the entry of the mob into the prison. Craig's comment is that we cannot 'see or hear anyone doing anything'. This is exactly half true: we hear and see rather a lot—sledge-hammers, rumors, one anonymous voice, crackling flames; the crowd, the smoke, the red glow on the façade, the anxious bystanders—but we do not indeed see any*one*. The passage shows us no individual because it is describing a collective action: that is its point. It is an historical point as well; lest we miss it, Scott appends a couple of long notes and documents explaining that the leaders of the Porteous Riot were never identified; no individuals could be held responsible. The point is that the event was a spontaneous but well-executed collective uprising against injustice; its participants are plural. Craig manages to miss the point because he demands to see some one person doing some one thing. Since he is not reading the text, he is hardly qualified to pass adverse judgments on its style.

The very invocation of 'style' in a normative and exclusive sense is but an excuse for not reading, a mask for a failure of attention that is ideologically motivated. If we can only pay attention to writers whom we can classify as great, then it is time so to reclassify Scott. His fiction not only repays analysis by whatever techniques we academic critics can bring to bear on it; it can also offer to a wider contemporary public a collective and social vision of life that is more applicable to our contemporary predicaments than the private vision of the tradition that replaced him. By predicaments, I mean three specific conditions that directly affect the structure and texture of our individual daily lives: 1) the planetary crisis of energy and ecology; 2) unstoppable worldwide inflation; 3) the doctrine, and hence the possibility, of mutually assured nuclear destruction. To alter these conditions, the individual consciousness and sensibility, no matter how finely cultivated, is impotent. Only social association in collective action can avail against these present threats to our collective, and hence individual, survival. It is precisely this historical dynamic—the necessarily social processes of change—that is modeled for us in the fiction of Scott, where its issue and purpose is, as Francis Hart has shown, precisely what has become of incomparably greater urgency for us today: survival.[16] To consider the compromises and sacrifices required by the historical process as Scott reveals it, as insuring the continued *co*existence of opposed parties, religions, or nations; to see the present as a product of the past at the same time as to see the past as necessarily altered if it is to remain a part of the present: I submit that there are no matters profounder than these to engage our reflection at this moment. That Scott presents them in settings of medieval Europe or eighteenth-century Scotland makes his fiction of no less immediate interest to us than the setting of ancient Britain makes *King Lear*. For Scott's portrayal, in whatever epoch, of the historical process as socially determined shows us the only way in which we can answer the question that history spared him but has posed for us, which is simply: will history continue? There will be neither past nor present if there is no future. And there will be no future if we do not, in the present, take collective action to change the conditions of the world we now live in.

In urging that Scott has plenty to say to us today, in opposition to the whole modern climate of literary opinion that finds him negligible, I have been stressing the unprecedented seriousness of his concerns for our generation. Without derogating from these, I must conclude with the shameless admission that Scott is also great fun to read. To combine pleasure with instruction, aside from being Scott's own modest boast, is perhaps the most venerable criterion of artistic merit in Western culture. We can learn from fiction, as Sir Philip Sidney averred, because we delight in it. That the learning and enjoyment that we derive from Scott may be different from those we derive from other novelists makes him no less great. The contemporary readers of Scott who placed him as an innovator in the epic tradition—in the company of Homer, Dante, Ariosto, Shakespeare, Cervantes and Fielding—were not wrong. For the really great tradition in fiction is all of it—all of it that contributes, in Leavis's own words, to our 'awareness of the possibilities of life', that is able 'to engage the critical attention of the adult mind'.[17] Very few writers make us aware of more such possibilities that more deserve our critical attention than Walter Scott. But in order fully to perceive and appreciate them, what we need—and I think the need is desperate—are attention spans and sympathies as wide and rich and all-embracing as his own.

Notes

1.   John Henry Raleigh, 'What Scott Meant to the Victorians', *Victorian Studies,* 7 (1963), 8.
2.   *The Secular Scripture* (Cambridge, Mass., 1976), 42.
3.   *The Great Tradition* (London, 1948), 6.
4.   *London and Westminster Review,* 1838, rpt. in *Scott: The Critical Heritage,* ed. John O. Hayden (London, 1970), 364–5.
5.   *Le National,* 1830, tr. in Hayden, 319–21.
6.   *North American Review,* 1864, rpt. in Hayden, 427–31.
7.   Quoted by James T. Hillhouse, *The Waverley Novels and Their Critics* (Minneapolis, 1936), 261.
8.   Quoted by Walter Allen, *The English Novel* (New York, 1954), who goes on to give a much fairer and more cogent assessment of Scott, 126ff.
9.   Arthur K. Moore, *Contestable Concepts of Literary Theory* (Baton Rouge, 1973), 218.
10.   Preface to *The American,* New York Edition, Vol. II (1907), rpt. in *The Art of Fiction,* ed. R. P. Blackmur (New York, 1950), 33. James's italics.
11.   I have argued elsewhere, in a wider historical context, that 'The "Autonomy of Art" is a Wish, Not a Fact', *Criticism,* 22 (1980), 341–56.
12.   *Sir Walter Scott* (1878), rpt. in Hayden, 489, 498.
13.   'Story as Historiography in the Waverley Novels', *ELH,* 47 (1980), 304–30.
14.   *The Historical Novel,* tr. Hannah and Stanley Mitchell (London, 1962; 1st ed. 1937).
15.   In *Scott Bicentenary Essays,* ed. Alan Bell (Edinburgh, 1973), 101–14.
16.   *Scott's Novels: The Plotting of Historic Survival* (Charlottesville, 1966).
17.   *The Great Tradition,* 226.

SCOTT, HISTORY, AND NARRATIVE

◆

The Rationalism of Sir Walter Scott

DUNCAN FORBES

1

Our picture of Sir Walter Scott has been created almost exclusively by critics and historians of literature for whom Scott is the central figure of the Romantic Movement. This interpretation of Scott as the 'King of the Romantics' is not entirely satisfactory even in literary annals; passively accepted and carried over into other spheres it may do further harm. Crane Brinton's account of Scott's political thought, or political attitude, for instance, is heavily coloured by the common but inaccurate notion of Scott as 'consistently romantic', a man of feeling rather than reflection.[1] He held 'impossible ideals' says Crane Brinton, 'he lived vicariously in the Middle Ages', he invested his loyalties with the 'cheating, consoling, steadying support of sentiment', 'he never thought of the feudal age of his ideals as on another plane of reality from the age in which he lived'. Can this really be believed of a man who was so practical-minded and forward-looking; an improving landlord, chairman of an oil gas company, president of the Royal Society of Edinburgh; who in defending Scottish legal procedure against the threat of reform on English lines could write: 'we are unalterably attached to that system of jurisprudence under the protection of which our native country has advanced from poverty and rudeness to prosperity and civilization'?[2] Scott had no illusions about the

From the *Cambridge Journal* 7 (1953):20-35. Reprinted by permission of Duncan Forbes.

Middle Ages. As A. W. Benn said: he had no tendency 'to seek for his ideal of human society in one period more than in another. If he had a preference, it was for the more civilized'.[3] Professor Brinton's chapter on Scott is ingenious, but he accepts the conventional interpretation of Scott's romanticism too easily, and pitches the key too high. He takes as typical of Scott's political mind a pamphlet issued anonymously in 1819. But it is agreed that Scott was inclined to panic in times of political crisis, and a pamphlet thrown off in such a moment is no more an indication of his real mind than a heated after-dinner speech. The political passion in the man contrasts strikingly with the calmness and objectivity of the writer. One of his earliest biographers (G. Allan: *Life of Scott*, 1834) pointed to the passage in *The Antiquary*, written in 1816, where Oldbuck likens the French Revolution to a hurricane which 'sweeps away stagnant and unwholesome vapours and repays in future health and fertility its immediate desolation and ravage',[4] and goes on to say that the whole spirit of Scott's writings furnishes a singular contrast to his political professions. 'The political bearing of the Scotch novels has been a considerable recommendation to them', wrote Hazlitt in 1825, in a paragraph conveniently truncated at this point by Crane Brinton to illustrate the fact that 'the world has not failed to discern' the political gospel of Conservatism in the novels. But the 'political bearing' that Hazlitt had in mind was Scott's cooling impartiality: 'the candour of Sir Walter's historic pen levels our bristling prejudices', etc.[5] Professor Brinton's account does not ring true because he forgets or ignores the dualism in Scott of hasty passion and calm judgment, romance and common sense. He sees only one side of the medal.

2

It is a commonplace of criticism to say that there is in Scott much that is typical of the rationalist eighteenth century; it is easy to point to obvious survivals from the Age of Reason: Scott's whole attitude to religion, for example—for him, the 'divine origin' of Christianity was 'proved by its beneficial effects on the state of society',[6] his concern with morality, his anti-clericalism (Harriet Martineau praised Scott for exposing 'priestcraft and fanaticism'), his treatment of the supernatural and so on. He rejected Ossian, quickly recovered from his early bout of *Sturm und Drang,* and disliked 'the gingerbread taste of modern Gothicizers'[7] (Abbotsford was planned as 'not Gothic by any means but an old fashioned Scotch residence'[8]); like Shaftesbury, he regarded ridicule as a useful weapon against 'enthusiasm'[9] and it is used to good effect, for instance, in the battle of the pulpit in *Woodstock,* and in the dole scene in *The Antiquary* (vol. II, p. 85); he thought the Crusades introduced a 'change for the worse . . . into the European character';[10] as A. W. Benn pointed out, his Saladin is a hero taken from the Rationalist Pantheon; and at the end of

Ivanhoe he shows us the old Jew and his daughter withdrawing from the benighted shores of Christian England to the tolerant civilization of Mohammedan Spain. A long catalogue of such things could be made out; but the view could still be taken that these things, though obvious, were unimportant, mere dead wood in a tree whose roots went deep into a romantic soil. The rationalism in Scott, however, is not just a heap of fossilized survivals from the eighteenth century.

Discerning critics have always rejected opinions like Bosanquet's, that Scott is 'the most unreflective of writers', and have directed attention to the hard vein of reflective writing in all his work, to 'his knowledge and not least, his very solid thinking' (Stephen Gwynn), to 'the large instructiveness, the stimulating intellectual air of Scott's historic tales' (R. H. Hutton), to his 'reflective power which atones sometimes . . . for his defects in creation' (Buchan), to 'his activity of thought' (Cazamian). Critics like these are dimly aware that there is a philosophy behind the pageant, a philosophy which is not of course original to Scott, who was no systematic thinker, but which equipped him with presuppositions, a manner of thinking and a historical method. If this eighteenth-century background is neglected, if the philosophical history of eighteenth-century Scotland is not taken into account, if the fact that Scott was a pupil of Dugald Stewart and a friend of Adam Ferguson,[11] and lived and worked in or near the metropolis of rationalist history—Edinburgh—is ignored, the story of the creation of the historical novel by Scott can only be half told.

The origin of the myth of the 'unphilosophical' Scott is perhaps worth noticing. John Mill, in his review of the *Life of Napoleon* in 1828, argued that Scott was unfitted to deal with a subject, like the French Revolution, which demands a 'philosophical historian'.[12] The fact was that in the work reviewed by Mill, Scott used the same weapon in the Tory interest that had been taken from the arsenal of conjectural history by James Mill for use in the service of radicalism. James Mill and Scott had both been educated in 'philosophical' history, both had been pupils of Dugald Stewart, but Scott used the master principle of 'philosophical' history, namely, the idea of the progress of society, as a Tory argument. 'Equalization', says Scott, appealing to conjectural history, is a 'ridiculous contradiction of the necessary progress of society . . . the savage may indeed boast a rude species of equality in some patriarchal tribes but . . . as society advances, the difference of ranks advances with it.' 'It is not too much to say, in conclusion, that excepting in the earliest stage of human society, there never existed a community in which was to be found that liberty and equality, which the French claimed for each individual in the whole extent of their empire.'[13]

On the other hand, to the romantics of the school of Coleridge and to Carlyle, Scott's 'philosophy' was not philosophy at all. In the same year in which John Mill was attacking Scott's 'Tory misrepresentations', F. D. Maurice also condemned Scott for lacking philosophy and depth. History for Scott, according to Maurice, is merely a brilliant pageant, a heap of facts of which he knows neither the why nor the wherefore.[14] Julius Hare described Scott's 'genius' as 'superficial', and Carlyle's harsh criticism is well known. Thus rationalists and romantics combined, for different reasons, to brand Scott a mere entertainer.

A modern critic who dismisses Scott as 'unphilosophical' is missing an important point: Scott was as 'philosophical' as the *Philosophes;* that is to say, his real concern was with life in society, his overriding interest was in the study of social man, and this meant also, in the eighteenth century, the empirical study of the 'principles of human nature.' His distrust of systems and system-building was typical of the eighteenth century; like a good 'Newtonian', he was an observer, especially an observer of human nature from the outside. He practised what the Scottish philosophers preached: he avoided the 'mist of metaphysics' and lived, by the light of common sense, a life of action and observation in society—the great laboratory of the *Philosophes*—the sort of life recommended by Adam Ferguson: full of 'bustle'.[15] Indeed his life is itself a monument to the spirit of the Scottish philosophy—for no great writer was less of a purely 'literary man' than Scott.

In his interests and in the turn of his mind he takes his place naturally in the great succession from Montesquieu and Adam Ferguson and the other founding fathers of sociology in eighteenth-century Scotland. When Adam Ferguson died in 1816, Scott described him as 'my learned and venerated friend . . . whom I have known and looked up to for thirty years and upward'.[16] This veneration is not surprising. There is in Ferguson, as in Montesquieu and in Scott,[17] a vein of Stoicism. He taught that life was a dangerous game of hazard, in which happiness cannot be a matter of calculation because it 'arises more from the pursuit, than from the attainment of any end'.[18] Life was more important than literature or learning.[19] War was not only natural but constructive of individual character and of society, for without it 'civil society itself could scarcely have found an object or a form'.[20] Ferguson was never tired of emphasizing that the strength of a nation is 'derived from the character not from the wealth nor from the multitude of its people',[21] nor of demonstrating from history the dangers in an advanced stage of civilization, especially the retreat of patriotism[22] and civic virtue before selfishness and political quietism. Similar views can be seen in whole or in part in Hume, Kames, Millar, Dunbar and other writers of the period. Dugald Stewart also ('eminently the psychological and ethical observer'[23]) was in many ways, as Allan pointed out, an ideal teacher for a man of Scott's temperament. His 'natural inclination is more to pluck the flower than to dig for the root', as Allan said of him.[24] Scott also attended the class of history taught by A. F. Tytler, and no doubt appreciated his warning against 'the prevailing propensity with modern philosophers to reduce everything to general principles', and against the construction of historical systems on insufficient knowledge of facts.[25]

The 'romantic' interpreters are inclined to make too much of Scott's lack of formal education and of his voracious reading of romances as a young man. It is true that in his autobiography Scott thought it necessary to apologize for his ignorance, when at High School, of 'names and dates and the other technicalities of history', and of 'the philosophy of history, a much more important subject . . .' He was, he says, assembling material, 'and when in riper years, I attended more to the deduction of general principles, I was furnished with a powerful host of examples in illustration of them'.[26] After all, Scott could not have been much more than thirteen at the High School. In 1790, when he was nineteen, he wrote a paper on the origin of the feudal system, which he submitted to Dugald Stewart and read to the Literary and Speculative Societies. This shows clearly the imprint of 'philosophical' history, for Scott attacked the view that the system was invented by the Lombards and 'endeavoured to assign it a more general origin, and to prove that it proceeds upon principles common to all nations when placed in a certain situation'.[27] This view of the origin of the feudal system, which is not original to Scott,[28] is more 'scientific' and less 'romantic' than that of Montesquieu, for whom feudalism is a unique event, 'un événement arrivé une fois dans le monde et qui n'arrivera peut-être jamais' (De l'Esprit des Lois, XXX, 1).

It is curious that in the study of Scott's pedigree of ideas, in the process of marshalling a host of 'influences' from the Sagas and Cervantes and Shakespeare to the eighteenth-century novelists, the Gothick school, Goetz von Berlichingen, Bürger's Lenore, Maria Edgeworth and Queenhoo Hall, the most immediate 'influence' of all, the intellectual atmosphere of eighteenth-century Scotland, should have been so consistently ignored; and the line that leads from Montesquieu to Waverley so neglected. For Montesquieu surely has as good a claim to be considered a spiritual ancestor of the Scotch novels as Goethe or Strutt. No Scottish lawyer could have escaped an influence so all pervasive as that of De l'Esprit des Lois—Montesquieu was a patron saint of Scottish lawyers, and Adam Ferguson an ardent disciple. (Laski described him, rather unkindly, as a 'pinchbeck Montesquieu'.) Scott had Montesquieu's (Œuvres in his library, naturally, and it is to Montesquieu that he appeals when he is arguing against the extension of English legal procedures to Scotland.[29] Anyone reading the Waverley Novels who pauses to consider just what it is that makes them 'historical' in a way in which the novels of Monk Lewis, Mrs. Radcliffe or Jane Porter's Scottish Chiefs are not, and who senses the determinism that makes the characters appear again and again like so many puppets, not only fashioned by their surroundings and by tradition—moulded by l'esprit général—but dominated and led into tragic conflict by historical forces outside their control,[30] must realize Scott's affinities with the spirit and doctrines of Montesquieu. To use Leslie Stephen's well-known phrase, it was not only Burke's philosophy, but that of Montesquieu and his Scottish sociological disciples that was 'put into the concrete' in the Waverley Novels.[31]

3

Scott's ideas on the scope and purpose of history are not radically different from those of the rationalist historians of the eighteenth century. He believed firmly in the usefulness of historical study both as a guide to the political future and a healing balm in times of internal dissension.[32] Scott's purpose was never merely entertainment. An element of conscious statecraft underlies his work. *Waverley* for instance, besides promoting sound morality, was to do for England and Scotland what Maria Edgeworth's Irish Tales had done for England and Ireland: to cement the Union in the hearts of men.[33] Marmion too, had a definite political object: to buttress morale in the Napoleonic struggle and dish Jeffrey and the Whig peacemongers. The novels were designed to be instructive as well as amusing, for Scott thought that in an advanced stage of civilization like ours when a 'half love of literature . . . pervades all ranks' and 'books are read for amusement rather than moral instruction',[34] a little history was better than none at all. 'The honey which is put on the edge of the cup induces many to drink up the whole medicinal potion; while those who take only a sip of that, have, at least, a better chance of benefit than if they had taken none at all.'[35]

Practical history meant "philosophical" history; Scott never believed, like Lingard, for instance, that the historian should confine himself to the mere reporting of events, to chronicle. On the contrary the historian should seek for parallels, compare events,[36] and endeavour to make out the general trend, 'the real and deep progress of opinions and events', beneath the surface conflicts. Histories which fail to do this, says Scott, are like a miller who is so busy among the clatter of his own wheels and machinery that he does not notice the rising flood which eventually sweeps him away. In his Memoirs, Sir George Mackenzie is so mixed up in petty political detail that he has lost sight of 'the great progressive movement of human affairs'.[37] Writing to his son Charles, on the value of reading history, he points out that man is a progressive animal because 'our eye is enabled to look back upon the past to improve on our ancestors' improvements and to avoid their errors. This can only be done by studying history and comparing it with passing events'.[38] (Scott, it should be noted, wrote a considerable amount of contemporary history, not only in his *Life of Napoleon,* but in the *Edinburgh Annual Register* and elsewhere).

He took it for granted that 'philosophical' history would form part of a young man's education. No doubt remembering his own experience at the High School, he wrote to Lord Montagu concerning the education of the young Duke of Buccleuch: 'I think I said before that I would be much more anxious to create the taste for the science of history in the outset than that my pupil should go through many books—in fact I would defer to the very last what is always taught first namely, the philosophy as it has been termed, of history. Let a youth get the leading and interesting facts fixed in his mind and the philosophy will come afterwards both with ease and pleasure. At the same time whenever the youth himself showed curiosity that way by comparing different natures or different stages in society, it will be a precious opportunity and not to be omitted by a tutor.'[39]

Although he considered writing a 'philosophical' history of Scotland in 1829,[40] Scott never actually wrote this sort of history—with the exception of the chapter on Civilization in the *Tales of a Grandfather.* But the important thing is that he never questioned its presuppositions. He accepted the leading principle of conjectural history: the law of the necessary progress of society through successive stages, and used it, as has been seen, as a weapon. For instance, against codification he argued that one cannot expect law to be simple in an advanced state of society.[41] Napoleon's conduct in war is condemned as tending 'to retrograde towards the brutal violence of primitive hostility',[42] and the Continental System 'consisted of the abolition of all commerce and the reducing each nation, as in the days of primitive barbarism, to remain satisfied with its own productions, however inadequate to the real or artificial wants to which its progress in society had gradually given rise'.[43] He looks forward to better relations with France because 'the enlarged ideas of commerce, as they spread wider, and become better understood, will afford, perhaps, the strongest and most irresistible motive for amicable intercourse—that ... which arises from mutual advantage; for commerce keeps pace with civilization'.[44] He prefaces his remarks on the tactics of Napoleon with a survey of the principles of war in the framework of the progress of society.[45]

Scott, as is well known, was not worried by historical inaccuracies, which are often gross. Such pococurantism in historical matters is characteristic of eighteenth-century 'philosophical' historians. It is all the more significant to find him disturbed by a 'gross defect', in *Marmion:* namely, the fact that Marmion's crime was forgery, 'forgery being the crime of a commercial, rather than a proud and warlike age'.[46] Sociological anachronism was unpardonable in a 'philosophical' historian; though forgery was not in fact unknown, as Scott pointed out, it was not typical of that state of society, and the typical was what mattered.

Like Kames, Adam Smith, Ferguson, John Millar and others, Scott had his doubts about the benefits arising from the progress of civilization. In 1829 he wrote: 'The state of high civilization to which we have arrived is scarcely a national blessing, since, while the *few* are improved to the highest point, the *many* are in proportion brutalized and degraded, and the same nation displays at the same time the very highest and the very lowest state in which the human race can exist in point of intellect . . .'[47] All the thinkers just mentioned issued warnings of this nature, with particular reference to the danger of the intellectual and moral debasement of the many produced by the division of labour in advanced societies. It did not prevent them from regarding progress as 'natural'. Thus in 1830 Scott wrote 'it is seldom that civilization having once made some progress can be compelled to retrograde, unless where knowledge is united with corruption and effeminacy.'[48] Progress in fact for Scott, as for the conjectural historians, is the organizing principle of history. As a social scientist he was always interested in the comparative study of different nations in similar 'states of society'. The essay on feudalism mentioned above was no mere college task; Scott was thinking along these lines all his life, for according to Lockhart, 'one of the last historical books he read before leaving Abbotsford for Malta in 1831 was Colonel Tod's interesting account of Rajasthan; and I well remember the delight he expressed on finding his views confirmed . . . by the philosophical soldier's details of the structure of society in that remote region of the East'.[49] In 1816 he described Elphinstone's *Account of the Kingdom of Caubul* (1815) enthusiastically as 'the best account of shepherd tribes which we have had for a long time',[50] and on his visit to France of that year he observed the Tartar soldiers among the Russian occupying forces with especial interest, noting, with the eye of the 'philosophical' historian, the 'cloaks of sheepskin, bows, arrows . . . and other appointments savouring of the earliest state of society'.[51] The Antiquary, in whom there is something of Scott himself, says: 'To trace the connections of nations by their usages and the similarity of the implements which they employ has long been my favourite study', and he tries to interest his nephew in a fisherman's funeral and in 'the resemblances which I will point out betwixt popular customs on such occasions and those of the ancients'.[52]

Scott, the social scientist, was therefore as much concerned with uniformities as with individuality. For this reason, the theory behind his balladhunting is not the same as Herder's. For Scott the ballads were not what they were for Herder: the revelation of unique, organic 'folk-souls'. He was interested in such 'Border Ballads as may tend to illustrate the ancient state of the Southern counties of Scotland',[53] but this 'state' was not a unique phenomenon, it was the 'partly pastoral, partly warlike'[54] state of society, in which 'the history, the laws and even the religion . . . are usually expressed in verse',[55] which is common to all mankind at a certain stage of social evolution. Although Scott regretted the dissolving of the 'peculiar features' of Scottish 'manners and character' into those of her sister and ally,[56] there is no national programme behind his ballad editing comparable to that of Herder and his disciples.

The Border, in fact, provides an instructive example of the misunderstanding of Scott that is liable to arise from the exclusively 'romantic' interpretation. It is moreover a crucial test, as all critics agree that the Border is the starting-point of Scott's literary journey; 'the taproot' as Sir Herbert Grierson says,[57] 'of Scott's later work as poet and novelist'. G. M. Young, for instance, writes: 'it is impossible to imagine Scott as anything but a Borderer, imbued from infancy with that sense of contrast, that feeling of something beyond, something mysteriously or magnetically different . . .'[58] But the Border for Scott was not only the national boundary—which hardly existed in a clear cut form in the Middle Ages—but the 'state of society' which cut across the national boundary, the contrast which originally fascinated Scott was not so much the contrast between England and Scotland, as the sociological contrast between the Borderers (both Scots and English) and their more civilized neighbours. He was especially interested in what the Borderers had in common. He quotes an original authority to show that in 1654 'there was little difference between the Northumbrian and the border Scottish'. He describes the intercourse between the English and Scots borderers: 'they met frequently at parties of the chace and football'.[59] Moreover his earliest explorations were on the English side, for as Dame Una Pope Henessy says[60]: 'Scott found the English border a great deal more exciting and important than the Northern side'—this is clear from his early letters. There was better evidence there of the state of society in which he was interested.

For Scott was no jealous guardian of the individuality and uniqueness, of anything peculiar to Scotland, in either the old Border or the Highland way of life. Thus the chieftains of the House of Douglas 'possessed the ferocity, with the heroic virtues, of a savage state'.[61] He wishes a work could be compiled dealing with the Highlanders 'with reference to the lowlands . . . and to all other countries'.[62] He is struck with the 'curious points of parallelism' between the Highland clans and the Afghan tribes as described by Elphinstone.[63] The names of the clans remind him of the sonorous names of the Brazilian tribes.[64] (Scott was reading Southey's *History of Brazil* at this time.) He compares the 'Constitution' of Scotland in 843 with that of present day Persia 'as described by Malcolm'.[65] Of the famous Andrea Ferrara swords he says: "Most barbarous nations excel in the fabrication of arms" (*Waverley*, II, p. 201[n.]), and Highland superstition is characteristic of 'all rude people'.[66]

It is this sociological interest that makes the *Waverley Novels* 'historical'. For they are not "historical" at the deeper levels of thought and feeling. For one thing, Scott believed with the rationalists in the essential uniformity of human nature. A long line of critics from Taine to Buchan has pointed out that Scott does not enter the mind of past ages, that he 'pauses on the threshold of the soul and in the vestibule of history'. Scott himself knew very well that 'he that would please the modern world, yet present the exact impression of a tale of the Middle Ages, will repeatedly find that he must . . . sacrifice the last to the first object . . . because he must, to interest the readers of the present time, invest his characters with language and sentiments unknown to that period . . .'[67] He made no attempt to sustain the *frisson historique*, because he knew that a novel which managed to do so would not find readers.

Scott's novels are 'historical' because the characters are so closely related to the relevant background of social and economic history that they seem to grow out of it. Even his wildest and most fantastic creations, like Meg Merrilees in *Guy Mannering*, for instance, succeed so long as they are studies in historical ecology, but are miserable Gothick failures—like Norna in *The*

Pirate—when they are not. As long as his 'romantic' imagination is ballasted by the sociological intellect of the rationalist historian, we have the unique mixture which is Scott. Otherwise, the result is merely a feeble aping of Fouqué or Mrs Radcliffe. For unlike these two authors, Scott's interest in the supernatural was sociological at heart, and he is at his best when he is most true to himself.

Lord David Cecil[68] pointed out that Scott is not primarily a writer of adventure stories. This is because the real hero is usually the particular 'state of society' which Scott is portraying, and as Leslie Stephen noticed,[69] it is only by a kind of happy accident when this interest in the surroundings does not put the chief characters out of focus. Scott himself was well aware of this. *Waverley* was not intended to be a 'story about the '45'. As two early critics noticed, Scott chose the '45 because his object being to illustrate the 'manners' and 'state of society' in the north in the earlier part of the eighteenth century, he fixed on an "era of turbulent events which drew into their vortex all classes of men".[70] Scott's work, no less than the Second Book of James Mill's *History of India,* is thus a 'grand sociological display', but Scott's sociology, unlike that of the Utilitarians, has all the zest and freshness of actual observation; his facts have often been gathered in the saddle, verified with his own eyes and ears, as in *The Pirate.*

Scott's stories do not hinge on psychological conflict, but on the contrast between different 'degrees of civilization' and 'states of society', especially between Highland and Lowland, barbarism and civilization, as in *Waverley, Rob Roy, The Fair Maid of Perth, Anne of Geierstein, The Two Drovers.* This contrast between Highland and Lowland, so sharply exhibited in eighteenth-century Scotland, the existence of a 'barbarous state of society', a sociological museum, at Edinburgh's back door, and the eruption of the Highlands in 1745, must have been a most potent factor in the outburst of sociological speculation after 1750, speculation which centred round the idea of the progress of society from rudeness to refinement. Adam Ferguson, hailed by some as the founder of sociology, was a Highlander who settled down near Edinburgh. Scott was fascinated by a character like Rob Roy, 'blending the wild virtues, the subtle policy and unrestrained licence of an American Indian . . . flourishing in Scotland during the Augustan age . . .' (*Rob Roy,* I, p. viii). He was especially interested in the transition period from barbarism to civilization, 'the most picturesque period of history'. This is the theme of *The Fortunes of Nigel.*[71] Kames had noticed that 'the period that intervenes between barbarity and humanity'—he is thinking of the sixteenth century—abounds with interesting psychological phenomena, 'surprising changes of temper and conduct' which 'in the present time are unknown'.[72]

That Scott was no mean economic and social historian is generally appreciated. In this, however, he was not unique: many lairds of his age were 'statistical' historians.[73] The letter on the depopulation of the Southern Uplands, mentioned with admiration by G. M. Young, is a fine example of such 'statistical' history, but there is nothing especially original in its method—this is the age of the 'statistical' accounts. Scott found this sort of economic and social history ready to hand, and applied it to the novel (his poems and the notes to them also impart statistical information),[74] and his surefooted knowledge in this sphere is another reason why his historical novels are so much more satisfactory than those of Dumas, for instance, or indeed than those of most other historical novelists. It is another vital legacy of the rationalist eighteenth century to the historical novel as fashioned by Scott.

A corollary of the sociological interest and knowledge that informs the *Waverley Novels* is another trait typical of a 'philosophical' historian: Scott decisively rejected the 'great man' approach to history. He shows us the great occupying high station or nobly enduring (like Mary Queen of Scots in *The Abbot*) but never in the act of consciously, rationally and decisively guiding events. His dislike of the 'crafty' politician, too, of Machiavellism generally, is typical of a *philosophe*. E.A. Baker has noticed how in *Quentin Durward* Scott chooses the very episode in which Louis XI overreached himself with perilous results as the cardinal incident in the story—'a curious way of making good the king's declared pre-eminence in statecraft.'[75]

4

Ultimately, the rationalist historians of eighteenth-century Scotland were interested in 'states of society' because they were students of human nature. They viewed the world as a vast laboratory in which an original element—human nature—was variously conditioned by different social states. In order to discover the real, abiding nature of man, it was necessary to make a comparative study of these various social compounds and to observe any 'experiments' which history had to offer. As Scott wrote to Southey in 1818: 'the history of colonies has in it some points of peculiar interest as illustrating human nature. On such occasions the extremes of civilized and savage life are suddenly and strongly brought into contact with each other and the results are as interesting to the moral observer as those which take place on the mixture of chemical substances are to the physical investigator.[76] He believed that the 'stamp which nature herself has fixed upon the manners of a people living in a simple and patriarchal state' is obscured 'by those peculiar habits of thinking and acting which are produced by the progress of society'.[77] The 'passions' are 'common to men in all stages of society . . . Upon these passions it is no doubt true that the state of manners and laws casts a necessary colouring; but the bearings, to use the language of heraldry, remain the same'.[78]

Because Scott's study of human nature was 'Newtonian', based on observation, it followed that the 'passions' could best be studied where men wore their hearts on their sleeves, that is, in primitive societies or what amounted to practically the same thing,[79] among the 'lower orders'. This is why Scott's 'polished' heroes and heroines are mere lifeless façdes; Scott, with his rationalist, 'Newtonian' equipment was unable to penetrate the polished surface of civilized men and women. He is notoriously unable to analyse motives in any but the simplest of minds. His Robespierre, for instance, is an incredible monster.[80] Allan says that in the novels Scott took his principal characters from among the humbler classes of society, 'who are the last to take on that polish which assimilates the manners of different nations'.[81]

Scott's antiquarianism, then, was not an end in itself; it was inspired not only by a sociology which cast a wide net, but by the study of human nature. He contrasted the antiquarianism of Ritson—whose pedantry was a source of amusement to him[82]—with that of Ellis who 'wished to be an architect, not a mere collector of stones and rubbish', and who 'avoids the great error of antiquaries who are too much busied with insulated facts . . .'[83] Edith Batho comments that for Scott the insulated facts are of importance only as contributing to the whole, and for Scott the whole is that understanding of the past which leads to a better understanding of man.[84]

It is said sometimes that Scott created a revolution in historical thinking because, as Dr. Trevelyan puts it, he 'first showed us how not only clothes and weapons, but thought and morals vary according to the period, the province, the class, the man'. 'It was he who first perceived that the history of mankind is not simple but complex.'[85] But nearly all the eighteenth-century historians were fascinated by the existence of these differences, by the 'variety of mankind' to use Hume's phrase. Adam Ferguson, for instance, wrote: 'the multiplicity of forms which different societies offer to our view is almost infinite . . . human affairs [have] a variety in detail which, in its full extent, no understanding can comprehend and no memory retain'.[86] This variety and complexity provided the great challenge to that rationalist generation, because it concealed, beneath the kaleidoscope, the essential uniformity of human nature. As Dunbar wrote: 'Human Nature, in some respects, is so various and fluctuating, so altered, or so disguised by external things, that its independent character has become dark and problematical.'[87] Scott's attitude does not constitute a revolution, for he too believed that, at bottom, human nature was uniform.

The *Waverley Novels* have been called 'the triumph of Romanticism' (Cazamian). But they could also be described as a triumph of the historical thought of the rationalist eighteenth century. In Scott, this thought blossoms, fertilized and bodied forth in concrete form by the imaginative grasp and creative energy of a great novelist. The result is that unique blend of sociology and romance, of 'philosophical' history and the novelist's living world of individuals, of the general and the particular, in which lies the peculiar genius of Sir Walter Scott. He is too big for any single label.

Notes

1.   *The Political Ideas of the English Romanticists.*

2.   *Edinburgh Annual Register* for 1808, vol. I, part II, p. 372.

3.   *History of English Rationalism in the Nineteenth Century,* p. 310.

4.   *The Antiquary,* vol. II, pp. 186-7. All quotations are from the 1860 edition of the *Waverley Novels.*

5.   Quoted in D. VEDDER: *Memoir of Scott* (Dundee, 1832), p. 39.

6.   *The Journal of Sir Walter Scott* (1950), pp. 453-4.

7.   Ibid., p. 406.

8.   *Letters* (ed. Grierson); IV, p. 282. Cf. VI, p. 323: 'modern Gothic, a style I hold to be equally false and foolish'.

9.   He quotes a case which Shaftesbury had used to make his point: the refugee Camisards in Queen Anne's reign, vide *Quarterly Review,* XVI, p. 474, and Shaftesbury, *Characteristics* (6th ed.), I, 26.

10. *Edinburgh Review,* VII, pp. 405, 409.

11. For the general intellectual background see GLADYS BRYSON: *Man and Society;* and for Adam Ferguson, W. C. LEHMANN: *Adam Ferguson and the Beginnings of Modern Sociology.*

12. Cf. *Westminster Review,* IX, pp. 252, 256.

13. *Life of Napoleon Buonaparte* (1827), I, pp. 213, 214; II, p. 89.

14. J. T. HILLHOUSE: *The Waverley Novels and their Critics,* p. 99.

15. An otherworldly, *'Der Traum ein Leben'* streak appears in Scott's Journal after the financial disaster and death of his wife.

16. *Letters,* IV, p. 181.

17. Vide A. W. BENN, op. cit., p. 312.

18. *An Essay on the History of Civil Society* (6th ed.), p. 81. 'The most animating occasions of human life are calls to danger and hardship, not invitations to safety and ease' (p. 74), etc.

19. *An Essay on the History of Civil Society,* pp. 48-51.

20. Ibid., p. 39.

21. Ibid., p. 101.

22. Cf. Scott. Noble, disinterested patriots 'belong to a less corrupted age than ours'. *Napoleon,* IV, p. 216.

23. LAURIE: *Scottish Philosophy in its National Development,* p. 223.

24. G. ALLAN: *Life of Scott,* p. 84.

25. *Elements of General History* (1801), I, pp. 43-4.

26. J. G. LOCKHART: *Memoirs of the Life of Sir Walter Scott* (1837), I, p. 37.

27. *Letters,* I, p. 17.

28. See, for instance, MILLAR: *Origin of Ranks* (3rd ed.), pp. 259-60; GILBERT STUART: *View of Society in Europe* (2nd ed.), p. 157.

29. *Edinburgh Ann. Regr.* op. cit.: 'Montesquieu has a chapter, of which the title is, *Qu'il ne faut pas tout corriger',* p. 335.

30. Cf. *The Monastery,* I, xxviii, for example. 'The numerous vessels of so many different sorts, and destined for such different purposes, which are launched in the same mighty ocean, although each endeavours to pursue its own course, are in every case more influenced by the tides and winds, which are common to the element which they all negotiate, than by their own separate exertions'. Louis Reynaud writes: 'Walter Scott, en dépit de son apparent idéalisme, part d'une conception de l'homme sourdement *déterministe et sensualiste.* Ses personnages ne sont pas libres. Ils sont presque exclusivement des produits de leur hérédité, de leur milieu, de leur profession, qui les dominent' quoted in E. A. BAKER: *History of the English Novel,* IV, p. 218, and cf. BAKER, op. cit., p. 213 et seq.

31. 'The Roman people, destined to acquire wealth by conquest . . . the Carthaginians, intent on . . . merchandise . . . must have filled the streets of their several capitals with men of

a different disposition and aspect.' A. FERGUSON, op. cit., p. 318. Such a remark shows clearly the link between Montesquieu and Scott; one can feel the sap of the *Waverley Novels* rising in it.

32.   Cf. *Letters*, VIII, p. 47.

33.   *Waverley*, I, p. xiii. *See Letters*, V, pp. 142-3.

34.   *Lives of the Novelists* (World's Classics), p. 21.

35.   *Quarterly Review*, XXXIV, p. 200.

36.   'Did you ever observe', Scott wrote to Southey in 1824, 'how easy it would be for a good historian to run a parallel betwixt the great Rebellion and the French Revolution, just substituting the spirit of fanaticism for that of soi-distant philosophy?' LOCKHART, op. cit., V, p. 359.

37.   *Letters*, VII, p. 98.

38.   *Letters*, VII, p. 34.

39.   Ibid., VIII, p. 104.

40.   *Journal*, p. 624.

41.   See *Napoleon*, VI, p. 55 et seq., on the Code Napoleon. There is nothing of Savigny, nothing of what the Utilitarians would have denounced as "mystical" about Scott's line of argument, which stresses practical considerations and is clearly the work of a lawyer with much actual experience of the courts. Rules worked out from imaginary cases 'can never have the same weight with precedents emerging in actual practice', he says. The Common Law of England may not be a showy warehouse built with much attention to architectural uniformity but it 'contains an immense store of commodities, which those acquainted with its recesses seldom fail to be able to produce . . .' Scott's argument is utilitarian in spirit in spite of his comparison of the Common Law to a Gothic cellar, for the point he is driving home is that the cellar is well-stocked.

42.   Ibid., III, p. 144.

43.   *Napoleon*, VII, p. 71.

44.   Ibid., IX, p. 50.

45.   Ibid., III, 88-9.

46.   Introduction to *Marmion* in *Poetical Works* (4 vols.), III, p. 4. On p. 199 (n.) Scott is afraid lest the reader 'consider the crime as inconsistent with the manners of the period'. For another example, see Note 34 to *The Lady of the Lake*, ibid., II, p. 211.

47.   *Letters*, XI, p. 128.

48.   *History of Scotland* (1830), I, p. 25.

49.   Op. cit., I, pp. 171-2.

50.   *Letters*, IV, p. 169.

51.   *Paul's Letters to his Kinsfolk* (1816), p. 368.

52.   *The Antiquary*, II, pp. 117, 120.

53.   *Letters*, I, p. 99.

54.   Preface to *Lay of the Last Minstrel, Poetical Works*, I, p. 14.

55.   *Edinburgh Review*, VII, p. 387.

56.   *Minstrelsy of the Scottish Border* (5th ed.), I, p. cxxxiii.

57.   *Sir Walter Scott, Bart.*, p. 73.

58.   *Sir Walter Scott Lectures* (1950), p. 84.

59.   See *Minstrelsy of the Scottish Border*, I, p. lxviii et seq.

60.   *Sir Walter Scott* (1948).

61.   *Poetical Works*, III, p. 249.

62.   *Letters*, III, p. 116.

63.   *Quarterly Review*, XIV, p. 288. Scott gives a list, and concludes: 'Similar examples may be derived from the history of Persia by Sir John Malcolm. But our limits do not permit us further to pursue a parallel which serves strikingly to show how the same state of society and civilization produces similar manners, laws, and customs even at the most remote period of time, and in the most distant quarters of the world', p. 290.

64. Ibid., p. 305. Mac Alisters, Mac Nabs, Mac Kechnies, etc., are compared with Tupinikins, Tupigais and Tupinambas. And this from the man who romanticized the Highlands.

65. *History of Scotland* (1830), I, p. 50.

66. *Poetical Works*, II, p. 207.

67. *Lives of the Novelists*, p. 203.

68. *Sir Walter Scott* (The Raven Miscellany).

69. *Hours in a Library* (1892), I, p. 154.

70. ALLAN, op. cit., p. 339. D. VEDDER, op. cit., p. 19.

71. See *Nigel,* I, p. vii.

72. *Sketches of the History of Man* (1774), pp. 268-9.

73. See *Paul's Letters,* p. 219, for example, where Scott refers to the Laird's 'statistical pursuits'.

74. To the Lochmaben Harper ballad in the *Minstrelsy,* for example, is appended a study of the King's rentallers, 'an extraordinary and anomalous class of landed proprietors who dwell in the neighbourhood. . . .'

75. Op. cit., p. 215. (For Scott's inability to portray statesmen, see p. 214). Napoleon's blunders are 'an awful lesson to sovereigns that morality is not so indifferent in politics as Machiavellians will assert', LOCKHART, op. cit., III, p. 116. In *Old Mortality,* I, p. 58, Claverhouse is described as 'profound in politics, and embued, of course, with that disregard for individual rights which its intrigues usually generate'.

76. *Letters,* V. p. 115.

77. Introduction to *Rokeby* in *Poetical Works,* I, p. 183.

78. *Waverley,* I, pp. 13-14. Cf. also *Quarterly Review,* V, p. 43.

79. See *Edinburgh Review,* VII, p. 403.

80. *Napoleon,* II, p. 26.

81. Op. cit., p. 385.

82. See *Letters,* I, pp. 355-6 for a good story against Ritson.

83. *Edinburgh Review,* VII, p. 413.

84. 'Scott as a Medievalist' in *Sir Walter Scott Today* (ed. Grierson), pp. 138-9.

85. *Clio, a Muse,* pp. 89, 166, also in *Ideas and Beliefs of the Victorians.*

86. Quoted in W. C. LEHMANN, op. cit., pp. 75-6.

87. *Essays on the History of Mankind in rude and cultivated ages* (2nd ed.), p. 1.

Story-Telling and the Subversion of Literary Form in Walter Scott's Fiction

INA FERRIS

In her recent study of Walter Scott, Jane Millgate draws attention to the puzzling fact that Scott—"this great originator"—consistently demonstrates a "profound distrust of innovation."[1] Millgate's observation affords an important clue to the question of generic innovation in the Waverley Novels, for it is precisely because Scott distrusts innovation that he is so innovative a novelist. This apparent paradox stems from the primary allegiance of his narrative imagination not to the literary form of the novel but to the preliterary form of story. Through story Scott opens up the nineteenth-century novel by introducing into the genre older forms of and motives for narrative. As is typical in Scott, his conservative impulse has radical implications, for it grows out of the historical mode of understanding that is the sign of his intuitive modernity. In one sense, story in Scott is the narrative equivalent of antiquarianism (itself a more complex activity for Scott than is generally recognized); in another (but related) sense, it both represents and encourages a historicist insight into the temporality and heterogeneity of cultures, an insight that challenges notions of uniformity, unity and universality. In narrative terms, story in both senses threatens the closural notions of authorship and of literary form on which the status of the novel as art conventionally depends.

The clearest recognition that Scott's narrative poses such a threat and that it does so through allegiance to story comes from E. M. Forster whose own formalist ideal of the novel renders him particularly alert to whatever may place it in question. Story for Forster is the source of the novel's generic weakness as a form of art, and Scott for Forster is the exemplary storyteller. The hostility to story in *Aspects of the Novel* is striking (it is the "low atavistic form" infecting the novel like a "tapeworm"),[2] and this hostility is generated by two characteristics of story. First, its origins in oral tradition ("the voice of the tribal narrator") contest the priority of the individual, literate imagination crucial to Forster's sense of art as civilized construct. Second, the linear, temporal nature of story ("saying one thing after another") undermines his modernist view of the novel as complex spatial form. As the "lowest and simplest

From *Genre* 18 (1985): 23–35. Published in *Genre,* copyright University of Oklahoma.

of literary organisms," story serves primarily to set off the "nobler aspects" of the "very complicated organisms known as novels" (pp. 27–28). It is less the evaluative assumptions of Forster's paradigm than his categories of definition that provide a useful point of entry into the question of the nature of Scott's narrative. Especially pertinent is his definition of story as syntagmatic chain. In contrast to current narrative theory, which tends to define story as paradigmatic core (structural, atemporal, even nonverbal), Forster identifies story with the narrative impulse itself: the desire to tell one thing after another. This impulse, acknowledging only "life in time," has for Forster no category of meaning ("life by values") to shape its energy into a coherent economy. Consequently, the story-teller is always at the mercy of another story, ready at any moment to abandon what he has begun and veer off to tell something else. "Unlike the weaver of plots," Forster remarks in the course of his discussion of Scott, "the story-teller profits by ragged ends" (p. 33). These "ragged ends" signal the dispersive impulse of story that accompanies its linear drive and not only resists but blithely ignores the integrative ideal animating the "weaver" of plots.

When Forster names Scott as paradigmatic story-teller, then, he effectively excludes him from the literary canon, and here Forster's move converges suggestively with that of Scott himself who typically locates his own novels outside the category of the properly literary. In particular, Forster's setting up the distinction between story and novel as a distinction between expansive and closural values in narrative recalls the terms in which Scott himself liked to distinguish his fiction from that of Henry Fielding, widely perceived at the time as the founder of the English novel and hence accorded a special status in the critical discussion of fiction by Scott and his contemporaries. While the popular novel of the period was regarded as beneath serious consideration (reviewers of *Waverley* felt compelled to distinguish it from what Francis Jeffrey called "the whole tribe of ordinary novels")[3], the fiction of the previous century was accorded rather more respect, as in Scott's own essays on his predecessors. And the highest respect was typically granted to Fielding, more particularly to *Tom Jones* whose plot Coleridge declared to be one of "the three most perfect plots ever planned."[4] What literary prestige the novel could claim at the beginning of the nineteenth century derived from the example of Fielding who, Scott notes, "had high notions of the dignity of an art which he may be considered to have founded. He challenges a comparison between the Novel and the Epic."[5] Repeatedly, Scott's discussions of fiction invoke Fielding as a model for "a story regularly built and consistent in all its parts" (*Prefaces,* p. 161), so that the very name of Fielding comes to stand for the formal unity which is itself a sign of high literary achievement. "The more closely and happily the story is combined," Scott generalizes in the Preface to *The Monastery* after recalling the "distinguished example" of Fielding, "the nearer such a composition will approach the perfection of the novelist's art" (*Prefaces,* p. 161).

But Scott himself is not interested in this kind of perfection. Throughout his prefatory material, within his novels, and in the *Quarterly* review of his early fiction that he coauthored, Scott draws deliberate and cheerful attention to the failure of his novels to meet the formal standards represented by a novel like *Tom Jones*. So the *Quarterly* article admits that the Waverley Novels lack "a clear and continued narrative," while the introduction to *The Fortunes of Nigel* playfully invokes a "demon" to account for the inevitability with which "the regular mansion" that Scott says he plans turns into "a Gothic anomaly" (*Prefaces*, pp. 14, 49). Yet Scott persists in writing the Gothic anomalies that resist the idea of a regular mansion, and his good-humored admissions of literary culpability serve mainly to underline the difference of his fiction from that to which he ostensibly defers. This is not to doubt Scott's admiration for Fielding; nor is it to suggest that he uses Fielding as a straw man. Rather, it is because Scott finds Fielding so compelling an example of formal literary values that he invokes him, for by doing so he can point to the value of his own fiction as lying outside the kinds of value structures embodied in Fielding.

To be sure, Scott began his novelistic career on a Fieldingesque note. The opening chapter of *Waverley* echoes the emphasis of *Joseph Andrews* on common human nature, as Scott asserts his interest in the typicality of "men" over the particularity of "manners."[6] But the historicity apparent even in these opening pages threatens that hierarchy, and the process of writing the novel finally overturns it. The Postscript concentrates exclusively on "manners" as the focus and motive for the fiction. Scott has discovered his own historicism, and his recognition of its incompatibility with the artfulness that Fielding's universalism encouraged is made clear by the Advertisement to *The Antiquary* where Scott announces that he has been "more solicitous to describe manners minutely, than to arrange . . . an artificial and combined narrative," adding his regret "that I have felt myself unable to unite these two requisites of a good Novel."[7] Quietly Scott abandons the "good novel," simply by choosing not to write one. When Robert Louis Stevenson considered the history of the English novel in 1874, he asserted that the Waverley Novels mark "a great enfranchisement." Significantly, he defined this "enfranchisement" in terms of a difference between Scott and Fielding. With Fielding, Stevenson writes, "the English novel was looking one way and seeking one set of effects," but "in the hands of Scott it was looking eagerly in all ways and searching for all the effects that by any possibility it could utilize" (*CH*, p. 476).

If there is a sense in which Scott's conservative political allegiance to the Hanoverian settlement makes him look one way and turns the Waverley Novels as a whole into one story,[8] his narrative conservatism—that allegiance to traditional story-telling signalled by the early publication of *The Minstrelsy of the Scottish Border*—looks quite another way: to unofficial rather than official history, to the margins rather than the centers of culture. And this more profound conservatism works by contrast to generate difference and irregu-

larity in the fiction through the storyteller's characteristic interest in particularity and singularity, in heterogeneous "manners" rather than homogeneous
"men." Attracted to the "quirks and quiddities" (*Prefaces,* p. 45) that resist the
generalizing impulses of the mind, Scott recognizes early in his first novel
that the energy of his narrative depends not on the power of unified vision
but on the irregular working of an imagination that prompts his pen to
"speedily change from grave to gay, and from description and dialogue to narrative and character" (*Waverley,* ch. 19, p. 172).[9] This imaginative bias lies
behind the decentering that marks the Waverley Novels, that flattening out
of the hero and his story which diverts attention to what Judith Wilt has
called "the brilliant periphery."[10] If (like Wilt) we now read Scott's main plots
with critical interest, his contemporaries typically read past them, ignoring
the implications that we find compelling. For them the Scott plot, moving
easily within the naturalized assumptions of the time, seemed so transparent
as to be hardly a plot at all, and it was the reassurance provided by this invisible plot that allowed Scott and his readers to surrender themselves to the dis-
persiveness that simultaneously challenged that reassurance.[11] With his passive hero Scott effectively empties out the conventional center as the focus of
narrative interest and blocks the centripetal drive of conventional novel reading. But his fiction maintains the categories of center and periphery in much
the same way that Scott's criticism maintains the norm of formal unity. The
Waverley Novels do not redefine periphery as center, just as Scott does not
displace Fielding as norm. They merely make the periphery central to their
reading, and in doing so they define the novel as less a construct of the individual imagination than a product of cultural memory.

The periphery of Scott's fiction typically recollects forgotten or almost forgotten types of historical being and language. Edie Ochiltree of *The Antiquary,*
Baron Bradwardine of *Waverley,* Meg Merrilies of *Guy Mannering*—all are remnants of superseded cultures, and their fictional vitality depends paradoxically
on their historical obsolescence, for Scott's imagination perceives the act of writing as a literal inscription.[12] Premised on the notions of loss and distance that
the idea of preservation implies, Scott's narrative operates disjunctively in that
it places narrator and reader alongside rather than inside the world it seeks to
represent, creating a gap which allows entry into but not fusion with the fictional world. The energy of that world animates both his and our imaginations,
but it remains—always—another world. The narrative thus itself embodies the
doubleness of memory in the sense that memory depends at once on an awareness of time present and of time past. Scott's concern is with the cultural form
of this awareness, and in the Postscript to *Waverley* he traces his concern to his
youthful experience with the alien culture of the Highlanders "of whose ancient
manners," he reports, "I have witnessed the almost total extinction." *Waverley*
was written "for the purpose of preserving" some idea of this vanishing world,
and Scott stresses that his "imaginary scenes" are based on "incidents which I
then received from those who were actors in them" (pp. 476, 44). The Lowland

characters of the novel, he adds, "are drawn from the general habits of the period, of which I have witnessed some remnants in my younger days, and partly gathered from tradition" (p. 477).

The emphasis in the Postscript on the oral concepts of witness and tradition points to the way in which Scott's fiction brings to the bookish, middle-class genre of the novel an older sense of the role of narrative. If Scott's notion of preservation is alien to Fielding (or, for that matter, to Radcliffe), it is quite familiar to the Gaelic bards whom Flora MacIvor calls "the poets and historians of their tribes" (*Waverley,* ch. 22, p. 188). Through his narrative allegiance Scott casts himself in a cultural rather than literary role, making tradition (with its connotations of inheritance and continuity) rather than literary convention (with its systemic overtones) the central category for his fiction. His novels exploit the oral forms of folktale, anecdote, and ballad, and they typically present themselves as compilations made out of bits and pieces of traditional lore. *Old Mortality* defines itself as grounded in the anecdotal, its fictional narrator, Peter Pattieson, claiming to have incorporated "into one compressed narrative" the stories told by the old Covenanter of the title.[13] Even *The Bride of Lammermoor,* frequently seen as atypical in its concentrated action, is typical in the fiction of its composition. Pattieson enters once again, this time to note that he "wove" his tale out of the "scraps" of writing and drawing handed to him by an old school friend.[14] Such strategies tend to locate the value of the fiction in the scraps and anecdotes rather than in the synthesis achieved by the novelistic imagination. That synthesis is not, of course, to be dismissed, but for Scott the fragments remain the reason for and core of the fiction. It is entirely characteristic that in preparing the Magnum Opus edition of his work, Scott should break up the integrity of his narratives by inserting notes at the ends of chapters. The Waverley Novels are not so much Fieldingesque vehicles for independent, enduring truths as historical gestures of cultural recollection, recording evanescent manners and moments whose endurance depends on the fiction. In a suggestive passage in *Waverley,* the narrator comments by means of a negative analogy on the study of family tradition and genealogical history. Such studies, he states, are

> the very reverse of amber, which, itself a valuable substance, usually includes flies, straws, and other trifles; whereas these studies, being themselves very insignificant and trifling, do nevertheless serve to perpetuate a great deal of what is rare and valuable in ancient manners, and to record many curious and minute facts which could have been preserved and conveyed through no other medium. (ch. 4, p. 79)

The passage recalls Scott's view of his own novels: his constant dismissal of them as trifles yet vigorous defence of their historical accuracy and fairness. The very reverse of amber, his narratives derive their value from their status not as artifacts but as acts of transmission.[15] And to so see the novel is to displace the novelist from originator to transmitter in a line of transmitters.

As such, the novelist is mediate and his stories are never final. Scott makes the point of mediation decisively (even excessively) in the editorial frames enclosing his novels and delaying entry into the fictional world. Perhaps the most elaborate of these is to be found in *The Monastery* where Captain Clutterbuck asks the Author of Waverley to edit a manuscript of "genuine Memoirs of the sixteenth century," the Memoirs having been "compiled from authentic materials of the period" by a recently deceased expatriate Scottish monk living in France. Incomplete at his death, the manuscript has been completed by a nephew who has turned the whole thing over to Clutterbuck for correction and editing. But Clutterbuck, bored by the task, now passes it on to the Author. Scott is having fun here, but his fun has a serious point. The tangled story of the manuscript draws attention to transmission as a sliding from sign to sign, and such sliding threatens the stability of truth. "That which was history yesterday," Clutterbuck remarks, "becomes fable today, and the truth of to-day is hatched into a lie by tomorrow."[16] Scott finds in such a perspective cause not for despair but for humility. For all of his confidence and ease in his own world, Scott knows that no version is final and that the important thing is to keep in play the *mélange* of facts, memories, legends, and biases—in short, the stories—that constitute a culture's knowledge about itself.

Scott's texts do this by remaining oddly unfixed *as* texts. With their proliferation of notes, appendices, prefaces, and prefaces to prefaces, they seem to be always open to addition, infinitely expandable as Scott discovers yet one more anecdote, one more fact, one more scrap of folk-lore that he must record. "I cannot help adding a note not very necessary for the reader," he tells us in *Redgauntlet*,[17] and the statement could well preface his notes as a whole, underlining a compulsion to keep adding which has little to do with the ostensible purpose of the documentation to establish the cognitive authority of the fiction. Scott's belief in the cognitive power of fiction was hardly firm, and his documentation, one suspects, represents in but another form the same attraction to the transitory and the fragmentary that marks his story-telling. Here too the desire to preserve is crucial, but Scott's documentary impulse works also to blur the boundary of any particular text by linking it directly to other texts, to Scott's own voice, to the recollections of other voices, to old songs and tales. Unlike the radical realist who seeks to make his words disappear as words, Scott emphasizes the linguistic nature of his medium, for only through words can the realities outside the here and now be recalled to memory and imagination. We live in a "talking world" says Peter Pattieson in the *Bride of Lammermoor* (ch. 1, p. 26), and reality in Scott is always in an important sense a matter of words, as the clash of languages in a novel like *Old Mortality* well illustrates. Scott's own texts, gathering as many words as possible, participate in "this talking world" as themselves a series of words in a historical stream of words with no fixed beginning or end.

Scott's favorite metaphor for the authoring of such texts is that of editor, a conventional motif in the novel from the time of Cervantes. But Scott elaborates the figure to an extraordinary degree in his introductory epistles, and his allegiance to historical tradition invests the metaphor with a literal charge. Uneasy as it often may be, Scott's authorial stance is a deliberate demystification of authorship, of writing as an original and privileged activity. So his notorious self-deprecation, for all its coyness, self-protectiveness, and even complacency, works to rebut literary claims of privilege.[18] Scott's self-conscious Philistinism—his insistence on "harmless amusement" as his goal, his emphasis on literature as a market, his mischievous manipulation of the mask of the Great Unknown—serves to puncture what he sees as the "cant" of art. In his most extended puncturing of "cant"—the Introductory Epistle to *The Fortunes of Nigel*—Scott sets up a debate between the Author of Waverley, who flaunts his commercialism, and Captain Clutterbuck, who stands appalled at an author's recourse to "the language of a calico-manufacturer." Scott's strategy, exemplified most clearly in the Author's economic argument that writers are productive laborers, is to place art inside the social matrix, to make it continuous with rather than different from other daily activities. Suggestively, the Author refuses "to disclaim the ordinary motives, on account of which the whole world around me is toiling unremittingly" (*Prefaces*, p. 55). Even as the Introductory Epistle recognizes that the writing of fiction is finally mysterious (regular mansions turn somehow into Gothic anomalies), it withholds the granting of any special status, and much of the warmth of the nineteenth-century response to Scott reflects his success in so integrating the novel and the novelist into ordinary social process. When the *Athenaeum*, for example, sought to define the particular effect of the Waverley Novels, it invoked the social context of after-dinner story-telling and distinguished Scott's informality from the air of "the professed *littérateur* with himself and his public before his eyes." Scott's novels, the article notes, are remarkable for "a total absence of self-consciousness . . . of a syllable which would seem to insinuate that the author was above his readers, or imagined himself to be engaged in anything very wonderful or splendid" (*CH*, p. 460).

The absence of this kind of "self-consciousness"—Henry James calls *Waverley* the first novel to be "self-forgetful" (*CH*, p. 429)—grows out of the seriousness with which Scott took the metaphor of fiction writer as editor rather than creator. Writing out of a context that identified art with originality and creation, Scott argues on behalf of a profoundly unoriginal art. Working in a genre whose very name defines its sense of itself as novel, Scott proclaims his lack of innovation. The *Quarterly* review stops to question the "originality of these novels in point of invention" and hastens to explain that in so questioning "we do not consider ourselves as derogating from the merit of the author, to whom, on the contrary, we give the praise due to one who has collected and brought out with accuracy and effect, incidents and manners which might otherwise have slept in oblivion" (*Prefaces*, p. 16). Again and again Scott stresses his lack of invention, and this is not simply the realist ploy of denying one's own artfulness but a sign of his commitment to a traditional view of the artist. When Scott says of his mottoes that "I drew on my memory as long as I could, and when that failed eked it out with invention" (*Prefaces,* p. 78), the remark (flippant as it is in context) could well stand at the head of the Waverley Novels which invert the conventional hierarchy of invention and memory to make the latter the energy for the fiction. For Scott writing is less creation than recreation, a type of reading in its widest sense. When Scott calls on the conventional metaphor of the book of nature in *Waverley,* he defines his fiction not as a copy of this "book" (as Fielding does in *Joseph Andrews*) but as a reading. "It is from the great book of Nature," Scott's narrator states, ". . . that I have venturously essayed to read a chapter to the public" (ch. 1, p. 66). The shift from copying to reading involves a subtle but significant shift from mimesis to repetition. Where the concept of mimesis highlights the artist's skill in creating a faithful but independent facsimile, repetition moves into the foreground the dependent status of the art work itself on something outside the artist's control. Copying and reading are both forms of reproduction, but a copy exists alongside the original whereas a reading perpetuates that which it reads. Responding to the kind of fidelity that Scott wanted to suggest through his metaphor of reading, William Hazlitt—himself an unsympathetic reader of Scott—summed up the Scottish novelist's achievement. "He has conversed with the living and the dead," Hazlitt writes, "and let them tell their story in their own way. . . . He is only the amanuensis of truth and history" (*CH,* p. 284).

By defining his authorial role in cultural terms, Scott identifies his resistance to formal unity as a political as much as literary act. Even as Scott supported the Union between Scotland and England, even as he affirmed the centralizing drive of British history, he sought through his fiction to counteract the erasure of difference that they implied. The appeal to cultural memory, Milan Kundera has recently reminded us, is an act of dissent. "The struggle of man against power," Kundera states, "is the struggle of memory against forgetting."[19] Scott, Macaulay shrewdly noted in 1838, made fiction out of "those fragments of truth which historians have scornfully thrown behind them" (*CH,* p. 309), and Scott exploits those discarded fragments in his Scottish fiction to stimulate the memory of his older readers and to create a memory for his younger ones. For Scottish readers, Scott makes clear in the Postscript to *Waverley,* he engages in an act of recovery, while for English readers he seeks to counteract stereotypes of Scotland, citing as an analogue for his effort Maria Edgeworth's undermining of English images of the Irish. It is no accident that *Waverley* is set in precisely the same period as is *Tom Jones.*

But in a more profound sense Scott's fiction acts for all readers as a sign of distinctive cultural memory and, more precisely, as a challenge to the forgetting which makes homogeneity itself a value. Writing out of a marginal culture threatened with absorption, Scott attempts to counter what he calls in the Advertisement to *The Antiquary* "that general polish which assimilates to each other the manners of different nations." In a revealing comment to his friend John Morritt, made shortly after finishing *Waverley,* Scott declared his preference for the conversation of "professional men" whose "peculiarity" of habits and study made them "so different from the people who are rounded and smoothed and ground down for conversation, and who can say all that every other person says—and no more."[20]

Scott's coordination of "rounded," "smoothed," and "ground down" reflects the bias of an imagination nurtured in a world whose peculiarities of historical being were eroding rapidly. "There is no European nation," Scott asserts at the end of *Waverley,* "which, within the course of half a century, or little more, has undergone so complete a change as this kingdom of Scotland" (Postscript, p. 476). Out of this felt awareness comes Scott's celebrated historicism, a historicism whose significance for narrative lies less in its general perception of culture as historical product than in its specific recognition of the sedimentation of a culture at any given historical moment. Interest in the linear implication of Scott's treatment of history has tended to turn attention from the way in which his narratives expose a cultural moment as coherent neither in its evolution nor in the relationship of its parts. Focusing typically on crisis, his novels reveal the fragility (even fictionality) of apparent social and historical coherence. So Henry Morton's journeying in *Old Mortality* uncovers a world of proliferating differences and alarming gaps,[21] its nature figured neatly in a linguistic encounter early in the novel when Lady Margaret's legal understanding of "warrant" comes up against Mause Headrigg's biblical interpretation of "warrant," and the feudal code that had hitherto defined the two women as part of the same world suddenly collapses. Exasperated by Mause's scriptural exegesis, Lady Margaret underscores the impasse that has been revealed with a question: "what had Nebuchadnezzar to do with the wappen-schaw of the Upper Ward of Clydesdale?" (ch. 7, pp. 118–19). Two languages, two versions of reality, confront one another, and no resolution is possible. Theirs is a metonymic relationship in which contiguity signals not the presence but the absence of connection. The world of *Old Mortality* is one in which proximity underlines difference, undercutting assumptions of cultural unity and cohesion. Even within groups identified under a single rubric—the Covenanting clergy are a prime example—differing languages contest the integrity of the notion that contains them.

Old Mortality is a particularly striking example of the representation of culture as obscurely and incoherently layered. But all of Scott's fiction makes the same point, replaying almost obsessively the encounter of Lady Margaret and Mause Headrigg in scenes of linguistic incomprehension, rivalry, and confusion. Replacing Fielding's static notion of ethical contrast with the historical notion of cultural contrast, Scott alters the perception of culture, making his contemporaries aware that singular concepts like culture, nation, and society cover plural realities. It is not just a matter of his reminding them of the difference of the actual present from the past but of his alerting them to the difference within any present. Scott jolted his readers out of their conviction of the unity of a given world, including their own world. One "great source of the interest" of *Waverley,* Francis Jeffrey commented in his review of the novel, is "the surprise that is excited by discovering that in our own country, and almost in our own age, manners and characters existed, and were conspicuous, which we had been accustomed to consider as belonging to remote antiquity, or extravagant romance" (*CH,* pp. 80–81).

By surprising his readers into such recognitions, Scott opened the way for the panoramic social novels of his Victorian successors who absorbed from the Waverley Novels the metonymic narrative method and the sense of the heterogeneity of culture on which their own fiction depends. Transferring his insights to the study of contemporary society, the Victorian novelists created the "loose baggy monsters" that so offended Henry James.[22] It is less to *Romola, Henry Esmond,* and *A Tale of Two Cities* than to *Middlemarch, The Newcomes,* and *Our Mutual Friend* that we should look for the impact of Walter Scott.[23] As Robert Louis Stevenson rightly saw, Scott's significance lies in his "enfranchisement" of the novel, Stevenson's political metaphor (with its double sense of liberating and endowing with civil privilege) pointing to the cultural model of fiction, rooted in a return to story, through which Scott renewed the novel for the nineteenth century.

Notes

1. *Walter Scott: The Making of the Novelist* (Toronto: University of Toronto Press, 1984), p. x.

2. *Aspects of the Novel* (New York: Harcourt, Brace, 1926), p. 26. All references to Forster are to this work and will hereafter be included in the text by page number.

3. *Scott: The Critical Heritage,* ed. John O. Hayden (New York: Barnes & Noble, 1970), p. 790. Cited hereafter as *CH* in the text.

4. "Table Talk," 5 July 1834, quoted in Frederick T. Blanchard, *Fielding the Novelist: A Study of the Novelist's Fame and Influence* (New Haven: Yale U. Press, 1926), p. 161.

5. *The Prefaces to the Waverley Novels,* ed. Mark A. Weinstein (Lincoln: U. of Nebraska Press, 1978), p. 45.

6. *Waverley* (London: Dent, 1969), p. 64. See also Henry Fielding, *Joseph Andrews and Shamela,* ed. Martin C. Battestin (Boston: Houghton Mifflin, 1961), Bk 3, ch. 1, p. 159.

7. *The Antiquary* (London: Dent, 1907), p. 1.

8. The most influential study of Scott from this point of view is Alexander Welsh, *The Hero of the Waverley Novels* (New Haven: Yale U. Press, 1963). For a counterargument to Welsh, see Harry E. Shaw's recent, *The Forms of Historical Fiction: Sir Walter Scott and His Successors* (Ithaca: Cornell U. Press, 1983). Shaw's emphasis on diversity in Scott's fiction accords with mine but grows out of a more specific interest in the problem of writing historical novels.

9. For a contrasting emphasis on the "drive for uniformity" in *Waverley,* see Richard L. Stein, "Historical Fiction and the Implied Reader: Scott and Iser," *Novel,* 14 (1981), 213–23.

10. "Steamboat Surfacing: Scott and the English Novelists,"*NCF,* 35 (1981), 461. Wilt contends that the identification of Scott's fiction with this "brilliant periphery" by later novelists constitutes a "psychodrama of sublimation and misreading."

11. George Levine argues that Scott's confidence in the intelligibility of history provided the security that allowed him to present "the muddles, the contrasts, the variousness of the simple facts of everyday life," *The Realistic Imagination* (Chicago and London: Chicago U. Press, 1981), p. 96.

12. See Sibyl Jacobson, "The Narrative Framing of History: A Discussion of *Old Mortality*," *JNT*, 1 (1971), 179–92.

13. *Old Mortality*, ed. Angus Calder (Harmondsworth: Penguin, 1974), p. 68.

14. *The Bride of Lammermoor* (London: Dent, 1906), p. 26.

15. In an article pertinent to this paper, Joseph Kestner argues that Scott's novels are studies of oral transmission. "Linguistic Transmission in Scott: *Waverley, Old Mortality, Rob Roy,* and *Redgauntlet*," *Wordsworth Circle,* 8 (1977), 333–47.

16. *The Monastery* (London: Dent, 1906), p. 26.

17. *Redgauntlet* (London: Dent, 1906), p. 446.

18. For an argument that Scott's playful authorial stance represents an ultimately debilitating unwillingness to take seriously the creative imagination, see Levine, *The Realistic Imagination,* pp. 81–93.

19. *The Book of Laughter and Forgetting,* trans. Michael Henry Heim (Harmondsworth: Penguin, 1981), p. 3.

20. J. G. Lockhart, *The Life of Sir Walter Scott, Bart.* 2 vols. (London: Caxton, n.d.), 1, 217–18.

21. See Shaw, *The Forms of Historical Fiction,* pp. 189–205 for a discussion of the sense of history in *Old Mortality* as one of "exclusion, loss, chaos." For Shaw this view of history stands counter to Scott's characteristic "rich, genial sense of historical memory."

22. Preface to *The Tragic Muse,* rpt. in Henry James, *The Art of the Novel* (New York: Scribner's, 1934), p. 84.

23. The standard analysis of the Victorian response to Scott remains J. H. Raleigh, "What Scott Meant to the Victorians," *VS,* 7 (1963), 7–34. For an approach to Victorian fiction that stresses its challenge to traditional notions of unity, see Peter K. Garrett, *The Victorian Multiplot Novel* (New Haven: Yale U. Press, 1980).

Scott's "Daemon"
and the Voices of Historical Narration

HARRY E. SHAW

In a mock-defense of his work as a novelist, Walter Scott laments his inability to keep to a single narrative thread and plan, blaming the problem on a "daemon who seats himself on the feather of my pen when I begin to write, and leads it astray from the purpose."[1] Scott, like many other self-deprecators, betrays at least as much self-satisfaction as remorse when he makes such comments: he glories in the imaginative fecundity that leads him and his stories astray. Perhaps this is why he tends to exaggerate his undeniable carelessness in composing. Scholarship, never content to take an author at his word, has recently hailed Scott as a "great reviser," which he sometimes was; in any event, we are beginning to realize that his narrative discontinuities may arise from causes more interesting than simple carelessness.[2] In what follows, I shall begin with a moment during which we can observe, thanks to the survival of the manuscript of *The Heart of Midlothian*, Scott's "daemon" at work, altering his narrative plans in mid-course. This moment has its own intrinsic interest; it also has larger implications concerning the representation of consciousness and the nature of realism in prose fiction. Even a "daemon" may work under constraints, and Scott's is hardly so erratic as he would have us believe. If we look carefully at Scott's revision, we shall discover that a set of tacit norms, based upon a recognizable vision of history and of the individual, guides its course. My purpose is to reveal these norms and to assess their significance.

In the fourth volume of *The Heart of Midlothian*, Jeanie Deans receives a letter from her sister Effie. Earlier in the novel, its readers will recall, Effie had disgraced herself and her family by bearing an illegitimate child, who mysteriously disappeared. Her lover turns out to be a wealthy English nobleman, Sir George Staunton; he subsequently marries her under circumstances that hide their indiscretion. But after they have been married for a number of years, the secret threatens to unravel. Effie must warn her sister against inadvertently betraying her; after years of ignoring Jeanie, Effie writes her a letter,

From *JEGP* 88 (1989): 21–33. Copyright 1989 by the Board of Trustees of the University of Illinois. Used with permission from the University of Illinois Press.

enclosing in it a fifty-pound note. Jeanie finds the letter moving but offensive. It is galling to learn that her erring sister has risen, in her new identity as Lady Staunton, to social eminence in London. It is insulting to receive the letter after years of silence, and only because Effie is worried that her mask will slip. It is annoying to be given fifty pounds as something very like a bribe. In the printed versions of the novel, Jeanie worries over the letter, wondering if she can show it to her clergyman husband but then realizing she can't, for fear of exposing Effie; and finally deciding that she had best keep the money. Her meditations are described in the following manner:

> Next morning . . . Mrs. Butler anew deliberated upon communicating to her husband her sister's letter. But she was deterred by the recollection, that in doing so she would unveil to him the whole of a dreadful secret, of which, perhaps, his public character might render him an unfit depositary. Butler already had reason to believe that Effie had eloped with that same Robertson who had been a leader in the Porteous mob, and who lay under sentence of death for the robbery at Kirkaldy. But he did not know his identity with George Staunton, a man of birth and fortune, who had now apparently re-assumed his natural rank in society. Jeanie had respected Staunton's own confession as sacred, and upon reflection she considered the letter of her sister as equally so, and resolved to mention the contents to no one.
>
> On re-perusing the letter, she could not help observing the staggering and unsatisfactory condition of those who have risen to distinction by undue paths, and the outworks and bulwarks of fiction and falsehood, by which they are under the necessity of surrounding and defending their precarious advantages. But she was not called upon, she thought, to unveil her sister's original history—it would restore no right to any one, for she was usurping none—it would only destroy her happiness, and degrade her in the public estimation. Had she been wise, Jeanie thought she would have chosen seclusion and privacy, in place of public life and gaiety; but the power of choice might not be hers. The money she thought could not be returned without seeming haughty and unkind. She resolved, therefore, upon re-considering this point, to employ it as occasion should serve, either in educating her children better than her own means could compass, or for their future portion. Her sister had enough, was strongly bound to assist Jeanie by any means in her power, and the arrangement was so natural and proper, that it ought not to be declined out of fastidious or romantic delicacy. Jeanie accordingly wrote to her sister, acknowledging her letter, and requesting to hear from her as often as she could.[3]

Ever since its publication, the fourth volume of *The Heart of Midlothian* has received a bad press: this passage suggests some of the reasons why. It is certainly objectionable to find Jeanie smugly shuddering at "the staggering and unsatisfactory condition of those who have risen to distinction by undue paths." Such a platitude, expressed in an entirely uninteresting variety of eighteenth-century genteel English, is not what we hear from Jeanie in earlier volumes, where her language and moral consciousness represent a rich synthesis of the possibilities of Scottish culture at a certain historical moment. Some have complained that in the fourth volume, Jeanie's "subjective world-view expands to take over the action."[4] (The model for such complaints must surely be F. R. Leavis's celebrated analysis of what goes wrong with *Middlemarch*.) Something rather different occurs in this passage. Jeanie's consciousness doesn't dominate; a bloodless, culturally alien translation of that consciousness suddenly appears, obscuring Jeanie herself. Not entirely, even here: as she talks herself out of returning the money to Effie, we can imagine that at least a watered-down version of Cameronian casuistry guides her. But enough offends in the sentence to make us aware that something is amiss. The voice that expresses Jeanie's thoughts is not her voice.

If we look at the manuscript version of the passage, we discover whose voice it is:

> Next morning . . . Mrs. Butler communicated to her husband her sister's letter. He read it over with a great deal of attention and called upon his wife to notice the staggering and unsatisfactory condition of those who have risen to distinction by undue paths and the outworks and bulwarks of fiction and falsehood by which they are under the necessity of surrounding their precarious advantages. But we are not called upon to unveil your sister's original history—it would restore no right to any one for she is usurping none—it would only destroy her happiness and degrade her in the public estimation. Had she been wise she would have chosen seclusion and privacy in place of public life and gaiety—but the choice may not be hers—The money he thought could not be returned without seeming haughty and unkind—Mrs. Butler ought to employ it in the educating their children better than his own means could compass or save it for their future portion. Her sister had enough was strongly bound to assist Jeanie by any means in her power and the arrangement was so natural and proper that it ought not to be declined. Jeanie accordingly wrote to her sister acknowledging her letter and requesting to hear from her as often as she could.[5]

As originally written, this passage embodies just those qualities lacking in the revised version. The sentiments and mode of expression that sit oddly with Jeanie fit her husband, an enlightened minister of the Kirk of Scotland. The tone and content of the passage further his general function in the fourth volume of the novel, in which he acts as the voice of the future, a role he plays when he refuses to countenance his father-in-law's sterner version of the Presbyterian faith and thereby saves an old woman from prosecution as a witch. Yet, as always in Scott, this growth in humanity, though admirable, is not without its drawbacks, here registered in Butler's solemnity as he works toward a conclusion from which his family will reap financial gain.

Scott originally wrote the passage we have been considering in a way that reflected his conception of Jeanie Deans and Reuben Butler as characters and historical representatives. But he quickly altered course, deciding that it would be better if Jeanie kept the letter a secret.[6] An author who strongly objected to wasting words already committed to paper, he revised his manuscript by making the minimum number of corrections and additions necessary to effect this change. In the process, he transformed into Jeanie's unspoken thoughts material he had originally intended to be the spoken language of her husband. Why did Scott make this revision? If Jeanie keeps the letter secret, he can create in the following chapter a kind of scene he relishes. Jeanie continues to receive the money from her sister for a number of years, saves it in a Bible she hides in a jar (or "pigg") in her cupboard, and produces it for her astounded husband when he wants to buy additional land for their farm. Their discussion of this miracle draws a pleasing contrast between the cultivated minister (whose excitement at seeing the money nevertheless causes him to drop into the Scots of "siller" before he recovers his urbane mode of speech) and his down-to-earth wife:

> "How on earth came ye by that siller, Jeanie?—Why, here is more than a thousand pounds," said Butler, lifting up and counting the notes. . . . "And I positively must not ask you how you have come by all this money?" said the clergyman.
>
> "Indeed, Reuben, you must not; for if you were asking me very sair I wad maybe tell you, and then I am sure I would do wrong."
>
> "But tell me," said Butler, "is it any thing that distresses your own mind?"
>
> "There is baith weal and woe come aye wi' warld's gear, Reuben; but ye maun ask me naething mair—This siller binds me to naething, and can never be speered back again."
>
> "Surely," said Mr. Butler, when he had again counted over the money, as if to assure himself that the notes were real, "there was never man in the world had a wife like mine—a blessing seems to follow her."
>
> "Never," said Jeanie, "since the enchanted princess in the bairns' fairy tale, that kamed gold nobles out o' the tae side of her haffit locks, and Dutch dollars out o' the tother. But gang away now, minister, and put by the siller, and dinna keep the notes wampishing in your hand that gate, or I will wish them in the brown pigg again, for fear we get a black cast about them—we're ower near the hills in these times to be thought to hae siller in the house. And, besides, ye maun gree wi' Knockdunder, that has the selling o' the lands; and dinna you be simple and let him ken o' this windfa', but keep him to the very lowest penny, as if ye had to borrow siller to make the price up."
>
> In the last admonition Jeanie showed distinctly, that, although she did not understand how to secure the money which came into her hands otherwise than by saving and hoarding it, yet she had some part of her father David's shrewdness, even upon worldly subjects. And Reuben Butler was a prudent man, and went and did even as his wife had advised him. (IV, 256—59)

The difference between Jeanie and Reuben, nowhere clearer than in the contrast between her Scots and his English, is finely noted here, and the greater substantiality of Jeanie, felt throughout the passage, is amusingly underlined by the Biblical phraseology with which it closes. Yet even for Jeanie, religion has felt the touch of worldliness; no longer will it spur action that transcends the social fabric but might also destroy it. As in the earlier passage, we recognize that far from dominating the fourth volume of the novel, Jeanie has become integrated into the social life it depicts, though she still maintains her saliency. Scott's instinct in revising to make this scene possible was sound, even if the form his revision took was less than ideal.

But was the form of this revision simply a result of Scott's celebrated haste and sloppiness? When he transformed Butler's speeches into Jeanie's thoughts, why did he not pause for a moment to render those thoughts in language more characteristic of her? I hope to show that this task would have been far from simple. His revision was partially guided by his normal conventions in representing consciousness; to follow them completely would have meant recasting the passage from beginning to end. A closer look at those conventions and their underlying assumptions turns out to have unexpectedly broad implications concerning the depiction of thought in fiction and even the nature of realism itself.

Jeanie's inner debate about whether she should reveal her sister's letter, as it appears in the printed version of the novel, takes the form of indirect discourse, tagged with such phrases as "she thought." Certain sentences, however, begin to move toward "free indirect discourse,"[7] as in the following passage: "But she was not called upon, she thought, to unveil her sister's original history—it would restore no right to any one, for she was usurping none—it would only destroy her happiness, and degrade her in the public estimation. Had she been wise, Jeanie thought she would have chosen seclusion and privacy, in place of public life and gaiety; but the power of choice might not be hers. The money she thought . . ." But nothing approaching free indirect discourse is achieved for very long here: it is as if the narrator is positively resisting the tendency of Jeanie's thoughts to enter this mode. The effect of all the reminders that Jeanie "thought" this or that is to suggest that we are listening to a *summary* of her thoughts, not to her *thinking* those thoughts: the reminders distance us from her thoughts, robbing them of the immediacy we would feel in true free indirect discourse.[8] Why does the narrator pull us back in this way? The answer is that Jeanie is a vernacular speaker. Even in the haste of imperfect revision, Scott's ear tells him that such a character's thoughts ought not to be rendered in free indirect discourse. But why?

Free indirect discourse is sometimes said to provide an ideal medium for conveying the idiolect of individual characters. But free indirect discourse can also tend toward a linguistic universality, or at least a class-based, "standard English" simulacrum of linguistic universality, as in Virginia Woolf. Thus free indirect discourse would appear to have the potentiality of moving in two different directions: one thick with particularistic and objective saliency, the other transparent, tending to merge with our own thoughts and the voice in which we think them. The former has the authenticity of a dialect we do not share; the latter promises to make palpable the way in which thought, all thought including our own thought, in very fact occurs.

If free indirect discourse can assume two opposite forms, these forms are in important respects unequal. Since the conventions of novel-writing tend to valorize genteel, literate narration, linguistic otherness can easily come to imply cultural inferiority. Represented thought couched in the idiom of the lower classes, for instance, runs the risk of appearing quaint and therefore trivial. To be sure, some modern authors avoid this problem: Dos Passos, whose novels are full of thought represented in idioms drawn from the most varied social positions, is a case in point.[9] But with an author like Dos Passos, we are aware of a certain stretching of the rules, because we inevitably read his works through our knowledge of the novelistic tradition in general. We interpret this stretching as an ideological statement: that characters are allowed to think in nonstandard English constitutes a political statement, an act of partisanship.

When we read novels, our sense of linguistic norms and proprieties is in constant play, resonating with presuppositions arising from age, from gender, and even from geographical situation, but perhaps centrally from social class.[10] Our sense of what is natural and proper in language comes in the first instance from our own cultural situations, but, as the example of Dos Passos indicates, it can be significantly modulated by the rhetoric of a work itself. For Scott, modulating linguistic presuppositions becomes a tricky problem indeed. Scott, as a historicist and particularist, wishes to create readers receptive to a wide range of dialects from the past. Yet the piquancy of such dialects arises in part from their difference from ours, and difference can always evoke condescension. Scott's ultimate aim is not simply to record history, but to make us accept as natural and inevitable, though regrettable, the movement from past to present. A proclivity to interpret linguistic difference as cultural inferiority can further such an aim. We will tend to accept the present as natural and inevitable because its speakers sound like us ("us" being the genteel readers implied by literary tradition), while those of the past do not.

The conflict between a wish to celebrate particularities in the past, interesting precisely because they are separated from us, and a wish to ratify the shape history has taken in producing the present, pervades Scott's fiction. This conflict makes itself felt with particular urgency in the various voices that enter Scott's novels, the voices of narration, spoken monologue and dialogue, and represented thought.[11] All these voices interact with one another, helping to create the set of conventions by which we read a Scott novel, and registering the ideology underlying those conventions. The presence of the medley of narrators and narrative frames informing *The Heart of Midlothian* may thus be explained as an attempt at once to value past uniqueness but also to privilege the voice of the present. In *The Heart of Midlothian,* historical specificity and cultural uniqueness are represented by the dramatized narrators Jedediah Cleishbotham and Peter Pattieson (respectively a stage Scotsman and a Man of Feeling), but the narrative presence soon settles into the recognizably "modern" voice of the Author of Waverley.[12] To be sure, the voices of Cleishbotham and Pattieson create a decorum in which we are more receptive to the culturally alien spoken language of Jeanie Deans. But there are limits to the part a Cleishbotham or Pattieson can play in narrating one of Scott's novels.

The depiction of speech and thought in Scott's novels shares the divided priorities guiding his choice of narrators. His genteel heroes and heroines link present readers with the past, partly through the language they speak, which echoes "modern" language. Yet in so doing they must avoid complete detachment from the world of the past. In one of many partial solutions to this problem, they voice their thoughts in set speeches that resemble nothing so much as stage soliloquies. The language of such speeches tends to be recognizably genteel and "modern," despite an overlay of tushery in novels, like *The Fortunes of Nigel,* which are set in the Renaissance or before. But imagining the voice of a character like Nigel filling a room in a seventeenth-century London lodging ties his language to the past as a matter of readerly experience, though hardly of logic. The vibrations of the voice we imagine connect the character with the scene we imagine, by simple metonymical juxtaposition.

When we hear a protagonist like Nigel voicing predominantly "modern" sentiments as he paces his seventeenth-century chamber (reflecting as he does so a "modern" view of Shakespearean soliloquizers like Hamlet), his thoughts nonetheless blend with the period setting. The overt use of theatrical artifice itself encourages an active, self-conscious mode of reading that invites us to sustain the effort necessary to imagine Nigel as existing in the past, instead of merging his world with ours. A less-stylized mode of representation would lose touch with the past more easily, would mingle more directly with thoughts of the present and therefore run the risk of being overwhelmed by them. The goal of a historicist mode of representation like Scott's is not to attempt the impossible task of insulating the past from the interests and determinations of the present, but to make possible a dialogue between past and present, by staving off the demands of the present for an imaginative moment. Scott seeks to create a space in which the past can emerge, before present interests reassert themselves.

Scott does not limit his use of soliloquies to genteel characters whose language and values resemble ours. In a passage which occurs shortly before the scene of the overhasty revision with which we began, he portrays Jeanie Deans's reaction to her sister's letter in a characteristic way:

What Jeanie least liked in the tone of the letter was a smothered degree of egotism. "We should have heard little about her," said Jeanie to herself, "but that she was feared the Duke might come to learn wha she was, and a' about her puir friends here; but Effie, puir thing, aye looks her ain way, and folks that do that think mair o' themselves than of their neighbours.—I am no clear about keeping her siller," she added, taking up a 50 l. note which had fallen out of the paper to the floor. "We hae aneugh, and it looks unco like theft-boot, or hush-money, as they ca' it. . . ." (IV, 230)

Scott's eagerness to give Jeanie's Scots the form of direct speech is amusingly apparent here, as she herself improbably glosses a word likely to puzzle an English reader ("theft-boot, or hush-money, as they ca' it"). Her voiced thoughts recall the soliloquies of Scott's genteel protagonists, but with a difference: here, Jeanie's own language resonates with just the cultural and historical specificity the setting must provide for the spoken thoughts of Nigel.

Represented thought in Scott takes forms other than soliloquy. The free indirect discourse the narrator resists in the case of Jeanie Deans, he more willingly employs to record the thoughts of her brother-in-law, Sir George Staunton. Staunton is a genteel character who inhabits a novel set much closer to the present than *The Fortunes of Nigel:* his "modern" language is therefore less likely to detach him from his historical period.[13] The following passage is notable for its lack of intrusive tagged references reminding us that Staunton is thinking this or that:

> Whatever might be Sir George Staunton's feelings in ripping up this miserable history, and listening to the tragical fate of the unhappy girl whom he had ruined, he had so much of his ancient wilfulness of disposition left, as to shut his eyes on every thing, save the prospect which seemed to open itself of recovering his son. It was true it would be difficult to produce him, without telling much more of the history of his birth, and the misfortunes of his parents, than it was prudent to make known. But let him once be found, and, being found, let him but prove worthy of his father's protection, and many ways might be fallen upon to avoid such risk. Sir George Staunton was at liberty to adopt him as his heir, if he pleased, without communicating the secret of his birth; or an act of parliament might be obtained, declaring him legitimate, and allowing him the name and arms of his father. He was, indeed, already a legitimate child according to the law of Scotland, by the subsequent marriage of his parents. (IV, 312–13)

Yet even here, the language that renders thought is not quite presented as the language of thought. Free indirect discourse characteristically combines, in proportions difficult to gauge, the idiolect of a character with the language characteristic of the narrative voice. Here yet another language supervenes, that of judicial summary and parliamentary report—the language Scott used in drawing up the summaries of judicial opinions that were his professional business as clerk of the Court of Session. This voice in Scott is usually submerged, though available to us if we are looking for it; it reasserts itself in an amusingly direct way when the right topic arises, as it does toward the end of the passage I've just quoted, with its discussion of the technicalities of legitimation.[14]

In introducing the language of law in this manner, Scott is focusing on social codes and conventions. Relatively uninterested in what the novels that followed him have taught us to consider the inner life, he tends to conceive of consciousness as existing at the intersection between the individual and larger social systems, as located, so to speak, from the skin outward, not from the skin inward. (This helps make set speeches appear to Scott a natural medium for what we would call "inner" thoughts.) Thus even genteel language is unlikely in Scott to seem entirely natural or fully transparent, in the sense of lacking social and historical mediation. When we hear George Staunton's thoughts merging with the language of judicial summary, we hear the law of a specific culture at a specific time speaking through him. We feel at such moments Scott's text resisting the promotion of any language to an ahistorical, universal, and natural status, even though the novel's larger rhetorical force depends upon just such merging and promotion. We feel, in short, the manifestation of an ideological contradiction with deep cultural resonances, scarcely resolvable within the confines of the work itself.

The voice of judicial or parliamentary summary is present in a mode of representing thought we have not yet considered. This mode provides a summary of the thoughts of a character, in a medley of reportorial forms (including direct descriptions, assertions that the character thought or felt something, and language approaching free indirect discourse but surrounded by the language of judicial summary), but it also includes reminders, direct and indirect, of the character's vernacular speech. This mixture of modes directs us to create a voice for the content of a character's thoughts, to imagine that we are hearing those thoughts in the vernacular—or at least to assume that they were or could be thought in the vernacular. In the process, the vernacular loses its potentially comic or quaint nature: because we imagine its possibility but do not hear its actuality, it gains the respectability and naturalness of our own inner language. If my own experience is any guide, a reader tends to remember such passages *as* free indirect discourse in the vernacular, but in turning to the text discovers they are nothing of the kind.

An inner debate, of which I shall quote only a small part, concerning whether Jeanie Deans should save her sister by betraying Staunton, exemplifies this technique.

> Jeanie, in the strict and severe tone of morality in which she was educated, had to consider not only the general aspect of a proposed action, but its justness and fitness in relation to the actor, before she could be, according to her own phrase, free to enter upon it. What right had she to make a barter between the lives of Staunton and of Effie, and to sacrifice the one for the safety of the other? His guilt—that guilt for which he was amenable to the laws—was a crime against the public indeed, but it was not against her.

> Neither did it seem to her that his share in the death of Porteous, though her mind revolted at the idea of using violence to any one, was in the relation of a common murder, against the perpetrator of which every one is called to aid the public magistrate. . . . With the fanaticism of the Scotch presbyterians, there was always mingled a glow of national feeling, and Jeanie trembled at the idea of her name being handed down to posterity with that of the "fause Monteath," and one or two others, who, having deserted and betrayed the cause of their country, are damned to perpetual remembrance and execration among its peasantry. Yet, to part with Effie's life once more, when a word spoken might save it, pressed severely on the mind of her affectionate sister.
>
> "The Lord support and direct me," said Jeanie, "for it seems to be his will to try me with difficulties far beyond my ain strength."
>
> While this thought passed through Jeanie's mind, her guard, tired of silence, began to show some inclination to be communicative. (III, 247–50)

The skill with which Scott here entices us to re-create in our own minds the movements of Jeanie's, to imagine them as having a separate but valid existence in a language alien to us, is remarkable. With such a passage, we seem to have reached a utopian state for the rendering of consciousness in historical fiction, where the claims of historical otherness can be fully registered and respected, because they are asserted in a voice produced by the reader. In fact, we haven't quite arrived at the promised land, we've only glimpsed it. For as we have seen, though we feel that Jeanie's mode of thought has dignity, we do not perceive it directly, much less share in it substantially. What we imagine is in the end a *structure*, a set of interlocking potentialities sufficient to create the thought of a character like Jeanie, not the substantiality of that thought, which because of its very historical difference must always essentially elude us.

Scott's practices and cross-purposes in rendering the thought of fictional characters have significant implications for our understanding of the realist novel. Critics have grown increasingly suspicious of the ideological baggage accompanying what once seemed the purely esthetic norms of Jamesian criticism, with its valorization of organic form, a disappearing narrator, and a strictly controlled point of view. The example of Scott can do nothing but deepen such suspicions. James himself once referred to the works of Scott as partaking in "l'enfance de l'art." We began by noticing an example of what appeared to be childishly careless revision, and such lapses are doubtless unfortunate. But there are moments when the child is father of the man. It is precisely by what would seem according to Jamesian standards a heavy-handed intrusiveness in narrative presence, a carelessness concerning consistency of point-of-view, and an attitude toward form better suited to a *bricoleur* than a craftsman, that Scott is able to make room for the representation of the past at all, and to imply the historicity of what in James might pose as the timeless, natural language of thought itself. Scott's practice, here and elsewhere, reminds us that realism in the novel is never a matter of what is inaccurately called a "photographic" immediacy, but instead always involves the self-conscious creation of a model of reality—or, perhaps more accurately, the creation of an audibly creaking machine for producing a simulation of the underlying workings of reality, which machine can work only in creative complicity with readers having access to the cultural tradition whose reality it seeks to capture. Since the reality with which realism is concerned is cultural and historical in nature, the central task of realism is not to produce organic form but to engage in the messier business of creating imaginative clearings in which reality can fitfully and fleetingly emerge, as it emerges when we nearly hear Jeanie Deans's historical voice and thereby nearly experience the cultural moment on which that voice depends.

Notes

1. "Introductory Epistle" to *The Fortunes of Nigel* (Edinburgh: Constable, 1822), I, xxvi.

2. On Scott as a reviser, see Mary Lascelles, "Scott and the Art of Revision," in her *Notions and Facts* (London: Oxford Univ. Press, 1972), pp. 213–29; G. A. M. Wood, "The Great Reviser; or the Unknown Scott," ARIEL, 2 (1971), 27–44; and Philip Gaskell, *From Writer to Reader* (London: Oxford Univ. Press, 1978), ch. 5. On the causes and significance of discontinuity in Scott's fiction, see Harry E. Shaw, *The Forms of Historical Fiction: Sir Walter Scott and His Successors* (Ithaca: Cornell Univ. Press, 1983).

3. I quote from the first edition of *The Heart of Midlothian,* which appeared as *Tales of My Landlord: Second Series* (Edinburgh: Constable, 1818), IV, 235–37; subsequent references appear in my text.

4. David Brown, *Walter Scott and the Historical Imagination* (London: Routledge and Kegan Paul, 1979), p. 124; Brown gives references to earlier critical commentary along the same lines.

5. This passage appears on leaf 287 of Scott's autograph manuscript of *The Heart of Midlothian* (National Library of Scotland MS. 1548). I am grateful to the Trustees of the National Library of Scotland for access to this manuscript and for permission to quote from it. Most of the longer revisions occur, as is usual with Scott, on the back of the previous leaf. In my text, I give Scott's initial attempt at revision. Scott in fact made further changes in the manuscript; the final version as it appears in manuscript is identical with that of the first edition, with the following exceptions, probably introduced in proof (I give first the version of the first edition, then that of the manuscript, and I do not note variants in spelling and punctuation): 1. "Butler already had reason to believe that Effie had eloped" / "He knew indeed that Effie had eloped as was believed"; 2. "robbery at Kirkaldy" / "robbery of Kirkaldy"; 3. after "re-assumed his natural rank in society," the manuscript continues: "He did not know this fact and no good could come to any one from imparting it to him"; 4. "to employ it as occasion should serve, either in educating her children better than her own means could compass, or for their future portion" / "to employ it in the educating her children better than his own means could compass, or to save it for their future portion."

6. Throughout the manuscript, the colors of ink employed suggest that Scott revised passages during the same writing session in which he created them.

7. For a useful survey of recent work on free indirect discourse, as well as a summary of the various names this stylistic feature has been given, see Brian McHale, "Free Indirect Discourse: A Survey of Recent Accounts," *PTL,* 3 (1978), 249–87.

8. It is an old complaint that Scott's depiction of character fails to capture the movements of the mind. As we shall see, this aspect of Scott's depiction of character involves rather more than simple omission.

9. I owe the example of Dos Passos to McHale.

10. Despite her reliance on the presocial and prehistorical framework provided by deep linguistic structures and her eschewal of the notion that free indirect discourse can be thought of as embodied in a voice, Ann Banfield has some interesting things to say about the class resonances of free indirect discourse—see *Unspeakable Sentences* (Boston: Routledge and Kegan Paul, 1982), pp. 250–53.

11. For a stimulating recent discussion of the narrative voices in Scott, see David Daiches, "Scott's *Waverley:* The Presence of the Author," in *Nineteenth-Century Scottish Fiction,* ed. Ian Campbell (New York: Barnes and Noble, 1979), pp. 6–17. The most thorough study to date of Scott's language, Graham Tulloch, *The Language of Walter Scott* (London: Andre Deutsch, 1980), points out that vernacular never enters the Author of Waverley's narrative voice; he concludes that this implies a demotion of vernacular speech, the kind of demotion I am arguing Scott employs for rhetorical ends.

12. The need to put "modern" in quotation marks points to further complexities. All narrators tend to become "period" narrators with the passage of time. I believe, however, that literary tradition and the conventions of novel-reading tend to make us view such narrators in a mode of connection and transparency: we may feel in their voices a period style, but we never impute to them the kind of historical difference we impute to a character like Jeanie Deans, unless the author has taken special pains to create such an effect. (In my own discussion, as the reader will have realized, I am calling "modern" the genteel state of society Scott imagined himself as inhabiting and wished to make his audience accept as inevitable.)

13. Staunton is of course closer to the genteel present than Jeanie, because of his class affiliation.

14. Roy Pascal's interesting analysis of a passage of free indirect discourse rendering Jeanie Deans's thoughts is in my view vitiated by his failure to recognize within it the presence of this language of judicial summary: see *The Dual Voice: Free Indirect Speech and Its Functioning in the Nineteenth-Century European Novel* (Manchester: Manchester Univ. Press, 1977), pp. 48–49. Pascal is troubled that Jeanie's thoughts include an adage in the past tense ("necessity had no law"), but for the language of judicial summary, a past-tense adage is perfectly in order. The passage Pascal cites embodies, I believe, an extension of the technique of incorporating in judicial summary echoes of a character's idiolect. Here, the translation is close to the original, so that we hear something like Jeanie's vernacular "needcessity" behind "necessity."

"By No Means an Improbable Fiction":
Redgauntlet's Novel Historicism

ROHAN MAITZEN

Sir Walter Scott . . . has used those fragments of truth which historians have scornfully thrown behind them in a manner which may well excite their envy," Macaulay observed in 1828, "But a truly great historian would reclaim those materials which the novelist has appropriated."[1] Scott's novel *Redgauntlet,* published in 1824, anticipates this objection to his fiction as a usurpation of material properly exhibited by historians. *Redgauntlet* celebrates narrative but foregrounds problems of historical composition, from the potential unreliability of sources to the subjectivity inherent in their interpretation; these issues alone make *Redgauntlet* particularly pertinent in the early nineteenth century, when historiography as a discipline was becoming increasingly self-conscious. But the elaborate mixture of fact and fancy in *Redgauntlet,* itself the story of an event that never took place, complicates its critique of historiography by insistently worrying the distinctions between historical and fictional narratives on which arguments like Macaulay's depend. Unlike Macaulay, Scott does not claim that history and fiction should be mutually exclusive but that, at the level of narrative, this distinction is impossible to sustain—and that even at the level of reference any representation of the past may benefit from its dissolution. Refusing a teleological or deterministic philosophy of history, *Redgauntlet* presents a complex and heterogeneous vision of the past, not as the triumphant linear progression towards the present so dear to Whig historians, but as the interspersion and collision of disparate desires and ambitions.[2] Some of these emerge as the constituent events of 'what actually happened,' but at the inevitable expense of alternative possibilities which, though equally real, are never realized. In the novel, a lost or aborted desire plays itself out in a project at once historical and imaginative, and in the process *Redgauntlet* proposes a special role for fiction in historical understanding, a move with implications Macaulay's defensiveness begins to foreshadow.[3]

In his essay "Narrative Form as Cognitive Instrument," Louis Mink proposes that "narrative is the form in which we make comprehensible the many

From *Studies in the Novel* 25 (Summer 1993): 170–83. Copyright 1993 by University of North Texas. Reprinted by permission of the publisher.

successive interrelationships that are comprised by a career." From his perspective, narrative is not a limiting and limited form, as some contemporary
discourse suggests; rather, it stands as "a primary and irreducible form of
human comprehension."[4] Throughout, *Redgauntlet* explores and appreciates
this power of narrative to explain and clarify the mass of details, episodes, and
relationships that make up human lives. For Scott's characters, narrative is
not artifice or bondage but a liberating force which helps them figure out (in
both senses) their experience. Darsie Latimer, for example, benefits from writing in his journal during his mysterious captivity:

> the exercise of the pen seems to act as a sedative upon my own agitated
> thoughts and tumultuous passions. I never lay it down but I rise stronger in
> resolution, more ardent in hope. A thousand vague fears, wild expectations,
> and indigested schemes, hurry through one's thoughts in seasons of doubt and
> of danger. But by arresting them as they flit across the mind, by throwing
> them on paper, and even by that mechanical act compelling ourselves to con-
> sider them with scrupulous and minute attention, we may perhaps escape
> becoming the dupes of our own excited imagination.[5]

In recording his adventures, Darsie brings his reason to bear on them, coun-
tering "vague fears, wild expectations, and indigested schemes" with specific
details and considered plans and resolutions. Most crucially, he avoids squan-
dering his energy in idle speculation: "it is better, in my present condition, to
exert my faculties in recollecting the past, and in recording it, than waste
them in vain and anxious anticipations of the future" (p. 164). "Arresting" his
thoughts results in a victory of realism over "excited imagination," of fact
over fancy, that the activity of narration makes possible.

Darsie's journal relieves his feelings but does not, in fact, help him overcome the exigencies of his situation; the empowering effects of the "rage of
narration" (p. 169) remain for him a fiction he is incapable of bringing to life,
and, while a hero in his prose, he remains a prisoner in practice. Darsie's failure does not completely undermine his idealization of narration as a tactic
enabling informed and thus effective action, but it does invite closer investigation of narrative's rewards in *Redgauntlet*. After all, one of the novel's most
striking features is its abundance of nested narratives: tap any characters in
the right place and out come their life stories. Many of the stories seem to
have the prosaic intent of contextualizing the present, "filling in the middle
between the temporal end-points of a change," which, as Arthur Danto suggests, is the primary role of narrative explanations.[6] Thus, Peter Peebles
recounts the history of his case before it reached Alan Fairford's hands; Nanty
Ewart explains how he, with his education and talents, came to be skipper of
the *Jumping Jenny;* Joshua Geddes tells Darsie his family history to account for
the transformation from the bloodthirsty ancestors of his heraldry to his own
Godly lifestyle; and Lilias Redgauntlet provides the details that unravel the

mysterious situation in which Darsie finds himself. All of these narrators recognize that conditions have changed, and they endeavor, through narrative, to elucidate the alterations.

Not all of the tales told have this overt end, though, and even those that have this practical purpose on the surface take on a different resonance in the telling. Wandering Willie's Tale, for instance, is an example of his storytelling skill as well as an ironic but prophetic "lesson" to Darsie, as Willie mockingly says, not to trust in strangers (p. 102).[7] Willie's narrative virtuosity is unmatched in the novel except possibly by that of Maxwell of Summertrees. Pate-in-Peril, as he is known, when he begins "to be sensible that the period of telling his story gracefully was gliding fast away" (p. 240), makes haste not to let the opportunity slip past. He is "much animated with the recollections which the exploit excited" (p. 243) and has to make an effort to restore "his usual manner, which had been a little disturbed towards the end of the narrative" (p. 244). Similarly, Nanty Ewart needs no prompting at all to privilege Alan with his history and, in the process of telling it, becomes increasingly affected and excited. For these men, as for Peter Peebles or Redgauntlet himself, retelling the past borders on reliving it, and the narrative's explanation matters less than the pleasure of the text. "Cut us off from Narrative," says Carlyle, "how would the stream of conversation, even among the wisest, languish into detached handfuls, and among the foolish utterly evaporate!"[8] *Redgauntlet* investigates narrative but also appreciates and celebrates it, as a fundamental and rewarding human activity.

Some of *Redgauntlet*'s characters construct narratives for a living. As an advocate, Alan Fairford occupies himself precisely this way: he gathers information and considers it with "scrupulous and minute attention" in order to represent it in a contained and coherent form. Faced with the "huge mass" of papers in *Peebles against Plainstanes* (p. 134), Alan sets to work until he can report to Darsie that he has "mastered the details, confused as they are; and ... I shall plead as well for Peter Peebles, as I could for a duke" (p. 140). Alan is "an accomplished advocate," as his unfortunately aborted defense of Peebles shows; he

> gives prominence to all the circumstances which support his case; he glides lightly over those which are unfavourable to it; his own witnesses are applauded and encouraged; the statements which seem to throw discredit on them are controverted; the contradictions into which they fall are explained away; a clear and connected abstract of their evidence is given.

These words are not Scott's, however, but Macaulay's, and they refer not to a lawyer but to the historian David Hume.[9] Lawyers and historians, as Scott and Macaulay both recognize, do much the same sort of work: they assemble documents or pieces of evidence; they evaluate their reliability and their usefulness; they organize them into a stable structure; and they present a verifiable or defensible case.[10] Macaulay is not praising Hume, though; for him, the legal parallel draws attention to the "partialities and prejudices" he believes are infecting contemporary historiography. "In the midst of these disputes . . . history proper, if we may use the term, is disappearing," he protests.[11] His deep distrust of the constructive and creative aspects of the historian's craft brings him perilously close to the specious belief that a "proper" historian allows the facts to write themselves; he is redeemed by his concern that while "our historians are practising all the arts of controversy, they miserably neglect the art of narration, the art of interesting the affections and present-ing pictures to the imagination"—he knows the historian's task involves more than transcribing objective reality.[12] Still, he aims to salvage "history proper" from the pernicious influences of legal sophistry or fictional embroi-dery. This project of separation and definition is the one with which *Redgaunt-let* is most actively and complexly engaged.

Redgauntlet seems to have the job of dismantling ingenuous assumptions about historiography that persist to the present day as straw figures for philosophers of history in search of something against which to define their own work: assumptions about the transparent relationship of a historical nar-rative to past events, for example, or about methodological questions such as the reliability of evidence or the unity of the 'true' story. It is hard to imagine that then, any more than now, any practising historian was guilty of such naivete, so the recurrent appearance in theoretical discussions of a phantom myopic historian going cap-in-hand to the archives suggests that any position needs some opposing figure against which to define itself.[13] Scott's underlying polemic, for instance, has a target: Dr. Dryasdust, whose "anxious researches" produce the material for *Redgauntlet* (p. 400). Dr. Dryasdust is devoted to documents and is skeptical of the kinds of ebullient personal narratives that form so much of the novel's content; instead of relating the old cadie's story with relish, as the narrator would have done, he says, with condescension worthy of Macaulay, that it "seems to refer to some inaccurate account of the transactions in which you seem so much interested" (p. 401). Scott's name for this tedious antiquarian confirms his status as a straw man in Scott's argu-ment, but he is nonetheless the touchstone for the novel's revisionist histori-ography.[14]

The novel most forcefully critiques the idea that historical narratives are examples of simplistically mimetic or transparent representation. The open-ing exchange of letters between Darsie and Alan immediately places prob-lems of accuracy and interpretation in the foreground; Alan mockingly points out the subjectivity of Darsie's accounts:

> Since the moon-calf who earliest discovered the Pandemonium of Milton in an expiring wood-fire—since the first ingenious urchin who blew bubbles out of soap and water, thou, my best of friends, hast the highest knack at making his-tories out of nothing . . . All that happens to thee gets a touch of the wonderful and the sublime from thy own rich imagination. Didst ever see what artists call

a Claude Lorraine glass, which spreads its own particular hue over the whole landscape which you see through it?—thou beholdest ordinary events just through such a medium. (p. 46)

This image anticipates a famous passage from *Middlemarch:*

> Your pier-glass or extensive surface of polished steel . . . will be minutely and multitudinously scratched in all directions; but place now against it a lighted candle as a centre of illumination, and lo! the scratches will seem to arrange themselves in a fine series of concentric circles round that little sun. It is demonstrable that the scratches are going everywhere impartially, and it is only your candle which produces the flattering illusion of a concentric arrangement, its light falling with an exclusive optical selection. These things are a parable. The scratches are events, and the candle is the egoism of any person now absent.[15]

With a prescience that rebukes modern detractors of realist fiction as well as of nineteenth-century historiography, both Scott and Eliot confront the problem of referentiality, the difference between the text and that which it claims to represent.[16] Both authors affirm the real presence of the referent, the landscape or the scratches on the glass, while pointing out that the spectator's subject position necessarily colors or illuminates its depiction. But, crucially for their novels as well as their larger claims about representation, this recognition does not obfuscate or nullify the effort to write a story faithful to this landscape. Eliot's ironic comment on Mr. Brooke's ideological flexibility is also a program for achieving historical objectivity: "it is a narrow mind which cannot look at a subject from various points of view."[17] Here the resonance of the kinship between legal and historical work for Scott becomes apparent: where Macaulay saw advocacy only as partisanship, Scott finds in it a model of judicious mediation between potentially dubious or contradictory pieces of evidence; and the historian's active participation in the narration, which for Macaulay threatened the production of "history proper," for Scott becomes the only means through which a 'proper' history can be written.

Redgauntlet also addresses the problem of the gaps even the most trustworthy sources may leave: "a genuine correspondence" that lays adventures before the reader "in the words of the actors themselves," the narrator says of Darsie and Alan's letters, "can seldom be found to contain all in which it is necessary to instruct the reader for his full comprehension of the story" (p. 141). Despite his exaggerated reluctance to pollute the "genuine correspondence" with additional material ("Heaven forbid it should be in any respect sophisticated by interpolations of our own!") (p. 141), the narrator proceeds quite blithely to replace it, or at least supplement it, with his own apparently omniscient voice. Again, Scott argues against effacing the narrator's participation in the form of his own narrative. The imaginative acts of authorship that link and arrange the miscellanea of the past into a story are an essential aspect of the historian's operations, something only the spectral 'bad' historicist would deny or pretend to work without. This particular trajectory of Scott's critique curves not so much towards the problem of objectivity as towards the relationship between historiography and fiction that the presentation of this whole critique in a novel must inevitably raise. The activity of a historical narrator may indeed resemble in innumerable ways the work of a novelist, but the fact remains that a historian can only hypothesize connections or relationships between events recorded as having taken place, while a novelist can, as Scott did in *Redgauntlet,* invent the events themselves. Historiography in *Redgauntlet* cannot be confidently distinguished from other forms of narrative explanation, including fiction. But, unlike many of the philosophers of history whose work has flourished in the late twentieth century, Scott does not then turn to analyzing historical writing as if it is only a special kind of story-telling, treating the difference between history and fiction as a "common sense"—and hence analytically or thematically uninteresting—distinction.[18] Instead, *Redgauntlet* focuses on that difference, examining its implications for the role of history in fiction and, more provocatively, of fiction in historiography.

Most significantly, each genre is characterized by a particular relationship to the conditions of historical possibility. Historiography tells of the realization of these conditions, possibility become fixed; fiction can depict the realization of alternatives contrary to the possibilities or, as in *Redgauntlet,* latent within the possibilities but forced to the margins of the narrative by what 'really' happened. Fiction of the latter sort, marked by its historical precision and particularity, can, according to the implicit claims of *Redgauntlet's* form and content, participate in a unique way in historiography. *Redgauntlet* itself is a fantasy, the story of a non-event, but, as Scott says in his 1832 note on the attack on Joshua Geddes's fishing station, it is "by no means an improbable fiction" (p. 409). *Redgauntlet's* claim is that if such an event had taken place, it would have happened as Scott describes it: *Redgauntlet* is not simply speculative, a playful working out of one of the infinite "what if" questions of history, but rather it is the true story of the Jacobite rebellion of 1765. The actual (non)occurrence of the rebellion matters only because it renders its history accessible through fiction alone. Macaulay himself acknowledged that a "history in which every particular incident may be true may on the whole be false";[19] Scott's insight is merely the inverse: that a history in which every particular incident is false may, on the whole, be true—as long as it respects the conditions of possibility.

Various characters in *Redgauntlet* present the possibilities latent in the historical moment preceding the non-rebellion of 1765.[20] Most of them believe that the time for rebellion is past and that only those caught in an antiquated vision of the country could see in it the loyalties and aspirations that fed the Jacobite uprisings of a previous age. Darsie scoffs gently at Fairford Senior, whose "impressions concerning the Highlanders are taken from the recollections of the Forty-five":

> Now, from all I can understand, these ideas, as applied to the present state of the country, are absolutely chimerical. The Pretender is no more remembered in the Highlands, than if the poor gentleman were gathered to his hundred and eight fathers, whose portraits adorn the ancient walls of Holyrood; the broadswords have passed into other hands; the targets are used to cover the butter-churns; and the race has sunk, or is fast sinking, from ruffling bullies into tame cheaters. (pp. 27–28)

He wonders at Redgauntlet's concern to hide himself from the government, observing pragmatically that "the government would scarce, at this time of day, be likely to proceed against any one even of the most obnoxious rebels. Many years have passed away" (p. 73). Much later, faced with his uncle's passionate interest in what seems to Darsie a lost and superannuated cause, he reviews the condition of the country as he sees it:

> I look around me, and I see a settled government—an established authority— a born Briton on the throne—the very Highland mountaineers, upon whom alone the trust of the exiled family reposed, assembled into regiments, which act under the orders of the existing dynasty. France has been utterly dismayed by the tremendous lessons of the last war, and will hardly provoke another. All without and within the kingdom is adverse to encountering a hopeless struggle. (p. 339)

"You'll as soon raise the dead as raise the Highlands—you'll as soon get a grunt from a dead sow as any comfort from Wales or Cheshire," says Nanty Ewart (p. 280). Even Lilias believes the bubble of the rebellion will "burst of itself" (p. 331).

Redgauntlet, however, through his own peculiar Claude Lorraine glass, sees the nation ripe for rebellion and the time propitious for the restoration of the exiled House of Stewart. He stalks the pages of the novel like a specter from the past, his dress, like his politics, "antiquated and unfashionable" (p. 49), a "decayed gentleman," as Darsie calls him, clinging "to a few of the forms and observances of former rank" (p. 39). In the early parts of the novel he seems to be a "Solecism Incarnate," as Carlyle called Louis XV.[21] But much of the interest of Redgauntlet (and *Redgauntlet*) lies in the inadequacy of this dismissive assessment of his place in history. "A strange delusion," Darsie says of his uncle's desire, "and it is wonderful that it does not yield to the force of reality." "Ah, but," Lilias replies, "realities of late have seemed to flatter his hopes" (p. 330). Darsie had, in fact, recognized earlier that aspects of the present time justified increased optimism and activity among Stewart sympathizers:

> There have . . . been rumours lately, as if the present state of the nation, or at least of some discontented provinces, agitated by a variety of causes, but particularly by the unpopularity of the present administration, may seem to this species of agitators a favourable period for recommencing their intrigues; while, on the other hand, government may not, at such a crisis, be inclined to look upon them with the contempt which a few years ago would have been their most appropriate punishment. (pp. 206–07)

Lilias reiterates this assessment in greater detail in her response to Darsie's skeptical remarks:

> The general dissatisfaction with the peace—the unpopularity of the minister, which has extended itself even to the person of his master—the various uproars which have disturbed the quiet of the metropolis, and a general state of disgust and dissatisfaction, which seems to affect the body of the nation, have given unwonted encouragement to the expiring hopes of the Jacobites, and induced many, both at the Court of Rome, and, if it can be called so, of the Pretender, to lend a more favourable ear than they had hitherto done to the insinuations of those, who, like my uncle, hope, when hope is lost to all but themselves. (p. 330)

Redgauntlet himself counters Darsie's analysis of the kingdom as "adverse to encountering a hopeless struggle" (p. 339) with his own reading of the historical conditions:

> The state of this nation no more implies prosperity, then [sic] the florid colour of a feverish patient is a symptom of health. All is false and hollow . . . Many eyes, formerly cold and indifferent, are now looking towards the line of our ancient and rightful monarchs, as the only refuge in the approaching storm— the rich are alarmed—the nobles are disgusted—the populace are inflamed— and a band of patriots, whose measures are more safe that their numbers are few, have resolved to set up King Charles's standard. (p. 340)

With the benefit of hindsight, of course, readers know now, as they knew when *Redgauntlet* was published, that no such standard waved over a Stewart victory in the 1760s, but, as the whole novel suggests and Scott's 1832 introduction and the editor's notes confirm, the realities were rich with insurrectionary potential as well as with the conservative forces that ultimately triumphed. The fitness of his plans to the moment makes Redgauntlet more than a fanatic pursuing "an antiquated and desperate line of politics" (p. 217), as Darsie's journal describes him. A full account of the past would acknowledge that the present emerged only through the subjugation and loss of other very real possibilities, and as one of these a Jacobite's aborted desire to see a Stewart once more on the throne deserves historical investigation and narration.

    Redgauntlet thus intersects in an important way with twentieth-century theories of history seeking to disrupt the alleged historicist tendency to read past events only as the roots or origins of the present. The compulsion to write the history of the present can be readily found in Victorian historians, including Macaulay: "No past event has any intrinsic importance. The knowledge of it is valuable only as it leads us to form just calculations with respect to the future"—that is, with respect to Macaulay's present.[22] In this respect, the phantasmic bones of Dr. Dryasdust retain some scraps of flesh. Scott illustrates a thesis in which much contemporary theory is heavily invested: by narrating possibilities as well as actualities, a historian can avoid privileging the winners, the dominant groups, and restore to those who conventionally appear only on the margins their full importance and presence in the historical moment. "We want historians," says Foucault, "to confirm our belief that the present rests upon profound intentions and immutable necessities. But the true historical sense confirms our existence among countless lost events."[23] It seems true, if unexpected, that in *Redgauntlet* Scott participates in at least one of the goals of New Historicism: the novel "disturbs what was previously considered immobile; it fragments what was thought unified; it shows the heterogeneity of what was imagined consistent with itself."[24] Darsie's and Redgauntlet's worlds are at once simultaneous and incompatible, and their juxtaposition reveals the heterogeneity, the fragmentation, that each individual narrative conceals.[25]

Scott also anticipates Foucauldian historicism in his refusal to privilege origins. By writing about an ending that is inseparable from a beginning—the fading of the Jacobite spirit and the confirmation of the Hanoverian dynasty—he accedes to Foucault's demand for a genealogy that will "never neglect as inaccessible the vicissitudes of history" but rather "cultivate[s] the details and accidents that accompany every beginning."[26] One crucial effect of this tactic is, again, to complicate a deterministic historiographical model by highlighting the "dissension of other things" that characterizes every historical moment.[27] Its other, equally important, effect is that, in pursuit of this history of an ending, Scott's rhetoric is one of mourning, most noticeably in the poignancy imbuing the failure of Redgauntlet's rebellion. *Redgauntlet* narrates a loss, the fulfillment of one set of historical possibilities at the expense of the others. The novel's denouement, with the almost comical irresolution of the conspirators followed by the commonsensical intervention of Colonel Campbell, has a bittersweet undercurrent; the possibilities that die with Redgauntlet's rebellion are those that, like Wandering Willie, speak of and from traditions that are passing away, and the replacement of old with new is not the less painful for being inevitable. The movement of time and the process of change are inexorable, however. Although Scott writes appreciatively about the good old days, there is never a sense in *Redgauntlet*—as there is, for example, in conservatively nostalgic texts such as Burke's *Reflections on the Revolution in France*—that it would be worth fighting to restore them: the past is the past and the Stewart cause is, as Scott says in his 1832 introduction to the novel, "a tale which [has] been told" (p. 10). The Jacobite rebellion fails because even the Jacobites are no longer prepared to rebel; Lilias's expectation that the rebellion is a "bubble" which will "burst of itself" proves prophetic (p. 331). All that is possible in 1765 is the attempt, and *Redgauntlet* is the historical narrative of this possibility. Thus the novel reins in the subversive potential of narrating a historical non-event by placing it within the story as it is always already known to have unfolded; its mourning is contained by its historicity.[28]

Scott does not evade the historiographical implications of treating non-events as valid historical subjects. In *Redgauntlet,* as in his other historical novels, he proves that fiction holds a substantive, not a parasitic, place in historiography. The claims he makes in *Redgauntlet* are more threatening to Dryasdust doctrine, though, than his demonstrations in novels such as *Waverley* that, in Carlyle's words, "the bygone ages of the world were actually filled by living men, not by protocols, state-papers, controversies and abstractions of men."[29] In *Waverley,* as in *Heart of Midlothian* and many of his other novels, Scott places a fictitious character in the midst of real historical events. The revolutionary impact of this move cannot be overestimated: it was "a great service, fertile in consequences, this that Scott [had] done."[30] But this project personalizes and animates what actually happened, which is different than writing about what did not happen as if it, too, were history. *Waverley* might well strike fear into the heart of Dr. Dryasdust, both because it accomplishes what is clearly a historiographical end and because it does it effectively and affectively, "in a manner which may well excite [his] envy."[31] But *Redgauntlet* suggests that a story of the past that tells only of actual events is likely, no matter how well told, to remain bound to a master-narrative that cannot do justice to impulses and events that were real but never realized. This project can be accomplished only through fiction saturated with but not limited by history. What Scott offers in *Redgauntlet* is a hybrid: historical fiction, steeped in "facts" but not tied to them, based on, as he said, "real or probable incident" (p. 3).

Macaulay wanted historians to "reclaim" the materials of history from Scott, to recover "those attractions which have been usurped by fiction."[32] In *Redgauntlet,* Scott undermines this argument by refusing the distinction Macaulay wants to sustain between historiography and fiction. More than that, with *Redgauntlet* Scott demonstrates a historical model in which the past, like the present, exists as a morass of conflicting possibilities. Narrative, Scott argues, is the means through which they become coherent and comprehensible, and historical narrative is not necessarily limited to those possibilities that materialize as events. The non-events can be part of that story as well, and because they are not amenable to conventional historical explanation they must be brought out through fictions. Scott delivers a playful, eccentric, yet profound challenge to Dr. Dryasdust and the hegemony of his historiography, throwing down *Redgauntlet* before him as Lilias casts her uncle's iron glove at the feet of King George's champion, in a style so compelling one almost regrets not knowing where to find such a historian so that Scott's celebration of narrative could succeed where Foucault's disparaging polemic could only fail. *Redgauntlet's* history is fantasy as well as fact, while its fiction is not just historical, it is historiography. The attendant claims could be the premises of a truly new historicism.

Notes

1.   Thomas Babington Macaulay, "History," in *The Lays of Ancient Rome & Miscellaneous Essays and Poems* (London: J. M. Dent, 1910, repr. 1963), pp. 1–39; p. 37.

2.   Surprisingly, Georg Lukács, probably this century's best Scott critic, describes Scott's art as present-centered in a much less ambiguous way than I think *Redgauntlet,* or even *Waverley,* supports: his "really great historical art," Lukács says, consists of "bringing the past to life as the prehistory of the present, in giving poetic life to those historical, social and human forces which, in the course of a long evolution, have made our present-day life what it is and as we experience it." *The Historical Novel,* trans. Hannah and Stanley Mitchell (Lincoln: Univ. of Nebraska Press, 1962), p. 53. In *Redgauntlet,* the possibility of other presents than our own is in some tension with historical necessity, which in Scott, as Lukács says later, is not "divorced from men" but is "the complex interaction of concrete historical circumstances in their process of transformation, in their interaction with the concrete human beings, who have grown up in these circumstances, have been very variously influenced by them, and who act in an individual way according to their personal passions. Thus, in Scott's portrayal, historical necessity is always a resultant, never a presupposition" (p. 58). Lukács never quite reconciles these statements, perhaps because Scott's novels, too, leave the issue ambiguous.

3.   In his article "Macaulay, Scott, and the Literary Challenge to Historiography" (*Journal of the History of Ideas* 50 [1989]: 117–33), Mark Phillips describes Macaulay's anxiety over the popularity of historical fiction, which reflected, Phillips argues, not just envy but also a "fear that fiction had captured a large part of the historian's traditional territory" (p. 128). Much criticism of *Redgauntlet* has underestimated or disregarded the novel's complex structure. Harry Shaw, Edward Mornin, and Margaret Criscuola, for example, all analyze the novel's depiction of historical change and process without troubling themselves over the rebellion's fictionality [Shaw, *The Forms of Historical Fiction* (Ithaca: Cornell Univ. Press, 1983); Mornin, " 'Bonnie Charlie's Now Awa' . . .': Charles Edward Stuart After the '45. On the Uses of History in Fiction," *Forum for Modern Language Studies* 24 (1988): pp. 97–110; Criscuola, "Constancy and Change: The Process of History in Scott's *Redgauntlet,*" *Studies in Scottish Literature,* ed. G. Ross Roy (Columbia: Univ. of South Carolina Press, 1985) 20: 123–36. James Kerr, in *Fiction Against History: Scott as Storyteller* (Cambridge: Cambridge Univ. Press, 1989), points out that by "eliding the historical referent he had supplied in the earlier novels, Scott shifts the emphasis of his writing, to a greater degree than ever, towards the processes of making historical narrative" (p. 102). Kerr, however, ultimately sees the novel's extensive metadiscourse and concern with narrative more as a negotiation between history and romance—and an assertion of Scott's own authority as a taleteller—than as an attempt to reconfigure the possibilities of historiography. In her recent study *The Achievement of Literary Authority: Gender, History, and the Waverley Novels* (Ithaca: Cornell Univ. Press, 1991), Ina Ferris analyzes the way Scott's novels opened up the historical field. Ferris does not discuss *Redgauntlet,* however, although its fictional rebellion is perhaps the most drastic example of this widening of the field, probably because she is more concerned with the subject matter of history and with gender than with genre.

4.   Louis O. Mink, "Narrative Form as Cognitive Instrument," in *Historical Understanding,* ed. Brian Fay, Eugene O. Golob and Richard T. Vann (Ithaca: Cornell Univ. Press, 1987),

pp. 182–203; pp. 185–86. For a careful analytical account of the explanatory power of narrative, see also Arthur C. Danto, *Narration and Knowledge* (New York: Columbia Univ. Press, 1985), especially Ch. 11, "Historical Explanation: The Role of Narratives."

5.   Sir Walter Scott, *Redgauntlet: A Tale of the Eighteenth Century,* ed. Kathryn Sutherland (Oxford: Oxford Univ. Press, 1985), p. 219. All subsequent references will appear in the text and are to this edition.

6.   Danto, *Narration and Knowledge,* p. 233.

7.   The *Westminster Review* called the Tale "the best thing in the book" (*Westminster Review* 2 [1824]: p. 186), and it has continued to attract its share of critical attention—see, for example, the discussion of it in Kerr, pp. 117–19.

8.   Thomas Carlyle, "On History," *Selected Essays* (N.p.: T. Nelson & Sons, n.d.), p. 232.

9.   Macaulay, "History," p. 31.

10.   Kerr too points out the "linkage between the figures of the lawyer and the taleteller" (p. 110).

11.   Macaulay, "History," p. 33.

12.   Ibid, p. 33.

13.   Foucault's scathing comments about "the surreptitious practice of historians, their pretension to examine things furthest from themselves, [and] the grovelling manner in which they approach this promising distance" provide a provocative example. "Nietzsche, Genealogy, History," in *Language, Counter-Memory, Practice: Selected Essays and Interviews,* ed. Donald F. Bouchard, trans. Donald F. Bouchard and Sherry Simon (Ithaca: Cornell Univ. Press, 1977), pp. 139–64; p. 156.

14.   Macaulay serves a similar purpose in my own text: even though his own work reflects nothing like the sharp division between history and other kinds of narrative that has come to be standard since the latter half of the nineteenth century, his unease with Scott's dismantling of generic categories makes him a useful counterexample.

15.   George Eliot, *Middlemarch: A Study of Provincial Life,* ed. Gordon S. Haight (Boston: Houghton Mifflin, 1956), pp. 194–95.

16.   Kerr says of the Waverley novels in general that Scott's "self-conscious playing with the procedures of historical representation anticipates a more modern preoccupation with the power and limits of the imagination as an instrument for writing history and with the problematic relationship between language and reality"—it is this feature of Scott's "historical reportage" that sets him off from earlier novelists such as Defoe (p. 104).

17.   Eliot, *Middlemarch,* p. 49.

18.   Hayden White's work, for example, examines history in this way. See especially *Metahistory: The Historical Imagination in Nineteenth-Century Europe* (Baltimore: Johns Hopkins Univ. Press, 1973); or, among his essays, "The Historical Text as Literary Artifact," in *The Writing of History: Literary Form and Historical Understanding,* ed. Robert Canary and Henry Kozicki (Madison: Univ. of Wisconsin Press, 1978), pp. 41–62. Ann Rigney also questions White's approach: "But to what extent would we be justified in concluding, as Hayden White does, that the literary activity of the historian constitutes a 'fictionalization' of history; that historical representation involves a 'translation' of 'fact' into 'fiction'?" "Adapting History to the Novel," *New Comparison* 8 (1989): pp. 127–43; p. 130. Her conclusions differ somewhat from my own (see n25 below). See also Mink, "Narrative Form as Cognitive Instrument." Mink dismantles the common sense distinction only to resurrect it in the end as our best way of understanding either history or fiction: "If the distinction were to disappear, fiction and history would both collapse back into myth and be indistinguishable from it as from each other" (p. 203).

19.   Macaulay, "History," p. 34.

20.   The length and detail of these accounts suggest Scott's concern that readers recognize the novel's historical specificity as well as the variety of ways in which even very concrete details or facts could be interpreted.

21. Thomas Carlyle, *The French Revolution: A History* (New York: Modern Library, n.d.), p. 18.

22. Macaulay, "History," p. 33. Another classic example of this tendency would be Burckhardt's *The Civilization of the Renaissance in Italy,* with its insistent focus on the creation of the modern individual as well as the modern state.

23. Foucault, "Nietzsche, Genealogy, History," p. 155.

24. Ibid., p. 147.

25. Here I take issue with Rigney, whose analysis of Scott's novels, especially *Old Mortality,* leads her to conclude that the fictional elements in his historical novels enabled him "to invest historical events with what [Hayden] White calls 'narrativity'; i.e. . . . with an imaginary coherence which they did not themselves possess" (p. 138). Rigney argues that the invented aspects helped Scott resolve heterogeneity into order, which would presumably move his novels further away from 'what really happened.' In *Redgauntlet* at least the opposite appears to be true: paradoxical as it seems, Scott's fictional intervention is in aid of a more faithful evocation of the past.

26. Foucault, "Nietzsche, Genealogy, History," p. 144.

27. Ibid., p. 142.

28. Mornin points out Scott's unidealized presentation of the Prince in *Redgauntlet* and suggests that it typifies Scott's attitude towards history in the novel, which shows an "awareness of the appeal of history and yet of the necessity of coming to terms with inexorable historical change" (p. 109). Kerr suggests that, through the variety of narrating characters in the novel, "Scott attempts to recast history, to recreate the past as he wished it had happened" (p. 122); this articulation implies an unambiguous nostalgia not really supported by the novel.

29. Carlyle, "Sir Walter Scott," *Selected Essays* (N.p.: T. Nelson & Sons, n.d.), p. 116.

30. Ibid., p. 116. Much Scott criticism has focused on this "service," including Lukács's classic analyses of Scott's "mediocre" heroes. Ina Ferris, for example, in *The Achievement of Literary Authority,* demonstrates how Scott's novels brought that "which was excluded from action and that which lay outside crisis" into the field of history (p. 197). In "Adapting History to the Novel," Ann Rigney emphasizes that Scott broke away from history's usual subjects ("courts and kings") to extend "the historian's territory into the truly historical" (p. 139); she goes on to suggest that changes in historical practice such as the rise of socio-cultural topics may be attributable to the influence of fiction, a point also made by Mark Phillips in "Macaulay, Scott, and the Literary Challenge to Historiography."

31. Macaulay, "History," p. 37.

32. Ibid., p. 36.

INDIVIDUAL NOVELS
◆

Scott's *Redgauntlet*

David Daiches

*R*edgauntlet is the novel in which Scott found the most adequate "objective correlative" for his feelings about Scottish history and for that complex attitude toward the relation between tradition and progress which explains so much of the workings of his mind and imagination. In his earlier novels dealing with Scottish history he had explored the relation between heroism and prudence in periods of civil and religious conflict in which noble fanaticism or anachronistic romantic loyalties were challenged by a prudence which sympathized with, yet in the end rejected, outdated patterns of heroic action. His gaze was on the great transitional period in Scottish history, the seventeenth and eighteenth centuries, when, against a background of violence and extremist views, there quietly emerged an unromantic commercial Scotland committed to the Hanoverian succession, to ever closer ties with England, to a "British" rather than a "Scottish" point of view. This for Scott was the wave of the future; this was where Scotland's material interests lay. Yet the appeal of Scotland's stormy and romantic past was insistent. Could one reconcile a passion for the picturesque violence of Scottish history and the traditions and rituals associated with Scotland's former existence as an independent kingdom with a sober appraisal of the realities of the present situation? Scott's best novels are projections of the dilemma involved in endeavoring to answer this question. All of them end with the reluctant victory of prudence over the seductive but in the last analysis anachronistic claims of romantic action. Thus Edward Waverley withdraws from his brief association with the Jacobites to become a respectable subject of King George; Francis Osbaldistone in *Rob Roy* returns in the end to his father's countinghouse after it has been shown that in the modern age the romantic hero is simply a shabby bandit and the future resides with the prudent Glasgow merchant, Bailie Nicol Jarvie; and in *The Heart of Midlothian* the spectacular heroics are left to criminals and desperadoes while the real heroine, a humble Scottish lass involved in a sordid family scandal, works her way out by quiet determination to find peace at last in facing the practical and economic problems of agricultural management.

From *From Jane Austen to Joseph Conrad,* Essays Collected in Memory of James T. Hillhouse, ed. Robert C. Rathburn and Martin Steinmann, Jr. (Minneapolis: University of Minnesota Press, 1958), 46–59. Reprinted by permission of David Daiches.

Scott's imagination was kindled most effectively not by the contemplation of life in distant times and lands—his novels of medieval life are cardboard affairs compared with those dealing with recent Scottish history—but by observing the immediate past of his own country and chronicling, with deliberate ambiguity of feeling, the transition from the age of heroic violence to the age of prudence. He is concerned with the mutations of heroism. When, in *Redgauntlet,* Darsie Latimer impugns (though good-naturedly enough) the courage of his friend Alan Fairford's father, Alan replies by contrasting useless military adventures with useful civil courage. "This is civil courage, Darsie; and it is of little consequence to most men in this age and country, whether they ever possess military courage or no." Military courage was once a useful virtue, but "in this age and country" it is no longer so. The modern world is a world of businessmen and lawyers, and modern battles are fought in the law courts.

But it is not quite as simple as this. Scots law retained its independence—in content, in ritual, in procedure, and in vocabulary—after Scotland had lost its political independence and become part of Great Britain, and in lingering over Scottish legal customs and terms Scott was emphasizing a *national* aspect of his country's life. This was one area where the old Scotland survived. Yet the dusty arguments of lawyers were a poor substitute for the lost heroic way of life. The legal profession in eighteenth-century Scotland was in large measure the guardian of Scottish antiquities. It was the lawyers who wrote monographs on ancient Scottish customs and argued about the origin of the Picts or the nicer points of heraldry. Lawyers and antiquaries were the new kind of Scottish patriots, and the part played by both these professions (often combined, as in Scott's own case, in a single person) in Scott's novels of Scottish life is highly significant. *The Antiquary* provides the most specific example of the movement from heroism to antiquarian study; the old heroic way of life is, by the latter part of the eighteenth century, only something to be argued over and written about. Scott himself—lawyer, antiquary, historian, novelist—is the perfect example of the shift from participation in the life of heroic adventure to nostalgic scholarship about it, and Abbotsford, that museum of Scottish antiquities, is the perfect symbol of Scott's dilemma.

Redgauntlet opens with a series of letters between Darsie Latimer and his friend Alan Fairford. Both are young men not yet twenty-one. Alan, son of an Edinburgh lawyer, lives at home with his widowed father who keeps him rigorously at his legal studies, for he is at the point of being called to the bar and his father, desperately anxious that Alan should become a legal luminary, combines paternal strictness with deep devotion to his only son. Darsie, a high-spirited, romantic youth, has lived with the Fairfords since early childhood; he is an orphan whose parentage is mysterious, but we do know that he is kept supplied with money by an agent of his deceased parents and that he has prospects of entering into a fortune at the age of twenty-one. The mystery of Darsie's parentage is a conventional plot device which Scott used also in *The Antiquary* and which belongs to those outward trappings of fictional technique which he borrowed from the tradition of the novel as he found it. The important thing is the difference in character between the irresponsible, adventurous Darsie and his hard-working and conscientious friend. Darsie, who has given up his legal studies since he will have no need to enter a profession in order to support himself, has gone on a jaunt to the southwest of Scotland, while his friend remains working for his bar examination at home. The time is the middle or late 1760's—just over twenty years after the failure of the 1745 rebellion and a few years before Scott's own birth, in 1771. It is the time when the active heroics of the Jacobite rebellion were rapidly fading into sentimental antiquarianism, a time which Scott knew about at first hand through conversations with his parents and with his older friends.

Alan Fairford is said to be a portrait of the young Scott himself, and there is no doubt that the portrait of his father, Saunders Fairford, is in all essential respects that of Scott's own father. Darsie Latimer is said by Lockhart to be based on Scott's friend William Clerk, but though there is clear evidence that Scott had Clerk in mind in a few scenes there can be little doubt that fundamentally Darsie represents another side of his creator. Scott was both Alan and Darsie, both the prudent loyalist and the romantic seeker of the "crowded hour of glorious life," just as he was both the modern man of business and the celebrator of Scotland's lost glories, sensible Hanoverian and nostalgic sentimental Jacobite (the term "sentimental Jacobitism" was coined by Burns to denote those who, while recognizing the anachronistic folly of the '45 rebellion, had a nationalistic emotional sympathy with it after it became a lost cause). The liveliness, the immediacy, the vivid sense of character and of place, displayed in the opening of the novel, are matched in no other of Scott's openings, which are notoriously slow and even labored. The epistolary method enables Scott to plunge *in medias res* in a way he never does elsewhere. He is personally involved here, to a degree and in a way that we never find again in his novels. It is almost as though the epistolary method was forced on him by his sense of participation and involvement in the scenes he is describing.

It is not only in the portrait of Darsie and the two Fairfords that Scott draws on his autobiographical experiences. There are many other echoes of Scott's own early life in the novel, including, in the portrait of Green Mantle, a reminiscence of his early, unsuccessful love affair, an experience which left a deep and permanent mark on him. In Andrew Lang's words, "*Redgauntlet* is, in part, a memory of first love, first friendship, and of filial affection." It is significant that Scott should employ an unwonted directness of style and draw to an unusual degree on his own autobiography in the novel in which he faces most directly the theme which lay at the center of his imaginative life.

Darsie, as the letters reveal, becomes gradually involved in adventures in the southwest of Scotland near the Solway Firth, which divides Scotland from England on the west side. In spite of warnings not to go to England, he hangs about near the English border and is eventually kidnapped by a mysterious man of noble bearing and stern demeanor. The story of his kidnapping and his treatment by his captor is told in a journal which Darsie keeps during his captivity. He is puzzled to determine the reason for his kidnapping and the intentions of his captor, who is melodramatically stern yet not unkind; but he is cheered by the intermittent appearances of a fair young lady in a green mantle. Meanwhile, Alan, at home in Edinburgh, receives and answers Darsie's letters while preparing for the great day (especially great for his proud and anxious father) when he is called to the Scottish bar. Alan is continuously surrounded by the language and the atmosphere of Scots law, while Darsie finds himself among a variety of picturesque characters—Wandering Willie the blind fiddler, Joshua Geddes the Quaker, and eventually the strange and exciting characters who preside over his captivity. Alan lives very much in the present, in the Edinburgh of 1766; Darsie gets drawn more and more into the past. Eventually Alan discovers his friend's plight and leaves his first case—the cause of an impoverished and crazy litigant, poor Peter Peebles, who has lost his substance and his reason in almost a lifetime of vain litigation—to hasten southwest in search of his friend. The novel now continues as straight narrative, with both the epistolary technique and the journal device abandoned. Scott had achieved his purpose in bringing the reader with force and immediacy into the action of the novel; now he continues more conventionally to unfold the remainder of the story.

Redgauntlet is in a sense the story of two worlds: the world of Alan Fairford and his father, which is the realistic, unromantic, modern world; and the world into which Darsie stumbles, a world of wild, romantic anachronism. For eventually Darsie discovers that his captor is his uncle, younger brother of Sir Henry Darsie Redgauntlet who was executed at Carlisle in 1746 for his part in the '45, and that he himself is Sir Henry's only son, Sir Arthur Darsie Redgauntlet. His uncle, who calls himself by a variety of names as well as by his real name of Redgauntlet, has ever since his brother's execution brooded fiercely over the injustices suffered by his country and his family, and has devoted himself to the ultimate restoration of the Stuart line. This is more than a matter of family pride or even of loyalty to a royal house: its basis is Scottish nationalism, a profound and even fanatical feeling for Scottish nationhood, which he identifies with the Stuart cause. When Redgauntlet finally tells his nephew something of the reasons for his kidnapping and of his family history, he opens like this:

> It was not of late years that the English nation learned that their best chance of conquering their independent neighbours must be by introducing amongst them division and civil war. You need not be reminded of the state of thraldom to which Scotland was reduced by the unhappy wars betwixt the domestic factions of Bruce and Baliol; nor how, after Scotland had been emancipated from the foreign yoke, by the conduct and valour of the immortal Bruce, the whole fruits of the triumphs of Bannockburn were lost in the dreadful defeats of

Dupplin and Halidon; and Edward Baliol, the minion and feudatory of his namesake of England, seemed, for a brief season, in safe and uncontested possession of the throne so lately occupied by the greatest general and wisest prince in Europe [Robert the Bruce]. But the experience of Bruce did not die with him. There were many who had shared his martial labours, and all remembered the successful efforts by which, under circumstances as disadvantageous as those of his son, he had achieved the liberation of Scotland.

Eighteenth-century Jacobitism is equated with fifteenth-century Scottish nationalism, and support of the Stuart cause is linked with the name of Robert the Bruce and the heroic actions of those who fought in the Scottish War of Independence against Edward I and Edward II of England to restore the independence and integrity of the Scottish nation and kingdom. The aftermath of the Union of Parliaments of 1707, which finally merged England and Scotland politically, was an increasing consciousness among Scotsmen of the lost glories of their once independent country—glories which appeared ever more glorious as time removed them further and further and they could be looked at with an emotion of romantic nostalgia. This emotion merged with Jacobitism after the final defeat of the Stuart cause at Culloden in 1746, and sentimental Jacobitism remained for generations a form of Scottish nationalist feeling even among those whose family traditions were Whig and Presbyterian. But it remained a feeling only; the cause was well and truly lost at Culloden, and though the consequences were disastrous to the cultural life and economy of the Highlands most Scotsmen, particularly urban Scotsmen in the Lowlands, who cherished vague Jacobite sentiments, were content to let them remain mere sentiments and bent their practical activities toward means of prospering under the by now thoroughly established House of Hanover. Scott himself is a perfect example of this. He sighed after Scotland's lost independence, exerted himself (with success) to discover and exhibit to the public Scotland's lost regalia, zealously collected and displayed at Abbotsford every Jacobite relic he could lay his hands on, and at the same time worked hard to make George IV popular in Scotland and in many other ways showed how committed he was to the modern view of Scotland as the north part of Great Britain. Beside Redgauntlet's reference to Bruce we can put a remark about the same king made by Darsie Latimer in a letter from Dumfries to Alan Fairford: "Neither will I take the traveller's privilege of inflicting upon you the whole history of Bruce poinarding the Red Comyn in the Church of the Dominicans at this place, and becoming a king and patriot, because he had been a church-breaker and a murderer." But the anti-romantic view is more often represented by Alan, who writes to his friend:

> View things as they are, and not as they may be magnified by thy teeming fancy. I have seen thee look at an old gravel-pit till thou madest out capes, and bays, and inlets, crags and precipices, and the whole stupendous scenery of the isle of Feroe, in what was to all ordinary eyes a mere horsepond. Besides, did I

not once find thee gazing with respect at a lizard, in the attitude of one who looks upon a crocodile?

Redgauntlet, in his recital of Scottish history to his nephew, is taking literally and seriously what to most eighteenth-century Scotsmen had become only a piece of emotional self-indulgence which had no relation to their practical lives. In showing this, and in modulating views of Scotland and Scottish history from Saunders Fairford through Alan Fairford and thence through Darsie Latimer to Redgauntlet, Scott is running the gamut of Scottish attitudes toward Scotland that were possible in the eighteenth century. And in bringing Darsie Latimer into the company of the last forlorn group of belated Jacobites, Scott is testing historical emotion by present fact. Redgauntlet's purpose in kidnapping his nephew was the quixotic one of persuading him to join the Jacobite cause, for his position as the head of the Redgauntlet family and the son of his father would, his uncle believed, bring hundreds of loyal Jacobites rallying to the cause. It eventually emerges that an actual conspiracy is under way, and that the Pretender himself has come over from France in the expectation of heading a new rebellion.

In describing the last Jacobite gathering Scott relentlessly exposes the widening gap between sentimental Jacobitism and active rebellion. The group of reluctant conspirators assembled at a shabby inn on the Solway Firth, brought there, as Charles Edward himself is brought there, only by the fanatical energy of Redgauntlet, are acutely embarrassed at having their professions put to the test so many years after the last fatal attempt at rebellion. Redgauntlet himself is the only one who unites theory with practice, sentiment with action, and it is his almost desperate activity in cajoling, flattering, urging, exhorting, that keeps the group together at all. None of the others— not even Charles Edward himself—believe any more in the practicability of rebellion. The picture of the slow disintegration of the meeting, of the embarrassment of the Jacobites when faced with the problem of reconciling their fierce protestations of loyalty to the House of Stuart with the realities of their present situation, is brilliantly done. The scene is one of the finest in Scott. The two worlds are finally brought together, and the romantic one disintegrates. The most poignant moment of all occurs when, as the result of betrayal by an informer, the Hanoverian General Campbell arrives, walking unnoticed into the midst of the wrangling assembly. He has, as they all know, troops to support him, and many in the Jacobite group, in a last surge of heroic action, are prepared to die fighting to cover the retreat of him whom they regard as their legitimate King. Death in this last desperate battle, or execution as traitors, seems now the only alternative. But these heroics prove unnecessary—worse than unnecessary, irrelevant. General Campbell calmly and politely informs them that they had better break up the party, since a gathering of people whose loyalty to the reigning house was suspect might be open to misunderstanding. Redgauntlet proudly asserts that "we are not men to be penned up like sheep for the slaughter," to which the general replies with a good-natured "Pshaw!" It takes him some time to convince them that his only objective is to persuade them to go peaceably home. There is going to be no battle. Nobody is going to be arrested or executed. They had presumably assembled here "for a bear-bait or a cock-fight" but it was really more sensible now for them to "return quietly home to their own houses." All were free to go. The dialogue continues:

> "What!—all?" exclaimed Sir Richard Glendale—"all, without exception?"
>
> "ALL, without one single exception," said the General; "such are my orders. If you accept my terms, say so, and make haste; for things may happen to interfere with his Majesty's kind purposes towards you all."
>
> "His Majesty's kind purposes!" said the Wanderer [Charles Edward Stuart]. "Do I hear you aright, sir?"
>
> "I speak the King's very words, from his very lips," replied the General. " 'I will,' said his Majesty, 'deserve the confidence of my subjects by reposing my security in the fidelity of the millions who acknowledge my title—in the good sense and prudence of the few who continue, from the errors of education, to disown it.'—His Majesty will not even believe that the most zealous Jacobites who yet remain can nourish a thought of exciting a civil war, which must be fatal to their families and themselves, besides spreading bloodshed and ruin through a peaceful land. He cannot even believe of his kinsman, that he would engage brave and generous, though mistaken men, in an attempt which must ruin all who have escaped former calamities; . . .'"
>
> "Is this real?" said Redgauntlet. "Can you mean this?—Am I—are all, are any of these gentlemen at liberty, without interruption, to embark in yonder brig . . . ?"
>
> "You, sir—all—any of the gentlemen present," said the General,—"all whom the vessel can contain, are at liberty to embark uninterrupted by me; but I advise none to go off who have not powerful reasons, unconnected with the present meeting, for this will be remembered against no one."
>
> "Then, gentlemen," said Redgauntlet, clasping his hands together as the words burst from him, "the cause is lost for ever!"

The heroic gesture cannot survive in the face of cool, good-humored, modern common sense. The Jacobite movement dissolves in the end because it is an unreal anachronism in the modern world. It does not really exist except as a sentiment. The victory lies with prudence and modernity.

Scott showed both courage and imagination in setting his novel in a period when the Jacobite movement was dwindling down to a trickle. Twenty years after the '45 rebellion Jacobitism had become, except for a tiny minority of die-hards, the merest emotional self-indulgence. It had produced a fine crop of songs, which showed Bonnie Prince Charlie's immense appeal to the folk (and not only the folk) mind and cast a fine romantic glow over the whole doomed enterprise; but in itself it was now more a matter of literature than politics. In *Waverley* Scott had brought his English hero into sympathetic contact with a group of Jacobites of the '45, who were shown in the end to be noble and heroic but at the same time histrionic and rather silly. Now, twenty years later, the essence of the movement was symbolized by its ultimate fate. It had been a foolish anachronism all along. And though a character like Redgauntlet arouses our admiration, his melodramatic posturings (which are not defects in the novel; Scott introduced them deliberately) reveal the essential unreality of the world he lives in. Like Helen MacGregor in *Rob Roy* he is not wholly real, and just as in the earlier novel Scott revealed this unreality by bringing the shrewd and realistic Bailie Nicol Jarvie into conversation with Helen, so in *Redgauntlet* Scott, in one of the master strokes of the novel, brings the half-crazed Peter Peebles, with his legal jargon and his utter indifference to anything except his own needs and problems, into conversation with Redgauntlet himself. Peter's brash accosting of the fanatical Jacobite (who at this stage is trying to keep himself anonymous, and who had been known in Edinburgh to Peter and others as Herries of Birrenswork) is true comedy—*critical* comedy, which both amuses and exposes:

"Ay, ay, Mr. Herries of Birrenswork, is this your ainsell in blood and bane? I thought ye had been hanged at Kennington Common, or Hairiebie, or some of these places, after the bonny ploy ye made in the forty-five."

"I believe you are mistaken, friend," said Herries, sternly, . . .

"The deil a bit," answered the undaunted Peter Peebles; "I mind ye weel, for ye lodged in my house the great year of forty-five, for a great year it was; the Grand Rebellion broke out, and my cause—the great cause—Peebles against Plainstanes, *et per contra*—was called in the beginning of the winter Session, and would have been heard, but that there was a surcease of justice, with your plaids, and your piping, and your nonsense."

"I tell you, fellow," said Herries, yet more fiercely, "you have confused me with some of the other furniture of your crazy pate."

"Speak like a gentleman, sir," answered Peebles; "these are not legal phrases, Mr. Herries of Birrenswork. Speak in form of law, or I sall bid ye gude day, sir. I have nae pleasure in speaking to proud folk, though I am willing to answer ony thing in a legal way; so if you are for a crack about auld langsyne, and the splores that you and Captain Redgimlet used to breed in my house, and the girded cask of brandy that ye drank and ne'er thought of paying for it, (not that I minded it muckle in thae days, though I have felt a lack of it sin syne), why, I will waste an hour on ye at ony time.—And where is Captain Redgimlet now? he was a wild chap, like yoursell, though they are nae sae keen after you poor bodies for these some years bygane; the heading and hanging is weel ower now—awful job—awful job—will ye try my sneeshing [snuff]?"

He concluded his desultory speech by thrusting out his large bony paw, filled with a Scottish mull of huge dimensions, which Herries, who had been standing like one petrified by the assurance of this unexpected address, rejected with a contemptuous motion of his hand, which spilled some of the contents of the box.

"Aweel, aweel," said Peter Peebles, totally unabashed by the repulse, "e'en as ye like, a wilful man maun hae his way; but," he added, stooping down and endeavouring to gather the spilled snuff from the polished floor, "I canna afford to lose my sneeshing for a' that ye are gumple-foisted wi' me."

Peter Peebles, on his first appearance in the novel, is an almost Dickensian figure, exemplifying the results of the law's delays. But he has other functions in the book. Scots law, which claims the attention of sober modern Scotsmen as the worthiest expression of Scottish nationhood after the Union, can also destroy and corrupt, and the legal language which comes with such force and dignity from the lips of Saunders Fairford trips crazily off the tongue of the obsessed Peter. If national feeling in an earlier, heroic age could break out into meaningless violence and cruelty, so in modern eighteenth-century Scotland the great national institution of Scots law could be used for destructive purposes. The realistic and critical mind is always necessary if national feeling and national institutions are to be properly guided. Though Peter Peebles is used in this scene to exhibit the melodramatic unreality of Redgauntlet, there is a sense in which Peter and Redgauntlet are the same character: Peter has long been obsessed with the unending legal case of Peebles against Plainstanes and can think and talk of nothing else, hoping still for a victory against Plainstanes, while Redgauntlet is similarly obsessed with the case of the House of Stuart against the House of Hanover and can think and talk of nothing else, hoping still for a victory against the Hanoverians. Here again the contrast between the older Scottish nationalism manifesting itself in military action and the modern Scottish nationalism represented by Scots law is clear.

Scott takes pains throughout the novel to remind his readers that this is a story of the *recent* past, dealing with the transition to the modern world of his own day. And the backward glances which he keeps sending to that past, the frequent references to dying customs and fashions which his older readers may remember, show with what reluctance he casts his vote for modernity and the wave of the future. And sometimes a Jacobite nationalist speaks for Scott himself, as when Pate-in-Peril declaims against modern female fashions:

"Can they not busk the plaid over their heads, as their mothers did? A tartan screen, and once a year a new cockernony from Paris, should serve a Countess. But ye have not many of them left, I think—Mareschal, Airley, Winton, Wemyss, Balmerino, all passed and gone—ay, ay, the countesses and ladies of quality will scarce take up too much of your ball-room floor with their quality hoops now-a-days."

The ambivalence of feeling even touches his handling of the Jacobite rebellion itself. He is of course against it, as prudence and realism and the whole theme of the novel is to show Jacobitism up as an unreal and sentimental anachronism; yet once the cause is totally lost, and the last Jacobite conspiracy evaporates, he allows some of his patriotic admiration for the cause to emerge. He even, most improbably, has General Campbell call the man who betrayed the conspiracy to him a "traitor." But it is in the character of Provost Crosbie that the ambiguities of Scott's attitude are most adequately reflected. Crosbie acts like a loyalist but has a strong tinge of rebellious feeling; prudence and generosity, a sense of the duties and responsibilities of his office and a desire not to offend or distress the dispersed Jacobites, fight within him. His wife is the true sentimental Jacobite with some touches of the active one too. Altogether the Crosbie family is an important link in that modulation from Saunders Fairford, Protestant, Whig, Hanoverian, lawyer, to Redgauntlet, Catholic, Tory, Jacobite, rebel.

Redgauntlet is perhaps best known to the general reader for the inset "Wandering Willie's Tale." Wandering Willie himself represents the fate of the old feudal retainer in the modern world. In the days when the Redgauntlets were feudal lairds, Willie had his function, his social position, and his economic security. Now he is a wandering beggar. The violent breakup of Scotland's long-lingering feudal pattern after the '45 was in most ways a good thing, yet it broke down that paternal relation between master and vassal which Scott could not help sighing after and which in some degree he tried to re-create between himself and his servants at Abbotsford. Darsie Latimer, discussing with his sister the unlikelihood of Redgauntlet's former tenants rallying to his cause at this late period, significantly remarks: "Whatever these people may pretend, to evade your uncle's importunities, they cannot, at this time of day, think of subjecting their necks again to the feudal yoke, which was effectually broken by the Act of 1748, abolishing vassalage and hereditary jurisdictions." The relation between Wandering Willie and his master in the old days, however emotionally satisfying to contemplate, also represented a "feudal yoke." Here again the ambivalence of Scott's attitude toward past and present reveals itself.

"Wandering Willie's Tale" is of course closely linked with the main theme of the novel. A brilliantly told story of the relation between a violent old feudal landlord and his piper and tenant, with enough of the supernatural brought in to give it the air of an old Scottish folk tale yet enough shrewd and humorous realism to make it also a *critical* piece about master-servant relations in old Scotland, it occupies a central position in the story. The piper was Wandering Willie's grandfather, and the lairds concerned were ancestors of Darsie Latimer and his uncle Redgauntlet—Sir Robert Redgauntlet and his son. In telling the tale to Darsie (who, as the heir of the Redgauntlets is, though neither of them know it at this stage, Wandering Willie's master if the feudal pattern is to be preserved), Willie is acting as a minstrel to his lord; yet he is but a wandering minstrel, picked up by chance by Darsie in his aimless travels. The tale involves the violence of the Scottish heroic past, but that violence is in the telling filtered through a shrewd and unromantic mind. It is also, of course, a perfect piece of story-telling in itself, a model of how to tell a tale dealing with the supernatural (allowing alternative, natural explanations, if the reader wishes to accept them, for all but one or two details), the perfect counterpart in prose, from the point of view of technique though not of content, of Burns's "Tam o' Shanter."

The language of the tale is a racy late eighteenth-century Scots. The tradition of Scots literary prose was quite dead by the eighteenth century; there had been a revival of Scots poetry, but the novel came too late to rescue Scots prose. All the great prose writers of eighteenth-century Scotland wrote in standard English, and some—like David Hume—had their manuscripts looked over by an English friend to be purged of "Scotticisms." Scots had long ceased to be a literary language with literary norms of its own and had degenerated into a series of regional dialects. The only way in which Scots could now be effectively used in literature was through dialogue, and Scott made the most of his opportunity here. The dialogue of his "low" characters—always so much livelier and more convincing than that of his formal heroes and heroines—contains some of the finest Scots of the century. "Wandering Willie's Tale," being an oral tale put into the mouth of a wandering minstrel, is told in a racy spoken Scots. It was a device to enable Scott to use more Scots in his novel than he would otherwise have found possible. For it never occurred to him to endeavor to restore a literary Scots prose by a deliberate conflation of dialects and standard English (as in some degree Burns did with Scots verse) and write his novels in that idiom. When Scott speaks in his own person in the novels he uses standard English, except for an occasional "Scotticism" of which he was unaware. After all, he aimed at an English audience.

The main defect of *Redgauntlet,* as of so many of Scott's novels, even his greatest, is that he uses the conventional plot patterns available to him to provide the external structure of his story, and these plot patterns are really quite unsuitable to the kind of exploration of the relation between tradition and progress which Scott is carrying out. Green Mantle, for all her autobiographical overtones, is just a nuisance; the love interest is perfunctory and unnecessary, and the theme of the lost and rediscovered heir (though handled here better and more organically than anywhere else in Scott) really otiose. Even a character like Nanty Ewart, the former student of divinity who goes to the dogs after carelessly ruining a girl, comes from the sentimental tradition of the late eighteenth century and has no business in this novel at all. And the Dickensian complications and resolutions of the plot, though done with considerable adroitness, are somewhat mechanical.

The real greatness of *Redgauntlet* lies in its dramatic investigation, through the interrelations of the appropriate characters, of the validity and implications of different attitudes toward Scotland's past and present. Nowhere else is this favorite theme of Scott's presented with such vitality and power. This vitality is felt even in the most ordinary of domestic scenes—

those describing the relation between Saunders Fairford and his son, for example, which are genuinely moving in virtue of the fully realized treatment of dialogue and action. Between sober routine and romantic melodrama, between daily domestic and professional life and the flamboyant crisis, between living in the world as it is and living in the world of the obsessed imagination, lies a whole gamut of attitudes and experiences. In creating a story which runs this gamut and explores all the crucial points on it Scott has written a kind of historical novel very different from what the historical novel is generally taken to be. He shows that attitudes toward history and attitudes toward the present depend on one another, and both depend on the character of the man who has the attitude, and that in turn depends in part on environment, which in turn is the product of history. We cannot escape from the past, for it has created us; yet we must escape from the past if we are to live in the real world. And the antiquarian can only write books; he cannot re-enact the past he writes about. And, in a profound sense, that for Scott was a tragic insight.

Old Mortality's Silent Minority

Peter D. Garside

*O*ld Mortality, in several respects the most *historical* of Scott's novels, could also claim to be his most *political,* and in a thoroughly direct and 'nineteenth-century' way. Recent emphasis on Scott's sense of historical process has drawn attention away from a contrary tendency towards direct historical parallelism. In a letter to Southey, Louis Bourbon's death automatically sparks off large-scale comparison:

> Strange times we have lived in! I am speaking of Charles X as a Frenchman of 1661 might have spoken of Charles II. By the way, did you ever observe how easy it would be for a good historian to run a parallel between the Great Rebel-lion and the French Revolution, just substituting the spirit of fanaticism for that of soi-disant philosophy. (*Letters,* ed. Grierson, VIII, 376)

Southey, taking the hint, encouraged Scott to write up just 'such a parallel,' though Scott had already sketched out some of his ideas in the *Edinburgh Annual Register's* 'History of Europe' for 1815, quoting Clarendon at length to establish a 'remarkable parallel' between the Bourbons' first re-accession and Charles II's restoration, and in *Paul's Letters to his Kinsfolk* (1816), where Eng-land in 1660 ('to which we almost involuntarily resort as a parallel case') serves to elucidate France in 1815. Governing much of this, too, was unques-tionably Scott's concern for present-day Britain: a yardstick of stability by which the French might learn, yet (less sanguinely) still needing guidance from past and near-contemporary experience. In fact, comparisons of this nature remained a prevalent feature of British thought from Waterloo to the Reform Bill debates of 1831–2. A good example of their operation in a fairly averagely 'alarmed' Tory mind in the 1820s is William Aiton's *History of the Rencounter at Drumclog and Battle of Bothwell Bridge* (1821), which moves from errors of fact in *Old Mortality,* through observations on a meeting of radicals held at Drumclog in 1815 (purportedly encouraged by Napoleon's escape from Elba), to 'Reflections' on the 'Folly and Dangers of the Lower Orders in Society becoming Politicians, and attempting to Direct the Government.'

From *Scottish Literary Journal* 7/1 (May 1980): 127–44. Reprinted by permission of the Association for Scottish Literary Studies and Peter D. Garside.

Considerable scorn is reserved for the protesters' naive sense of precedent, though Aiton himself freely offers the Independents' ascendancy over Presbyterianism in the Civil War as a salutary warning to latter-day Whigs against dallying with radicalism. Heavy in application (the 'labouring classes' are advised to 'fear God; honour the King; and to avoid them that are given to change'), Aiton's parallels still seem to derive from a well-established habit of thought, capable of moving fluently between the Civil War, French Revolution, Napoleon, and contemporary Britain. Moreover, though never directly invoked, there is every indication that Aiton considered *Old Mortality* a fully supportive document, written by a fellow Tory, borderer and sheriff in the wake of a recent and still ominous local disturbance.

Nor was Scott likely to have quarrelled with the response, though at the time of writing he would almost certainly have seen his position as 'moderate,' and by no means reactionary. Both the 'History of Europe' and *Paul's Letters* hold out the hope of a 'constitutionalist' France, though clouded by the possibility of an outbreak of old extremisms, with 'moderate' opinion particularly vulnerable in any impending 'collision of parties.' *Old Mortality,* written shortly after *Paul's Letters* and while Scott was researching materials for the *Annual Register,* sets out a comparable situation, though with less indifferent 'moderates' and stronger *British* connotations. In Chapter 29,[1] the 'moderate' royalist Evandale, alarmed by 'the fanaticism and violent irritation of both parties,' wishes 'every Whig as moderate as Morton'—the same Morton who two chapters earlier is found rallying 'the moderate party among the insurgents,' convinced that their petition will find sympathy 'even among the royalists,' particularly with the 'moderate' Duke of Monmouth. Scott clearly thought himself a 'moderate Tory,' and liked to claim affinity with the 'moderate Whig;' his political statements are filled with the ill-effects of party spirit and dangers of Whig-radical alliance. It is easy at the best of times to underestimate the political message locked in all the Waverley Novels. But I suspect that in 1816, as the euphoria of Waterloo faded and internal divisions started to show, Scott waited with particular keenness for news of his novel's success with the Whigs, and must have relished John Murray's account of its overpowering (even gout-quelling) success at Holland House (see *Letters,* ed. Grierson, IV, 318n). If we are alive to this kind of possibility, all sorts of lost topicalities are likely to emerge. Evandale and Morton can be seen as surrogate 'moderates,' drawn into open conflict in an atmosphere of increasing party enthusiasm; the more extreme Covenanters could be Scott's radicals, embroiling, then overwhelming more orthodox Whigs while inciting 'the mob of the insurgents, always loudest in applause of those who push political or religious opinions to extremity' (Ch. 26); while Claverhouse might easily embody a genuine fear of a new High Toryism, militarist, autocratic, even bureaucratic. Clearly it would be misleading to claim a full political allegory, a kind of Regency *Animal Farm;* but the unrelenting 'historicist' bent in much Scott criticism has undoubtedly obscured a whole range of *contemporary* significance, and any fresh reading of the novel must be prepared to face this full on.

Another singularity lies in the novel's unmistakable 'exuberance of dialogue.'[2] Lady Louisa Stuart cheerfully observed how the *cognoscenti* first thought it not Scott's since lacking 'that constant description of scenery that makes him so tiresome,' while Scott's contemporary reviews, including his own *Quarterly,* were quick to point out 'the peculiar excellence of the *dialogue*' (*Letters,* ed. Grierson, IV, 345n; *Quarterly Review,* XVI, 469). Modern critics have generally followed suit, Angus Calder praising Scott's 'ventriloquist's gifts,' R. C. Gordon noting a never-to-be-excelled 'vitality' in 'the speech of the characters,' Alexander Welsh and Francis Hart both mounting complex analyses on the difficulties faced by Morton in self-expression (Introduction to the Penguin *Old Mortality* [Harmondsworth, 1975], p. 34; *Under Which King?* [Edinburgh, 1969], p. 53; *The Hero of the Waverley Novels* [New Haven, 1963], Ch. 9; *Scott's Novels* [Charlottesville, 1966], pp. 78–80). But the prevalence of speech *in the text,* and more particularly the latter's constant signalling of the speech-act itself, have largely gone unnoticed in Anglo-American criticism. Yet 'speech' is the main token by which characters judge each other: Claverhouse, Morton ('your language corresponds with all I have heard of you' [Ch. 13]); Morton, Burley ('I must remind you that you are unnecessarily using dangerous language in the presence of a mere stranger,' 'much of this sort of language, which, I observe is so powerful with others, is entirely lost on me,' 'I know no reason you have . . . to use such uncivil language' [Chs. 5, 21, 26]); the Covenanters, Morton ("Macbriar . . . instantly recognized the words" [Ch. 33]); Cuddie, the Covenanters ('They are wild Western Whigs . . . I ken by their language' [Ch. 33]); Bothwell, ironically, Mause ("The finest language I ever heard" [Ch. 8]). It also works as a 'test' in both camps: 'He hath spoken the word . . . he hath avowed his carnal self-seeking and Erastianism,' 'again hath his mouth spoken it,' 'If they speak a word of cant or fanatical nonsense, let them have a strapping with a shoulder-belt,' 'We shall know . . . how to make you find your tongue' (Chs. 33, 14, 36). Scott's direct narrative, too, is often heavily involved, noting in turn 'the virulent strife of tongues' after Drumclog and 'violence in language' before Bothwell Bridge, accentuating the spoken word down to its expiratory source ('the first words he uttered,' 'having uttered these words,' 'as she uttered these words,' 'collecting the last effort of respiration to utter these desperate words, and expiring as soon as they were spoken'), focusing likewise on the physical appurtenances of speech (a remorseful Jenny wishing her 'tongue . . . cuttit out' [Ch. 28], Lauderdale 'lolling out a tongue which was at all times too big for his mouth' [Ch. 36]), sometimes allowing an unusual precedence to 'words' over 'expression' ('Lady Margaret was little able to reply to a *speech* so much in unison with her usual *expressions* and *feelings*,' 'His *words* became distinct, his *manner* more earnest and energetic' [Chs. 20 & 18, my italics]). In several respects, *Old Mortality* bears a striking resemblance to Mikhail

Bakhtin's 'dialogic' (or 'polyphonic') novel, which is dominated by a 'plurality of independent and unmerged voices' (*Problems of Dostoevsky's Poetics,* tr. R. W. Rostel [Ann Arbor, 1973], p. 4 and *passim*). Scott's authorial voice, admittedly, asserts a detached authority; but his narrative base often seems unusually sparse and isolated—at points even threatened by theoretically extraneous voices, themselves hectically dominant in a kind of secular Pandemonium.

This might seem a long way from political allegory, and is liable to remain so unless we are prepared to look more closely at Regency 'moderacy' and the nature of Scott's involvement. Here again a useful pointer is provided by a document virtually contemporary with *Old Mortality,* the pamphlet record of *The Speeches and Public Addresses of the Right Hon. George Canning, during the election in Liverpool . . . 1816.* Canning, freshly returned from a frustrating ambassadorship in Lisbon, and facing the constant threat of radical Whig opposition, stood at a crossroads in his political career, and in a much-reported campaign was careful to project himself as the unflappable 'moderate,' firm to Commerce and Constitution while ever vigilant against 'the influx of foreign theories.' Like Scott, he frequently warns about the vulnerability of 'moderacy:' 'I take leave of you this evening; exhorting you to maintain that moderation which you have displayed hitherto, without, however, at all relaxing that firmness which has caused your moderation to be respected' (op. cit., p. 25). At the same time, one notices Canning's constant attempt to reify his equilibrium in distinctly verbal and stylistic terms, an endeavour made explicit in the Introduction: 'Mr. Canning's style may be termed emphatically an *English* one, as contradistinguished from that florid and fanciful oratory which is clearly of Irish origin, and which abounds in violent metaphor, forced allusion, and tumid diction, more than can be reconciled to the rigour of English taste. Mr. Canning's speeches are wholly free from these ambitious absurdities. They exhibit great vigour of thought, and exquisite eloquence of expression' (ibid., p. 5). Anxious while asserting confidence, insistent that the interests of 'true' Whigs and Tories are the same (the opposition is identified as 'Burdettism rather than Whiggism'), half-conscious of a concealed anarchism needing only verbal encouragement ('the subtle arts of restless demagogues') to materialise, the document takes us to the heart of orthodox politics in 1816, and is perhaps most remarkable for its ultra-consciousness about language, in the wrong hands a lord of misrule, correctly used a token of time-honoured standards. Scott's own contemporary observations frequently reveal a similar suspicion of 'strong language,' a distrust reflected in his historical judgements, particularly of the seventeenth century. Moreover, as I argue in an article entitled 'Scott's Political Speech,' which will appear in a future number of *Scottish Literary Journal,* there are signs in his make-up of a peculiarly *psychological* dependence on an idea of a silent 'moderacy,' deeply rooted in his own sense of a relative inarticulateness in rapid debate and oratorical statement. Two of his main activities, the mastership of

Abbotsford and silent authorship of the Waverley Novels, can be interpreted as part expressions of a consciously non-voluble Tory constitutionalism. If Abbotsford ideally embodied a tangible world of 'real' action and active social relations, the Waverley Novels strove from that security to communicate an essentially quietist 'moderacy' through the hubbub of political controversy. Yet both were prone to moments of self-doubt. Just as Abbotsford could appear a dream or vanity, so the novels and their audience of honorary 'moderates' might appear an illusion, the sustaining message merely a collection of 'words.' In such ways the linkage of politics and language was vital for Scott, and is likely to prove crucial in so tersely political a work as *Old Mortality*.

With this in mind it is worth turning to one of the novel's most celebrated sequences, the succession of sermons which follows on the Covenanters' unexpected victory at Drumclog. Strictly speaking this is not a continuum, but occurs in two distinct sections: the first (Ch. 18) involving two main speakers, Kettledrummle and Macbriar; the second (Ch. 22) dominated by the arch-extremist Mucklewrath. But it is still legitimate to think of a concerted gradation, and with special importance for Scott. Historically, it undoubtedly reflects three main categories in his sources, the homely prolixity of the field preacher, the more intense metaphor of the testimonies, and the fierce declamatory style of the Cameronians' 'declarations.' In more contemporary terms, too, there plainly resides a fairly straightforward message about the perils of accelerating radicalism, with Scott's 'essentially plebeian'[3] Presbyterians never far distant from the 'demagogues' of his Tory imagination. Both readings are entirely valid, but the complexity of Scott's narrative encourages further investigation, perhaps into areas where 'intention' is less obviously decisive. Several distinct strands are worth temporarily isolating. (i) The decline of the general narrative voice, originally broadly 'philosophical,' then more 'aesthetic' in its judgements, finally muted or uncertain. Kettledrummle is controlled by neo-Johnsonian censure, Macbriar elicits a more Wartonian response, but Mucklewrath emerges straight from the text unhindered by overt literary stricture. (ii) An associated movement from indirect to direct speech. Kettledrummle is largely contained in scathingly ironic third-person reportage; Macbriar, though mostly paraphrased, is finally allowed a sizeable flourish of direct rhetoric; but Mucklewrath appears abruptly and in full cry, 'a shrill, broken, and overstrained voice from the crowd,' his speech direct and *in toto*. (iii) The declining physicality of the speakers, matched by a growing potency in 'voice.' Kettledrummle's 'square face' and 'unanimated features' are immediately set against Macbriar's 'thin' and 'worn out' look, though the latter's 'words' gradually gain a more devastating effect. Mucklewrath's features, however, 'extenuated by penury and famine, until they hardly retained the likeness of a human aspect,' appear only after his initial outburst, a natural adjunct to 'such a voice and such language.' (iv) The declining 'objectivity' of the speeches. Kettledrummle's heavy burlesque gives his a decidedly referential air, but Macbriar works almost exclusively in rapid and elevated metaphor. Mucklewrath continues in a metaphoric vein, though his fiercer language tends to cut backwards at an already established reality, its implication clear from our fresh memory of the Bellendens: 'take the daughters and the mothers of the house and hurl them from the battlements of their trust, that the dogs may fatten on their blood as they did on that of Jezebel . . .' (v) The response of the listeners, a process leading back to Burley's instigation of the speeches as a means of diverting the army's unavailing 'clamour . . . for bread and other necessaries.' Kettledrummle offers 'cake of the right leaven,' Macbriar 'heavenly manna' (his audience 'elevated above the wants of the world'), but Mucklewrath forges a new determination for action ('We receive the command; . . . as he hath said, so will we do'). (vi) The final vulnerability of 'moderacy', when its spokesmen finally emerge in Chapter 22. Poundtext, a doughty opponent in the opening 'din' of debate, wilts before Mucklewrath's scream 'ere he could articulate a word;' while Morton manages only one exasperated protest ('This is utter abomination and daring impiety') before staggering away, 'Astonished, disgusted, and horror-struck at what he had . . . heard!'

Isolated in this way several of these elements might seem to possess a more obvious, even trite, function (e.g., the potentially clichéistic association of emaciation and fanaticism). Yet reassembled the pieces form a more than averagely engaging pattern. From a starting-point in action 'words' are deliberately deployed to obscure 'reality' so that action (of a sort) can continue; yet so potent do those 'words' prove that they end by creating their own 'reality', and become themselves a motive for action. At the same time, an originally controlling and diachronic narrative appears to lose weight in the face of alien and predominantly metaphoric speech forms. Naturally one should be wary of underestimating Scott's urbanity and powers of manipulation, and at one level the depth of the nightmare adds strength to the intended moral and actively endorses the author's control. Nevertheless, it is still a *nightmare,* and more than the extremity of his situation could lie behind Morton's frailty. A similar intensity underlies the novel's other main physical engagement at Bothwell Bridge. Before the event (Ch. 30), 'words' are constantly asserted in the face of Morton's desire for conciliation or, failing that, action: Macbriar elevates 'the Word' above all secular considerations, the Cameronians make their unhistorical entrance 'morose and jealous in communication.' Rejoining the army (Ch. 31), Morton finds a Babel of party contention, 'their pickets and patrols . . . more interested in defining the limits of Erastian heresy than in looking out for . . . their enemies', with Mucklewrath again the strongest 'speaker'. 'Names' now openly challenge 'reality': for Mucklewrath, Morton is 'one of those men of Belial who, in the words of his text, had gone out amongst them'; 'a lukewarm Presbyterian', to the Cameronians, is 'little better than a Prelatist, an Anti-Covenanter, and a Nullifidian'; others are wryly observed 'moderating a harmonious call, as they somewhat improperly termed it.' One of Morton's rare 'heroic' speeches calls for action not words:

'Silence your senseless clamours; yonder is the enemy!' But even in direct conflict language remains a decisive factor as Morton, in pursuit of vital reinforcements, suffers incapacitating verbal misrepresentation 'ere he could speak his errand or utter his orders.' With the effective disappearance of 'moderacy' as a communicable ideology, both in field and council, Morton clings more anxiously to a realm of action, where 'union' might still be achieved in the face of a common enemy. But the threat is indigenous, and 'words' and disunion continue to prevail. Throughout, in effect, one senses Scott's *current* insecurities as much as the proposed historical event. And perhaps what is ultimately most at threat is the validity of his novel as a vehicle of 'truth,' its authorised signifiers never quite reaching the desired signified, while alien voices move arbitrarily in their own 'dangerous' world.

It is by now a critical commonplace that a similar scale of extremism exists in the Royalist camp, though it has not been fully observed how much this is conveyed in speech. Gudyill's bibulously loyal wish that Bothwell succeeds in 'raking this country clear o' Whigs and Roundheads, fanatics and Covenanters' chimes, for example, with Kettledrummle's equally inhumane sloganising when exhorting the Covenanters to 'expel from the land' all 'Papists, Prelatists, Erastians, assuming the name of Presbyterians, Independents, Socinians and Quakers' (Chs. 9, 18). As hostilities intensify, Major Bellenden reaches a metaphoric pitch not so distinct from Macbriar: 'I ought to have been aware that I was nursing a wolf-cub, whose diabolical nature would make him tear and snatch at me on the first opportunity' (Ch. 25). There is even evidence of a third degree of intensity in Claverhouse's reaction to news of rebellion:

'When the adder crawls into the daylight . . . I can trample him to death; he is only safe when he remains lurking in his den or morass' (Ch. 12),

which is later matched by Mucklewrath's verbal assault on Tillietudlem:

'I say take the infants and dash them against the stones . . . Slay utterly, old and young, the maiden, the child and the woman whose head is grey. Defile the house, and fill the courts with the slain.' (Ch. 22)

But from here the resemblance fades, as Claverhouse's language becomes increasingly literal and non-figurative (in the Privy Council [Ch. 36] he even tells Lauderdale to proceed 'without further metaphor'). His orders at Tillietudlem are uncompromisingly abstract, the solitary figure sharply metonymic, moral consideration firmly subject to the 'word':

'You are to behave bravely, soberly, regularly, and obediently . . . In case of mutiny, cowardice, neglect of duty, or the slightest excess in the family, the provost-marshal and cord—you know I keep my word for good and evil.' (Ch. 20)

The same toneless commingling of moral disparates is apparent after Bothwell Bridge:

> All these various orders—for life and death, the securing of his prisoners, and the washing his charger's shoulders—were given in the same unmoved and equable voice, of which no accent or tone intimated that the speaker considered one direction as of more importance than another. (Ch. 34)

At this point Mucklewrath rises from the floor to predict Claverhouse's death: 'Wilt thou trust in thy bow and in thy spear, and in thy steed and in thy banner?' The contrast of styles seems total, but in opposition lies a similarity. Claverhouse will shortly ridicule the Covenanters' misapplication of text, though his own judgements are surprisingly text-centred: orders stem from the strict letter of military law; his personal bible is Froissart; campaigns are accompanied by a 'black book' record of opponents' names 'arranged in alphabetical order.' An equivalent linguistic divergence also allows a similar extremism in action—particularly the sentence of death, which Claverhouse and Mucklewrath so frequently proclaim. 'The word thou hast spurned shall become a rock to crush and to bruise thee' (Ch. 33). 'Take the other three down to the yard, draw out two files, and fire upon them; and d'ye hear, make a memorandum in the orderly book of three rebels taken in arms and shot' (Ch. 34). In such a framework, the two meanings of 'sentence'—the linguistic and legalistic—are virtually indistinguishable.

Claverhouse and Burley, who make more obvious strange bedfellows, also show similar habits in sentence-forming. Claverhouse's arbitrary and often negative sentences usually move downwards to enclose and nullify the sentimentally-suggested private feeling. 'Let it be your first task to subject to the public interest, and to the discharge of your duty, your private passions, affections, and feelings' (Ch. 13). Or reversing the pattern: 'I hope my private affections will never interfere with my public duty' (Ch. 15). And more heroic at first sight: 'I will not yield to my own feelings a deeper sympathy than I have given to those of others' (Ch. 20). Theocratic rather than autocratic, Burley's syntax works in the same unmysterious way. 'No . . . we are enjoined to smite the ungodly, though he be our neighbour, and the man of power and cruelty, though he were our own kindred and the friend of our bosom' (Ch. 6). 'But our carnal affections will mislead us . . . They must be as earnest in their struggles as thou . . . that would shake themselves clear of the clogs and chains of humanity' (Ch. 30). Apart from perfunctory indications of tone, most of such statements appear to spring fully-armed from the text, so that each character is effectively denied full subjectivity. Though in Burley's case, when he is found sleeping at Milnwood, there is an interesting half-exception:

> The perspiration stood on his brow, 'like bubbles in a late disturbed stream', and these marks of emotion were accompanied with broken words which

escaped from him at intervals: 'Thou art taken, Judas—thou art taken—Cling not to my knees—hew him down!—A priest? Ay, a priest of Baal, to be bound and slain, even at the brook of Kishon.—Firearms will not prevail against him—Strike—thrust with the cold iron—put him out of pain—put him out of pain, were it but for the sake of his grey hairs'.

Much alarmed at the import of these expressions . . . , Morton shook his guest by the shoulder in order to awake him. The first words he uttered were, 'Bear me where ye will, I will avouch the deed!' (Ch. 6)

Here there is evidence of three distinct stages. The first posits an emotion-based conscience. The second appears to indicate an inner discourse of 'broken words,' some subjectively emotional (e.g., Sharpe's 'grey hairs'), others more text-centered and anaesthetic in effect. Whilst the third, materialising in the fully-coded sentence, instantly shuts off the supposed starting-point. 'Words,' in this way, actively engage against the 'sentimental' and its alleged subjective base.

In contrast, the mouths of the 'moderates' are filled with 'sentimental' language, its connotations ranging from an amorphous eroticism to Anglican benevolism: 'warm affections' (Edith), 'energetic humanity' (Evandale), 'those feelings of natural humanity which Heaven has assigned to us as the general law of our conduct' (Morton) (Chs. 29, 6). At the same time, the general narrative works hard to emphasise the degree of feeling accompanying speech. 'Expression' frequently colours 'words' ('the noble warmth which dictated her language', 'the temporary animation which accompanied her language' [Chs. 24, 29]), or 'words' fall short of 'feeling' ('The manner, differing from the words, seemed to express a feeling much deeper and more agitating than was conveyed in the phrase he made use of' [Ch. 12]). Characters earnestly observe each other's expressions, Edith earnestly scrutinising her uncle's 'looks' and 'manner' during his 'earnest intercession' on Morton's behalf (Ch. 12). Sometimes 'words' fail altogether ('she . . . twice strove to speak, but her . . . mind refused to suggest words, and her tongue to utter them' [Ch. 13]), while sentences started can be difficult to finish ('as she hesitated how to frame the exception with which she meant to close the sentence,' 'He stopped, and his companion continued the sentence;' 'She paused, unable to bring out the word which should have come next' [Chs. 12, 22, 10]). Texts, particularly of a threatening sort, are few and far between. Major Bellenden, barring three stock exceptions, has 'not read a book these twenty years', and his scorn for Edith's diet in French romance ('One to three is as great odds as ever fought and won . . . these d---d books put all pretty men's actions out of countenance') is soon vindicated by Scott's more 'real' action, most glaringly in Bothwell's death after 'killing three men with his own hand' (Chs. 11, 16). Even Bothwell, who 'did not altogether want sympathy' (Ch. 13), leaves behind relics of a 'blighted affection', allowing Morton to moralise on the perversion of 'our best and most praiseworthy feelings' (Ch. 23).

Such sentiments find their safest haven in Scott's direct narrative, but once Morton is enticed by Burley into the novel's harsh political world it becomes necessary that he should formally 'speak'. Yet how slowly he is drawn in—a sense of something 'repulsive' in Burley's manner prevents him from 'opening the conversation'—and how stronger a speaker is Burley when he 'abruptly' begins. At the end of their first exchange (Ch. 5), Morton's response is characteristically internal and associationist ('A thousand recollections thronged on the mind of Morton at once'). And were it not for earlier promptings on his behalf, his attempt at self-justification next day would seem almost half-hearted:

> There was little conversation between them, until at length Burley suddenly asked Morton, 'Whether the words he had spoken over-night had borne fruit in his mind?'
> Morton answered, 'That he remained of the same opinion which he had formerly held, and was determined, at least as far and as long as possible, to unite the duties of a good Christian with those of peaceful subject.'
> 'In other words,' replied Burley, 'you are desirous to serve both God and Mammon . . .' (Ch. 6)

Burley's tirade leaves Morton stranded, his own contribution advancing no further than this first shorthand statement, so awkwardly locked in a hybrid of direct and indirect speech. Hart argues the difficulty of the liberal among extremists, forced to speak in 'an abstract, formal coldly detached way' (*Scott's Novels*, p. 79), though this might easily beg a prior question about the *reality* rather than the expressibility of Morton's 'opinion'. Consider his subsequent soliloquy:

> 'Farewell, stern enthusiast', said Morton, looking after him; 'in some moods of my mind, how dangerous would be the society of such a companion! If I am unmoved by his zeal for abstract doctrines of faith, or rather for a peculiar mode of worship (such was the purport of his reflections), can I be a man and a Scotchman, and look with indifference on that persecution which has made wise men mad?' (Ch. 6)

At first Morton is shown 'speaking,' but the qualifying parenthesis almost immediately suggests paraphrased 'reflection'; from which point Morton spirals downward from a sense of public to private alienation ('I am sick of my country, of myself, of my dependent situation, of my repressed feelings'), before ending with an operatically vocal determination to follow fame abroad:

> 'But I am no slave', he said aloud . . . 'Perhaps some lucky chance may raise me to rank with our Ruthvens, our Lesleys, our Monroes, the chosen leaders of the famous Protestant champion, Gustavus Adolphus; or, if not, a soldier's life or a soldier's grave.' (Ch. 6)

Welsh, sensing a fatal dichotomy between 'social' and 'erotic' urges, sees the final outburst as raucously and unacceptably 'social' (*Hero of Waverley Novels,* p. 243). But, considered as a whole, the sequence's *arrangement* could just as well reflect a larger and more formal disparity between 'thought' and 'speech'. What Morton so badly needs is verification for his political ideology and, more pressing, the language in which it is expressed. Yet almost immediately his terminology is forced back into 'subjective' narrative. From there the movement is inward, as Morton searches for a meaning anterior to 'words' while (paradoxically) validating his own chosen 'word'. The desired goal, it seems, is an essentially pre-verbal 'thought'; more specifically, a subjectively knowable altruism, capable of moving outward through a range of social 'affections'. But what Morton ultimately faces is the prospect of a *nothingness,* making thought empty, words translucent, and other sign-systems potently self-justifying. This helps explain the abrupt movement back into language spoken 'aloud'. If 'heroic', it is an unsatisfactory and unsatisfying heroism: half shared and half observed by Scott, and significantly framed in autonomous-sounding 'speech'.

Later soliloquies reveal Morton in similarly indeterminate 'moods of mind': 'half speaking to himself', unable to 'utter . . . names even in soliloquy', 'arranging his reflections betwixt speech and thought' (Chs. 14, 39, 41). Likewise in more open situations he often appears tongue-tied: lost for the right word, unable to end what he has begun (the latter making him easy prey for Claverhouse and Burley, both of whom have a nasty habit of finishing other people's sentences). Temporarily re-united with Edith under threat of death at Tillietudlem, 'words' prove his least adequate means of expression:

> loading her with a profusion of thanks and gratitude which would be hardly intelligible from the mere broken words, unless we could describe the tone, the gesture, the impassioned and hurried indications of deep and tumultuous feeling, with which they were accompanied. (Ch. 10)

Again, under the Convenanters' sentence, only the formal code is available to fill the vacuum:

> It was with pain that he felt his mind wavering, while on the brink between this and the future world. He made a strong effort to compose himself to devotional exercises, and unequal, during that fearful strife of nature, to arrange his own thoughts into suitable expressions, he had, instinctively, recourse to . . . the Book of Common Prayer. (Ch. 33)

Morton *in extremis* reaches for established religion in the same way that elsewhere he clings to the language of Constitutionalism. Yet how can he be sure his own code is better than others, and what bearing has its formal stability on the confusions of his inner experience and equally confusing 'real' world?

Probably his most deliberate attempt at self-explanation occurs in his letter to Tillietudlem, accompanying the Covenanters' surrender terms. Both Scott's prefix ('It was couched in the following language') and the immediate positioning between the Covenanters' slogans and Bellenden's new-found metaphor point to the peculiar importance of the words chosen:

> I have taken a step, my venerable friend, which, among many painful consequences, will, I am afraid, incur your very decided disapprobation. But I have taken my resolution in honour and good faith, and with the full approval of my own conscience. I can no longer submit to have my own rights and those of my fellow-subjects trampled upon, our freedom violated, our persons insulted, and our blood spilt, without just cause or legal right. (Ch. 25)

The private ('*I* have taken a step, *my* . . . friend') strives for contact with the abstract ('honour and good faith'), the individual with the communal ('my *own* rights and those of my *fellow-subjects*'); a rise in emotion, metaphorical and reminiscent of Claverhouse ('trampled upon . . . our blood spilt'), is levelled and apparently contained by the general concept ('just cause or legal right'). Above all the passage aims for synthesis, for a vital meeting-point between Conscience and Constitution. Yet its language remains formal, the medium (a letter) adds distance while claiming authority, and the communication is exclusive to the charmed circle of 'moderacy'. In more assertive moments there is even a hint of stridency, a suggestion in the tone of what one *wished* one had said. 'You have thought it worth your while to bestow particular attention on my private affairs and personal attachments; be so good as to understand that I am as constant to them as to my political principles' (Ch. 26). 'My interference would have been the same from common humanity . . . ; to your lordship it was a sacred debt of gratitude' (Ch. 17). The impulse is to establish the essential *sameness* of things, the private 'friendship' and larger moral ruling, local attachment and a wider patriotism. But the words are still 'official'; while the model, more 'Augustan' this time in its compulsory balances, seems strained. Besides, nobody bothers much to listen.

In his post-Revolution sequel Scott returns to a more familiar *narrative* mode, the first task of which is to assert a new public stability and revived attention to 'private affairs'. Nevertheless, the quietism which is so obviously approved in Cuddie's case acquires a darker hue with Niel Blane's apolitical acquisitiveness ('politics . . . mine host did not care to mingle in his theme' [Ch. 41]), while Morton remains hopelessly insecure. Moreover, in a series of chapters critics agree are far from Scott's best, the most challenging sequence—Morton's quest-like journey to Burley's cave—culminates in a revived preoccupation with language. Armed with his talismanic 'benevolence', Morton ends his search at a waterfall (Ch. 43), amid the 'tumultuary sounds' of which he distinguishes Burley's 'shouts, screams, and even articulate words'. Far from the sub-Coleridgean hokum alleged by Welsh (ibid., p.

260), topography and movement combine to suggest a more probing return to the source of 'dangerous' speech. Even as Burley is perceived, 'sound' remains a dominant concern:

> His figure, dimly ruddied by the light of the red charcoal, seemed that of a fiend in the lurid atmosphere of Pandemonium, and his gestures and words, as far as they could be heard, seemed equally violent and irregular. (Ch. 43)

As at Milnwood, Burley's 'wild exclamations'—'What mutterest thou of grey hairs? It was well done to slay him'—quickly harden into that 'cold, determined manner which was peculiar to his ordinary discourse'. Again, too, the self-referential emphases of the speakers ('In a word', 'Sayest thou?', 'I do say so') signify no ordinary flyting. Burley's mounting idiosyncrasies lead to unprecedented syntactical gyrations, a kind of obverse of Morton's attempts at synthesis:

> 'The heathen virtues of such as he (Evandale) are more dangerous to us than the sordid cupidity of those who, governed by their interest, must follow where it leads, and who, therefore, themselves the slaves of avarice, may be compelled to work in the vineyard, were it but to earn the wages of sin.' (Ch. 43)

Morton, forced into oral defence, achieves a steadier movement than before:

> 'I will not dissemble with *you* . . . even to gain a good end. *I* came in hopes to persuade *you* to do a deed of justice to *others,* not to gain a selfish end of *my own*. *I* have failed; *I* grieve for *your* sake more than for the loss which *others* will sustain by your injustice.' (Ch. 43, my italics)

The style, a measured progression through pronouns, allows a new and vital *formal* security. Projecting a 'real' subjectivity, it gives tangible expression to Scott's ideal society of concentrically-developing 'affections'. Secure in its own dialogic self-containment, it offers a paradigm for the novel's communication of 'truth', from author (I), through 'words' (your), to audience (others). Morton can now jump safely from 'words' to life, whereas Burley, despite contract-burning and a final flurry of violence, is from here surprisingly mute, his hands perhaps significantly round his last opponent's *throat*.

But if Morton gains reassurance he hardly finds relaxation. Only in conversation with social subordinates does he ever seem to approach a meaningful reciprocity. While his own 'elaborated' code moves anxiously out from the first person, Cuddie and Ailie's more 'restricted' type,[4] grounded in dialect and folk culture, descends smoothly from communal awareness to individual commitment. As with Ailie at Milnwood:

> 'And when cam ye here, hinny? And where hae ye been? And what hae ye been doing? And what for did ye na write to us? And how cam ye to pass yoursell

for dead? And what for did ye come creepin' to your ain house as if ye had been an unco body to gie poor auld Ailie sic a start?' she concluded, smiling through her tears. (Ch. 39)

Together, too, the styles form their own distinct and self-generating pattern, from personal to communal and back to personal—a flexible and more satisfying version of Morton's singular progressions. Also the communal voice, local and organic, appears as much threatened as Morton by the externally blank third person: 'they are heading and hanging among us, and trailing us after thae blackguard troopers, and taking our goods and gear as if we were outlaws. I canna say I tak it kind at their hands' (Ch. 14). But most important is the sense of a silent communication, initiating and then shading dialogue. This is apparent right at the start of Morton's longest conversation with Cuddie, Morton characteristically in 'deep dejection':

Instinctively he turned his head back to take a last look of a scene [Tilli-etudlem] formerly so dear to him, and no less instinctively he heaved a deep sigh. It was echoed by a loud groan from his companion in misfortune, whose eyes, moved, perchance, by similar reflections, had taken the same direction. This indication of sympathy on the part of the captive was uttered in a tone more coarse than sentimental; it was, however, the expression of a grieved spirit, and so far corresponded with the sigh of Morton. In turning their heads their eyes met, and Morton recognised the stolid countenance of Cuddie Head-rigg, bearing a rueful expression, in which sorrow for his own lot was mixed with sympathy for the lot of his companion. (Ch. 14)

The notion of an innate 'sympathy' provides Scott with his strongest weapon in the war of 'words'. As in Smith and Hume, it argues a basic transference in sentiments, a psychological interdependence by which Morton can transcend the perils of subjectivity. The centrality of the idea can be gauged in another resonant immediate moment, Ailie's archetypal 'recognition' of Morton at Milnwood (Ch. 39). Morton is again lost in subjectivity, 'confounded', 'confused', linguistically alienated ('I have almost forgotten my own language'), awkwardly reticent ('he would have had difficulty in answering her, even if he had known well what to say'). Ailie in turn is non-committal. Until Morton is recognised by, and instinctively names, the household dog: 'Ye ken our dog's name ... And the creature kens you too ... it's my ain bairn!' Our equally immediate resistance to canine loyalists and selflessly devoted housekeepers only half dulls the consummation. The instinct precedes the word, but the instinctual word is necessary for final human recognition. And from this Morton gains a brief verbal confidence, a foretaste of the style which will shortly overcome Burley: '*I* do indeed live ... and ... rejoice that there is at least one *friend* to welcome me back to my *native country*.'

It is easy with hindsight to be scathing about Scott's hopes. His ideal 'sympathy' sometimes smacks of the palliative, alleviating class differences which now seem desperately unfair. Undeniably, too, Scott uses the novelist's full prerogative to make his own ideology central while casting others to a dehumanising fringe. In identifying 'words' as the source of political unrest he also effectively turns attention away from any underlying social or economic factor. But most of all the search for a satisfying style reflects the uncertainty of a class hegemony, identifying and attempting to stabilise itself through a language held always to be more 'social' than 'political', resisting while travestying alternatives beyond that pale, finding half-comfort in the tones of a suppliant yet suitably 'clownish' peasantry. A recent advertisement for Citroen cars invites the potential buyer to 'join the silent minority'— appealing no doubt to the individual's craving in a mass society for *exclusiveness*. Conversely, Scott's *minority* society wanted so badly to feel itself truly a majority, the hub of national well-being, less noisy than it *could* be. Such objections might seem carping, or simply beside the point, but there is an at least equal danger in too casually taking Scott's text as a source of detachable truth. Besides, an awareness of limitation helps clarify those impulses which do survive: Scott's fear of a text-bound totalitarianism; his accompanying belief in a society flowing from the individual and toward local communities; above all, his abiding (and I would suggest motivating) faith in an inherent and encourageable altruism. Of course generosity meant loyalty, and Scott pinned his colours to a dubious and fated mast. At the height of Reform agitation in 1831, feeling obliged to 'speak' in his own locality, he was badly mauled by a Jedburgh gallery which must have seemed uncomfortably close to his own Covenanter-radicals. Next day he wrote to Henry Scott, M. P. for Roxburghshire, his letter coming to life with one poignant detail. 'I had the misfortune to lost [sic] little Spice through the carelessness of a dunce [sic] servant who let her escape in the tumult which has kept me a little busy . . . I fear little chance of her finding her way back' (National Library of Scotland, MS 1752, f. 241).⁵ As defeat looms large, one senses the disintegration of several of those elements—the loyal servant, momentarily a 'dunce', the faithful pet, now 'lost' in a 'tumult'—by which Scott had endeavoured to sustain and invigorate his chosen world. But the destruction of the myth's shell need not distract us from the reality it might easily contain.

Notes

1. All quotations are from vol. 5 of the Border edition of the Waverley Novels, ed. Andrew Lang (London, 1901).

2. The phrase is from ch. 1 of *The Bride of Lammermoor.*

3. See Lockhart's account of a conversation in 1818, in which Scott describes the Scottish Reformation as both 'plebeian' and 'republican' (*Life of Scott,* ed. A. W. Pollard [London, 1900], III, 227.)

4. I am conscious of using terms from Basil Bernstein's *Class, Codes and Control,* vol. 1 (London, 1971), though it must be added that Bernstein's model is anticipated by Scott's liter-

ary prototypes, the ballad and "sentimental" novel. It is worth considering generally how much Bernstein's "results" reflect a long-established *literary* presentation of class differences. Roger Fowler, *Linguistics and the Novel* (London, 1977), p. 115, takes the tradition back as far as Lawrence; Smollett might have been a better starting-point.

    5.   Scott has deleted 'dunce' in the MS.

Real and Narrative Time:
Waverley and the Education of Memory

MARILYN ORR

Beginning in *Waverley,* Scott the novelist sets himself "the task of tracing the evanescent manners" of the traditional culture of Scotland, for "there is no European nation which, within the course of half a century or little more, has undergone so complete a change as the little kingdom of Scotland."[1] Conscious of the completeness of this change, he writes in order to make readers "aware of the progress we have made" but also of the loss that this progress has entailed; and his novel is meant to help focus this change for the "we" who "fix our eye on the now distant point from which we have been drifted" (*W,* 72:364).[2] Scott does not try simply to memorialize the difference of the ancient culture or figuratively to bring this "distant point" closer by enhancing the affinities between past and present. Instead "the Author of *Waverley*" compels his hero and challenges his readers to become active in the process by which "we have been drifted"—passive, despite our progress—by the movement of time. As the first of what will become his exemplary historical novels,[3] *Waverley* radically redefines the relationship between individuals and history, not by inviting readers to observe its hero in relation to history, but by employing narrative to analyze the nature of time itself, activating the memories of its readers to draw them into the process by which history emerges out of the interrelation of time and memory.

In the novel Scott sets his notoriously passive hero to work out his relationship to time: he must learn to set his private time according to the public time of history. Simultaneously, Scott sets his readers the congruent task of working out a relationship to time through their reading of *Waverley* and of its hero.[4] Although the history that is the novel's subject is past history for the reader and contemporary history for Waverley, both character and reader confront this history as public time, a sphere that is distinct from, yet related to, the private time of individual experience. While for Edward Waverley, individual, private time is reset according to the public time of history, for the readers of his story the adjustment works in the opposite direction, a resetting of the sense of the public time of history according to the private time of indi-

From *Studies in English Literature 1500–1900* 31/4 (Autumn 1991): 715–34. Reprinted by permission.

viduals. While Waverley moves from his experience to an understanding of history and of his place in history, readers move from their accustomed perception of history as inscribed event (or text) to an understanding of the experiences out of which history has emerged.[5] For both Waverley and the reader, this changed perspective is accomplished in the process by which memory changes the relationship between self and time.

I

Underlying Scott's understanding of the process of memory are two related distinctions: a distinction between two kinds of memory (voluntary versus involuntary) and a distinction between two kinds of time (real versus narrative). Although the two kinds of memory are not actually differentiated until *Chronicles of the Canongate* (1827) and the two kinds of time are never explicitly differentiated, both distinctions are implicit from the beginning of the Waverley Novels. In *Waverley* the hero comes to understand what Scott in this novel calls "real time" and learns to distinguish it from what I will call "narrative time." Edward Waverley's ability to make this distinction is linked to his learning to respond to his involuntary memory and to recognize its distinction from his voluntary memory. It is the latter that may then be activated to narrate his time.

Scott introduces the concept of "real time" very late in the novel as a rather transparent gloss on the hero's realistic chastening. In chapter 70 readers are informed that "considerably more than two months" of "real time" elapse before Waverley's wedding, a delay of the conventionally romantic conclusion of his story. This "real time" obstructs by virtue of being "occupied" by "law proceedings" and the tedious inconveniences of travel (*W,* 70:348). Reflecting the overall movement of the novel towards moderation and compromise, real time modifies the romantic passion and the romantic resolution. The "important matters" that delay the marriage, the narrator notes, "may be briefly told in narrative," and they are so told, occupying little narrative time (*W,* 70:348). But Scott refuses to allow the narrative time they *may* take to replace or obscure the real time they *do* take. For the eager bridegroom, the fact that the delay may be so briefly told provides no consolation as he endures the real time of waiting. For readers, the negative correlation of our reading time and *Waverley*'s real time is a reminder that what is narrative time to us is unrelenting real time to him. Scott's deliberate drawing of attention here to the two kinds of time, a conventional technique of eighteenth-century novels, takes on a special pertinence in a historical novel which necessarily confronts more literally the problem of the transformation of experiential time into narration. And since readers of *Waverley* have been made aware of themselves as historical beings, located in time as historical change, the disjunction here between real time and narrative time implicitly locates the reader's own real time within potentially narrative time and suggests that our "important matters" may also turn out to be simply dead time for narrative.

In discussing the narration of history, Hayden White states that it is in historiography that "our desire for the imaginary, the possible, must contest with the imperatives of the real, the actual." Because "narrative becomes a problem only when we wish to give to real events the form of story," he says, historiography best exemplifies the process in which "narration and narrativity [function] as the instruments by which the conflicting claims of the imaginary and the real are mediated, arbitrated, or resolved in a discourse."[6] One might further contend that since individual, private time is always to some extent contingent upon public time and because the individual does take a narrative stance towards one's experience, the individual produces a "discourse" of one's time by a parallel process of narration. This personal narrative mediates, arbitrates, or resolves the conflicting claims of one's own imagination and reality. One's personal narrative also negotiates, however, the conflicting claims whose negotiation produces one's understanding of the official story that is read as history. This text of public, social, narrative time provides the context for private, individual, narrative time.

Although inherently fictional, narrative time—public and private—can be authentic or false depending on its relation to real time. Insofar as narrative time takes real time into account, it achieves consequentiality by at once substantiating its own narrative structure and ordering the otherwise amorphous material of experience (real time). At both a public and a private level, achieving consequential narrative time involves activating and properly coordinating the faculties of consciousness. Edward Waverley initially impedes the process and renders his time inconsequential: his imaginative powers are so highly developed that real time is falsified and the understanding is subverted. In the course of the novel, he must learn not only how to appreciate real time but also how to narrate his time authentically, that is, in a way that takes real time into account.

II

Scott takes pains in the early chapters of the novel to make clear that Waverley is peculiarly handicapped in undergoing the conventional realist "education."[7] As a child his experience of real time is fragmented because his time is divided between the two diametrically opposed worlds of his father and his uncle. Because his education is "regulated alternately" by these divergent minds (W, 2:17), Waverley's experience is rendered curiously insubstantial, as the real time spent in one household is systematically negated in the other.

Under these circumstances, the boy not only learns but virtually imbibes a radical sort of neutrality of spirit, which deprives him of a footing—a point of view—from which to narrate his time. Thus divided between two worlds and accountable to neither, with neither accountable for him, Waverley undergoes an education that is notably misguided or unguided because of this "relaxation of authority" (*W,* 3:19). And, as a consequence of the "desultory style of his studies," he emerges without "any fixed political opinion to place in opposition" to the emotional forces he later confronts (*W,* 4:25).[8]

In his studies, as in his upbringing, Waverley moves at will from one work to another in order to avoid effort and engagement. In part a kind of metonymy for his faulty upbringing, his faulty education also has a substantial significance of its own. "Alas!" sighs the narrator in chapter 5, Edward, permitted to read only for amusement, "foresaw not that he was losing forever the opportunity of acquiring habits of firm and assiduous application, of gaining the art of controlling, directing, and concentrating the powers of his mind for earnest investigation,—an art far more essential than even that intimate acquaintance with classical learning which is the primary object of study" (*W,* 3:20). Because he does not learn to read well, Waverley is without the habits of mind which would enable him to read or interpret his experience wisely and to narrate his time appropriately. This disability manifests itself, not surprisingly, in a confusion between life and literature and in inappropriate modes of narration. A romantic youth naturally has a penchant for "romantic literature," and his imagination, predictably, constitutes "the predominant faculty of his mind." But Waverley is also betrayed by the dangerous confusion that results from the intermingling of memory and imagination. His imagination is fed not only by his own "memory of uncommon tenacity" but also by his uncle's memory of "family tradition and genealogical history" and his aunt's romantic nostalgia for family glory (*W,* 3:23, 4:27). Vaguely remembered family "legends" excite "fancies" that call for clandestine re-enactment in an "ideal world" (*W,* 4:29, 30). We are told in this chapter that Waverley reads French memoirs that can be taken for romances and romances that can be taken for memoirs. Such texts both literally foster and metaphorically underline his more profound generic confusion of memory and imagination. Thus tainted by "that more common aberration from sound judgement which apprehends occurrences indeed in their reality, but communicates to them a tincture of its own romantic tone and colouring" (*W,* 5:32), Waverley emerges from his upbringing and education without having learned the use and significance of time. On the one hand, his experiential, real time is falsified by his unaccountability: because he never has to account to any authority for his time, it is not subject to the "imperatives of the real" and it is therefore not itself real. On the other hand, the time that is for him subject to narration is the time spent in the "ideal world," time which the imagination narrates in terms of romance. His time never achieves the consequentiality that results from struggling to reconcile the conflicting claims of imaginative desire and a given reality, because reality is never imperative to him and there is therefore no conflict. Desire, without any real imperatives to define it, dictates a false, inconsequential narrative. And, separated like this, both kinds of time are unreal. Waverley ventures into the world, then, without ever having been faced with that "problem" that White identifies as commensurate with a wish "to give to real events the form of story." And he is further handicapped in learning to narrate real time by the resemblance of the "real world" into which he ventures to the "ideal world" of his imagination. In one world, as in the other, real events seem to take the form of story on their own, producing a false congruence of real time and narrative time that further militates against their proper relation.[9]

The dangers of Waverley's irresponsible education become manifest when he sets out from home, in that the geographical and epistemological journey he then begins follows the pattern established by his course of reading. Quickly becoming disenchanted with a military role that requires him to "judge of distance or space" (*W,* 7:57) in the real world, Waverley moves on to the more promising terrain of more isolated parts of Scotland. Taking one generational step back, he first visits a friend of his uncle's youth. Here he moves, as he did at home, from his uncle's memories into the land of legends. In Rose Bradwardine, Waverley is astonished to find himself talking with someone whose experience in real time corresponds to his experience in the purely narrative time of "day-dreams" and "ancient times." Instead of appreciating Rose's experiences in terms of real time, however, Waverley can see them only in terms of the narrative time they tell to him, and he responds like a reader of romance whose "curiosity" and "sense of danger" are piqued (*W,* 15:136). Because it "seemed like a dream to Waverley" (*W,* 15:137) that the violence of the Highland clans should occupy real rather than narrative time, he becomes involved like one in a dream, and only gradually awakens to the sobering truth that mistaking real time for narrative time can be a matter of life and death.

Like one in a dream, Waverley is drawn deeper and deeper into an unknown world as he moves farther and farther into the Highlands.[10] Journeys within journeys enact his deepening entanglement in circumstances and events beyond his control. All his comings and goings serve merely to reinforce his helplessness, and all the activity merely to ratify his neutrality of spirit into a confirmed passivity.[11] This passivity that has the air of activity is dramatized forcefully when his injury places him in very much a dream-like state: wounded, blind, and unconscious, he is carried about in an unknown place by unknown beings, who could be enemies disguised as friends or friends disguised as enemies. This incident could serve as a metaphor for the paradox that defines Waverley's situation: any action he takes is negated or inverted by his ignorance of or removal from its context. However well-intentioned, all his actions are ineffectual because they are always untimely and ill-informed. He is victimized by time both as the monolithic force of official history, in whose hands he is a pawn, and as the random medium of mundane social life, when he suffers because of delayed and waylaid letters and newspapers. His ignorance and absence then allow for interpretations that condemn as treachery what really is simply bad timing.

Waverley's vulnerability to treacherous interpretation is enacted in different forms of narrative as the time and space that separate an action and its context (or consequences) are used to produce false interpretations until he finally begins to appreciate the difference between real time and narrative time. Only then, when he finds himself falsely written into the narratives of others—characterized as a traitor and a parricide in letters and newspaper articles, for example—does he begin to feel impelled to narrate his own time. But to become the narrator of one's own story at this late date—and, more important, in the middle of an ongoing story—proves impossible. There is no such thing as a simple personal narrative, Waverley learns, as even his own narratives betray him. Written as they are from a false position, his letters renouncing his commission serve merely to ratify a false position. Even more incriminating, his stolen seal is being used to authorize the false narratives of others. Then, when he is arrested on his way to correct false reports, his story becomes the subject of the two conflicting interpretations, an ambiguity in which he is complicit since he still compares himself to the hero in Flora's romantic narrative. All these narratives underline Waverley's naive inability to interpret his experience, as he is overcome by seeing "circumstances of truth" become the context for "gross falsehoods" (W, 31:20).[12]

Significantly, Waverley cannot recognize and begin to rectify the falseness of his position until he materially inhabits it and finds himself literally clothed in its garb.[13] Carried passively back into the Highland ranks once more, and then "personally solicited for assistance" by a prince who "answered his ideas of a hero of romance," Waverley is virtually compelled by circumstances (and certainly by Scott) to enact the role he must ultimately reject (W, 40:85). Once again, real time and narrative time seem to converge as real events take the form of story. Face to face with a prince and caught up in the emotion of the moment, Waverley is again without the perspective required to narrate real time. As real time and narrative time are compressed together in this single climactic moment, experience and story become as one for him. "The time," says the narrator, "admitted of no deliberation" (W, 40:86). There is no time for choice when there is no differentiation between time-as-experienced (real time) and time-as-told (narrative time).

In this moment when Waverley meets the Prince and commits himself to his cause, the public time of history and the private time of Waverley's personal life also converge. A real historical prince becomes a figure in his personal life, and for the first time Waverley begins dimly to sense the historical reality in which he is involved. Although this moment disallows reflection, it is only once he has used this moment to take a side in the conflict (and thus make his real time count) that he gains a foothold that allows him the perspective necessary to have a choice. Only then does Waverley gain the point of view that he needs in order to narrate his time and to begin to gain some understanding of his experience. This process starts in the very next chapter, "The Mystery Begins to be Cleared Up," when Fergus explains Waverley's time with Donald Bean Lean. With this narrative, Waverley begins to gain the understanding necessary for him to begin to narrate his own time.

Even as Scott carefully dramatizes the conspiracy of time and circumstances that undermines Waverley's ability to make a significant choice, he dramatizes just as carefully the contrary reality that Waverley does make a choice—and a choice of momentous consequences. Only when he makes this choice does the physical impression of its incongruity provoke a change. The two battles of the campaign mark the two crises that propel Waverley out of what has become his untenable position as a follower of the rebel cause and back to the world from which he came, but with a new sense of its historical context and of his own place in history. The working of both voluntary and involuntary memory is crucial here, as Scott dramatizes what he will later analyze more explicitly in *Chronicles*. On the eve of the battle of Preston, Waverley's memory of his home is sparked by an encounter with a man from his troop who addresses him with the "common phrase" by which Waverley had been known at home. Like Chrystal Croftangry, Waverley finds that the contrast between an alien setting and a familiar impression (initially auditory for Waverley and later visual, like Croftangry's) stirs his involuntary memory, susceptible as it is to sensuous promptings. The sound of Houghton's voice "now thrilled to his heart with the thousand recollections which the well-known accents of his native country had already contributed to awaken." The remembered sound, together with the explanation the dying man brings, "forced many unavailing and painful reflections upon Waverley's mind" (*W,* 45:132, 134).[14] Shortly thereafter, Waverley's memory prompts another revelation. As the English troops approach for battle, his memory is stirred by the familiar sights and sounds of his former troop, and "[i]t was at that instant, that, looking around him, he saw the wild dress and appearance of his Highland associates, heard their whispers in an uncouth and unknown language, looked upon his own dress, so unlike that which he had worn from his infancy, and wished to awake from what seemed at the moment a dream, strange, horrible, and unnatural" (*W,* 46:139–40). Memory draws much of its power, in both these incidents, from the sensuous impressions which make the past concrete. Drawn by the familiar sights and sounds (which he has set himself against) and repelled by the unfamiliar sights and sounds (which now command his allegiance) Waverley is overcome by a sense of discontinuity with his very self, as memory delineates a jarring contrast between past and present.

In both these incidents, memory registers the falsity of Waverley's position by allowing him to step back from his immediate experience in order to view it from a different perspective.[15] In other words, with memory comes a separation between the percipient and the event which allows for the possibility of seeing in two ways and therefore for the possibility of choice. In a kind of epiphany during the battle, memory illuminates for Waverley his own nature and the absolutely "unnatural" nature of the world he has joined. What has been until now involuntarily summoned to consciousness, prompted primarily by an emotional response to sensuous impressions, now becomes the material for the working of the voluntary memory, which demands a rational, moral, and volitional response. The opportunity for choice is posited but still not offered to Waverley in the climax of this incident when one of his associates takes aim at Colonel Gardiner, and "ere [Waverley] could say 'Hold!' " another choice is made for him (W, 46:140). Here, prompted by memory's forcing the incongruity of his position upon him, Waverley is able to imagine himself an "unnatural" parricide and, in revulsion from that image, to make a gesture towards a fully conscious voluntary response. He is still allowed only to see the choice he would make, however, rather than to choose. Nevertheless, combined with Colonel Talbot's report of the negative effects of his actions on his family, these incidents at Preston begin to provide Waverley with a context and a perspective which radically alter the narrative of his experiences that he had composed.

The culmination of this change comes with the skirmish at Clifton when the Highland army is in retreat, and Waverley makes his own retreat from the stage of history. Circumstances again act for him. Having lost his place with the Highland troop (chap. 59), he begins to find another self, a process that is underlined when he is mistaken for another Edward: "Edward, is't thou man?" (W, 60:250). He is indeed becoming another Edward, one who will take up the narrative of his own time instead of merely acting out the parts assigned to him in the narratives of others. When "a tremendous fall of snow" forces him to remain for "more than ten days" in a "lonely and secluded situation," the conspiracy of time and circumstance to render him inactive and reflective is complete (W, 60:254–55). Thus withdrawn from active experience Waverley reads of public events in the narrated form of sporadic newspaper reports. Now, however, the separation in time and space from the events of which he reads provides a safe and necessary distance that affords a perspective for understanding.

Waverley makes use of this period for the "deliberation" that time had not "admitted" before. He reflects not only upon the public events but also upon his own personal history as it has intersected with public history. What takes "more than ten days" of Waverley's real time occupies very little of the novel's narrative time because of the minimum of action and event with which he is filling it. Instead he fills it with reflection: a mental repetition of the preceding action of the novel. Waverley is reviewing his experience from the perspective of his new understanding in order to realize it in a way that he had not done at the time of experiencing. In other words, he is exercising his memory in order to transform his experience in real time, which has been narrated only in the terms of others or in terms of romance, into his own narrative time. As Waverley activates his memory to narrate his experience, he learns what his program of random and passive reading could not teach him, and he acquires "a more complete mastery of spirit tamed by adversity." Experience itself—real time—is not enough to shape a spirit: only in the process by which one narrates real time, negotiating what White calls "the conflicting claims of the imaginary and the real" to produce a discourse, does one account for one's time and oneself. At this point, Waverley negotiates these opposing claims by resolving to denounce the claims of the imaginary and to embrace those of the real: he decides "that the romance of his life was ended, and that its real history had now commenced" (W, 60:256). But the accompanying "sigh" is telling, of course, and Waverley never has to forsake his ideal world completely.[16] Instead, by learning to re-order the relation between memory and imagination so that imagination serves memory, he achieves a reconciliation of the imaginary and the real that is more salutary than either romance or real history.

These ten days, as Jane Millgate has pointed out, are a crucial turning point for Waverley in a number of ways.[17] When he activates his voluntary memory to review his experience, he for the first time realizes (in an active sense) the real time that makes up history, the real lives that are lost. He also learns here to use his memory to narrate his experience: to contain, order, and tell it in a form that can be incorporated as narrative time into the real present and future. In a sense, Waverley is also here refusing to accept the received narrative of official history, which does not take real time into account, and is instead taking up the responsibility of negotiating the opposing claims of public and private life, as well as those of real time and narrative, to produce a consequential discourse. Because voluntary memory works by means of narrative, mediating experience through a kind of discourse, such memory by necessity changes experiences, translating action and event into word with the help of imagination. With imagination no longer the "predominant faculty" of his mind, then, Waverley learns that it is nonetheless a necessary and salutary adjunct of his memory.

Imaginative capacity, in fact, distinguishes the members of the community of survivors at the end of the novel.[18] Lacking this imaginative capacity, Fergus and Flora do not survive, because their literalism makes them unable to separate values and beliefs from a particular mode of representation (the Stuart claim), and they lose their lives rather than accept an alternative embodiment of the ideals by which they define themselves. The Baron, by contrast, is the consummate survivor because he can separate ideals from particular embodiments by accepting symbols as substitutes for the realities that cannot subsist in the present in any but symbolic form.[19] Waverley, too, survives because he accepts substitutes—a barren aunt and uncle as surrogate parents, a domestic Rose for the archetypal Flora, and, of course, a "substitute" King. For him, accepting substitutes is also a matter of accepting words as substitutes for deeds—a substitution that for Scott typifies the modern world and will be requisite for all his survivor heroes. The execution of Fergus represents the death of the possibility of heroic action,[20] and the text stresses that Waverley's alternative is words when it focuses on his transforming the event of Fergus's death into narrative in letters to Rose. Waverley's technique here signifies the way in which he will survive by framing his memories in imaginative terms. The "impression of horror" which he receives from Fergus's death is "softened by degrees into melancholy—a gradation which was accelerated by the painful, yet soothing task of writing to Rose." Disregarding his own feelings, he changes the impression of the event for her, endeavouring "to place it in a light which might grieve her without shocking her imagination."[21] His tendency to romanticize has been overcome by his sense of shocking reality, and that sense, in turn, has been subordinated to his concern for Rose. Concern for Rose, in its turn, then motivates a different exercise of his imagination from the kind in which he had indulged at the beginning of his adventures.[22] This process of narration is salutary for them both, as if the very act of narrating the impression is an experience that creates another impression with an effect of its own. The result of Waverley's narrative efforts is that the "picture he drew for her benefit he gradually familiarised to his own mind," and he is able to turn his mind cheerfully to the future.

Imagination also comes into play when Edward is received home as one of "the vaunted heroes" of the Waverley line, and all "real circumstances" which would have "tarnished" his image are eschewed (*W*, 70:345, 348). But although survival in *Waverley* necessitates imaginative adaptations of the past, memory persists, resisting a complete remodelling of the past. Amid the solace of "Dulce Domum," Waverley retains the memory of a grim experience. Once again, memory is stirred and sharpened by contrast, this time between the "verdant, populous, and highly cultivated country," and the "scenes of waste desolation, or of solitary and melancholy grandeur" that have been the places of romance and strife (*W*, 70:344). Here the familiar scene of home is enhanced by the contrast, and Waverley's appreciation of it focuses the change that has occurred in him since leaving home.

Scott draws attention to the persistence of memory and the inadequacy of imagination by heightening the sense of temporality in the last stages of the novel when Waverley is entering upon a new life. This sense of time is largely translated into spatial movement: just as Waverley has journeyed into the public world of romance and history, so he has to travel back into the private world of mundane domestic life. These return journeys, however, are noteworthy for their uneventfulness and their pedestrian but salutary motivations. During the journey from Carlisle (scene of Fergus's execution) to Waverley Honour, for example, Waverley gradually adjusts to his friend's death, and the time it takes is measured in geographical terms (which, since he is journeying from a hero's death homeward, are also metaphorical): "Edward had reached his native country before he could, as usual on former occasions, look round for enjoyment upon the face of nature" (*W,* 70:344). This is but one stage of Waverley's return from the land of dreams, a return which involves a long and complicated series of journeys—to London, to Tully Veolan, to Carlisle, to Waverley Honour, back to London, back to Tully Veolan. All these journeys do lead to the conventionally comic conclusion of hero and heroine's marriage, but by the very time it takes to achieve this end Scott makes clear that Waverley is learning to value real time. For all his "urgency," real time—represented in the real space Waverley must traverse— cannot be hastened or curtailed. Commensurate with this experience, Waverley also learns, however, to narrate this time with the help of memory and imagination in a way that allows him to move forward into a future that is chastened and enhanced by the sense of the past that he carries with him.

III

The reader of *Waverley* sets out on the novelistic journey knowing history in terms of narrative and public time. Scott employs various tactics in order to break down the reader's sense of narrative time so that one might know the past in terms of its existence as real time. In the closing paragraph of the introductory chapters, just before Waverley is about to set out on his journey from home, Scott invokes the conventional metaphor of reading as a journey. This geographical image makes the reader's situation comparable to Waverley's, of course, but it also converts the temporality of reading into spatial terms. While engaging "to get as soon as possible into a more picturesque and romantic country," the narrator warns readers that they will make the journey, not in "a flying chariot," but in "a humble English post-chaise." The latter vehicle, he notes, is subject to all the "terrestrial retardations" that will later delay Waverley's "romantic" journey (*W,* 5:42–43): "My plan," the narrator says, "requires that I should explain the motives on which the action proceeded; and these motives necessarily arose from the feelings, prejudices, and parties of the times" (*W,* 5:42). In conventional realist fashion, Scott refuses to narrate the time of the novel in romantic terms that do not take the real time of character and reader into account. Even as the reader's romantic desires must defer to the exigencies of terrestrial grounding, the character's actions and motives will be seen to be functions of his social and historical context. Scott is here making a double epistemological and generic claim. On the one hand, he is claiming fidelity to historical reality; on the other, fidelity to a truth achieved by what he calls in a late chapter the "narrative" of "events," as opposed to the "duller medium of direct description" of characters in abstract and static terms (*W,* 70:347). It is by such a concrete, dynamic, and circumstantial narrative that Scott tries to take real time into account.

For the reader, of course, the actions and events of the novel and of history are purely narrative and do not constitute one's real time. But while Waverley learns to use his memory and imagination to compose a consequential narrative of his time, the reader, who has begun the novel with a sense of history as purely narrative time, gains from its unfolding a sense of the real time of the past. By sharing Waverley's narrative journey, the reader's sense of narrative time becomes reconstituted, incorporating a sense of the private real time of individuals. Scott's aim, we recall, was that he and his contemporaries "fix our eye on the now distant point from which we have been drifted." Another way of putting this is to say that he asks his readers to experience history as real time. Scott's main tactic in this strategy involves our being introduced to Waverley in a way that encourages us to associate with him. The "earlier events" of the novel are "studiously dwelt upon" (*W,* 70:347) so that "we fix our eye" on him and then begin with him to see his world. But although readers are informed of "the feelings, prejudices, and parties of the times" (*W,* 5:42) as these impinge upon the Waverley family, they also accompany Edward in an upbringing and education which seem designed to decontextualize him in "real time" and allow him to fabricate for himself a purely narrative context in the "ideal world" of romance. Even as Scott is busy at the seemingly conflicting but actually dialectical tasks of historicizing and dehistoricizing Waverley's context, he is at work on the congruent task of historicizing and dehistoricizing his readers. Partly in order to make credible Waverley's ahistorical perspective (especially incredible for a period like 1745 and for his contemporary readers), Scott begins in the very title of the novel to simulate for the reader a sense of this dehistoricized context. Wishing to activate readers' "preconceived associations" as little as possible (*W,* 1:1), he self-consciously entitles the novel with as neutral a name as possible and proceeds to catalogue the literary genres to which it does not conform. His subtitle acts in a parallel way to neutralize readers' expectations for a work of history.[23] Unlike the charged "1745," which would provoke an automatic and even perhaps violent response in most of his readers, "'Tis Sixty Years Since" disarms them by assuming a connection between them and a past time that is at once accessible and remote, datable and indefinable. "'Tis Sixty Years Since" renders the narrative time of official history in terms of the real time of personal memory. The crucial "since" both establishes the pastness of the past and places it in what Lukács calls a "felt relationship to the present."[24] It also implies that the writer and his readers are products of this time and able to perceive it only in a way that is inevitably retrospective and contingent.

This mutual position of writer and reader becomes all the more ambiguous when it is seen to be contingent upon the "fixing" of a date that is itself entirely contingent. When Scott resumed the writing of *Waverley* after a hiatus of some nine years, he chose to retain the present of his initial writing, declaring to his readers of 1814 that he was writing from "this present 1st November, 1805" (*W,*1:3). This undoubtedly preserves the poetry that would have been spoiled by a prosaic "'Tis Sixty-Nine Years Since" and be-speaks an equally poetic reluctance to tamper with what is written. But this redefinition of the readers' present may also suggest a bid (however playful) to disorient readers in an effort to prevent their automatic "fixing" on unwanted historical associations that would mitigate the novelty of first impressions. Of course, the consequent disorientation is only temporary, as even the most naive of readers, then and now, is led to the realization of that historical date, 1745. At the same time, in maintaining the discrepancy between the writing present and the reading present, Scott is writing into his narrative the evanescence of the "now" that will inevitably be written into it by time. Scott's historical subject certainly is a particular, identifiable one for which "the '45" can serve as a kind of metonymy, but the blatant varying of the ostensibly fixed time of the story brings into focus the more abstract underlying subject: the relative or proportionate distance between the readers/writer of the tale and its "actors." "Sixty Years Since," in its highly fictionalized truth, becomes a metaphor for the ideal time for memory's knowing of the past, the time during which memory is converting real time into narrative time, experience into history.[25]

This tactic of withholding the crucial date of the action and playing with the date of the writing and reading present has the effect of demythologizing history and drawing the reader into an unusually intimate relationship with the past. That relationship is in large part a function of Scott's attempt to break down the reader's conventional categories of order, of his deliberate disorientation of his readers as well as of his hero. Like Waverley, readers are deprived of the crucial names, dates, places, and circumstances that would provide the historical context and significance of events. Without the privileged understanding that comes with historical perspective, the reader has only Waverley's experience to go on. As Waverley is being carried about by unidentified persons or lying disabled without being permitted a look at his captors, the reader, also blind and in the hands of an unknown narrative, shares his experience. Bereft of their sense of history and perspective and usual categories of time and place, friend and enemy, the readers of *Waverley* come to know the past in a new way. Along with its hero, readers learn only retrospectively through the activity of memory where they have been and what they have been involved in.

Scott further breaks down the reader's sense of history (experience known as narrative time—1745) into real time (experience that comes within the range of memory—sixty years since) by disrupting the conventional categories of time. Throughout the novel he strives to open up the closed book of history—to challenge the reader's perception of history as finished and irrecoverable, like time already narrated—by recovering the sense of the potentiality of time as it is experienced. He enriches the reader's understanding of historical time in both the national and personal sense by re-investing time with a sense of latent possibility that makes any event or action at once decisive, in that it determines what follows it, and arbitrary, in that it is one of a multitude of might-have-beens. The narrator makes clear, for example, that it is because of fatal timing that Fergus MacIvor exemplifies a tragic heroism that establishes his status as a historical figure: "Had Fergus MacIvor lived sixty years sooner than he did," he would have lacked the sophistication that makes him such an unusual chieftain; "had he lived sixty years later," his world would not have afforded the circumstances for his remarkable powers of leadership (*W,* 19:175). Only at that particular moment do time and circumstances intersect to produce his fatal character, just as they have intersected to make Waverley what he is.

Throughout the novel, readers are reminded that history is only a temporal configuration: only the unaccountable play of time and circumstance makes history out of moments. One such moment occurs at the beginning of the novel when Sir Everard comes close to changing his will and signing over his heritage to the family's traditional enemies. "Had Lawyer Clippurse . . . arrived but an hour earlier," the narrator says, Sir Everard would have done the deed, spurred on by the impulse of the moment. But "an hour of cool reflection" allows him to go beyond the immediate situation, to employ the larger perspective of memory and of future prospect. Even so, his decision is finally determined non-rationally and by misinterpretation when he reads reproach in the lawyer's innocent action of producing materials for writing and then himself looks up to see the sun lighting up the family crest. His legacy remains in the family and eventually, through a combination of other such circumstantial moments, falls to Waverley. "All this was the effect of the glimpse of a sunbeam," the narrator wryly comments, "just sufficient to light Lawyer Clippurse to mend his pen" (*W,* 2:11–12). Thus in a moment of what is later called "real time," so slight as to hold the mending of a pen, history is made. In the novel, Waverley and the reader come to see history as always consisting of "real time" and "real time" as always consisting of potential history. It is only with the narrative prospect afforded by memory that one can understand the conjunction of real time and narrative time.

The point is made especially clear in Scott's next novel, *Guy Mannering,* where the young hero, Harry Bertram, returns home after an absence of seventeen years. The novel dramatizes his return as a recovery of lost time, filling in what he experiences as a "blank" (*Mannering,* 50:249) and the narrator describes as a "gap" and a "space" (*M,* 11:99). Easily covered in narrative time, these seventeen years remain abstract: because they have not been made concrete in real time, the seventeen years (lived under false pretenses) in real terms have not happened. The attempt of the simple Dominie, whose understanding is concrete, to "resume" the past ("to take up Harry pretty nearly where he had left him" [*M,* 51:259]) focuses on the irrecoverable loss of this time. But the narrator shows how narrating the time can recover, though never replace, that time. As in *Waverley,* space fills in time. Scott's epigraph for chapter eleven of *Guy Mannering* is a quotation from *A Winter's Tale* in which Time expresses his role in terms of space: "I slide / O'er sixteen years, and leave the growth untried / Of that wide gap." The narrator immediately echoes the epigraph and, in the echo, suggests again that the completed literary text mediates between space and time: "Our narration is now about to make a large stride, and omit a space of nearly seventeen years" (*M,* 11:99). This position assumes both the privileges of "narrative time," striding over "real time," and the liabilities entailed in omitting growth and change. But the narrator suggests that the "gap" can be filled (that is, that narrative time can be realized) if the reader draws from his own experience. As in *Waverley,* a comparison between the character's "real time" and the reader's reading time discloses the potential for narrative in real time and the substance of real time in narrative. "The gap is a wide one;" the narrator says, "yet, if the reader's experience in life enables him to look back on so many years, the space will scarce appear longer in his recollection than the time consumed in turning these pages" (*M,* 11:99). Real time is at once both substantial and ephemeral enough that it can be "consumed," if only by reading; narrative time, on the other hand, is so insubstantial and abstract that, isolated from real time, it can itself be only a gap. Memory brings real time and narrative time together by negotiating their mutual claims. While involuntary memory stores the sensuous data of real-time experience, voluntary memory narrates this material, collecting and completing it (as Chrystal Croftangry finds) so that it is both preserved and benevolently changed. When memory brings the two kinds of time together, narrative time converts real time into something abstract enough to be called "space." In the conjunction of real time and narrative time a space is made which memory fills by its "recollection." Memory converts time into something comparable to reading time in which a whole world unfolds during the course of a few hours and, conversely, a few hours expand to encompass a world of experience.

Notes

1.   In the absence of a standard scholarly edition of Scott's novels, there is no common method of citation. All quotations are drawn from the Border Edition (48 vols., ed. Andrew Lang [London: John C. Nimmo, 1892–94]). To facilitate reference, I cite the chapters as consecutively numbered in most modern editions, followed by page number. All citations are incorporated parenthetically in the text.

2.   Claire Lamont draws attention to the fact that in the manuscript Scott originally wrote "we set out," changing it to "we have been drifted" for the published text. Walter Scott, *Waverley,* ed. Claire Lamont (Oxford: Clarendon Press, 1981), p. 417.

3.   Lukács established Scott as the exemplary historical novelist, arguing that the distinction of his work lay in his presentation of the past both in its own terms and as the "prehistory of the present." Georg Lukács, *The Historical Novel,* trans. Hannah and Stanley Mitchell (London: Merlin Press, 1965), p. 53.

4. Richard Waswo shows that Scott's "literary activity" projects in fiction "a vision of the past the basis of whose creation is enacted in the continual present of every reader." Richard Waswo, "Story as Historiography in the Waverley Novels,"*ELH* 47, 2 (Summer 1980): 304–30, 326.

5. Shaw identifies the underlying pattern whereby readers, along with Edward Waverley, "move from spectatorship to an unsettling engagement with the past, but they make a crucial retreat back to spectatorship again." Harry E. Shaw, *The Forms of Historical Fiction* (Ithaca: Cornell Univ. Press, 1983), p. 185.

6. Hayden White, "The Value of Narrativity in the Representation of Reality," *CritI* 7, 1 (Autumn 1980): 8.

7. For a discussion of the realist disenchantment plot of *Waverley,* see in particular George Levine, *The Realistic Imagination: English Fiction from Frankenstein to Lady Chatterley* (Chicago: Univ. of Chicago Press, 1981), chap. 4.

8. Millgate notes that having completed his education, Edward is "almost totally lacking in historical awareness, or, for that matter, in any very adequate means for proceeding from the particular to a more general understanding of what he observes." Jane Millgate, *Sir Walter Scott: The Making of a Novelist* (Toronto: Univ. of Toronto Press, 1984), p. 37.

9. Levine notes that Waverley "is hardly mistaken in thinking the world corresponds to his dreams . . . the narrative seems almost to sanction the romantic dream while making us aware of its absurdity." Levine's analysis of the novel as a whole stresses the way in which it "transforms action into dream, drives a wedge between narrative and desire, between language and action." Levine, pp. 83, 84.

10. Welsh notes the prevalence of dream in romance, but points out the ambiguous nature of the dream and Scott's use of the motif. "Though the total action of the romance may be construed as a wish-dream," notes Welsh, "the incidents affecting the hero are usually fearsome or unpleasant." The experiences of the Waverley hero, he argues, "are more like fragments of a nightmare than logical constructions of a hopeful dream." For Welsh these nightmarish experiences are symptomatic of the anxiety characteristic of the Scott hero, who "propitiates authority and represses all unacceptable passions." Alexander Welsh, *The Hero of the Waverley Novels* (New Haven: Yale Univ. Press, 1963), pp. 151, 174.

11. See Welsh for a full exploration of Scott's passive hero.

12. Waswo cites this incident (Waverley's appearance before the stern Major Melville and the more sympathetic Mr. Morton) as an example of "the inexorable importance of reputation, the conferring of identity and value by social interpretation" in the Waverley Novels (p. 316). Bruce Beiderwell also analyzes this scene in terms of Scott's sense of the complexities of justice and civil disobedience. Bruce Beiderwell, "The Reasoning of Those Times: Scott's *Waverley* and the Problem of Punishment," *Clio* 15, 1 (Fall 1985): 15–30.

See also Judith Wilt's provocative discussion of Waverley's loss of identity and reputation. Judith Wilt, *Secret Leaves: The Novels of Sir Walter Scott* (Chicago: Univ. of Chicago Press, 1985), pp. 32–34.

13. Welsh comments that "dress figures in *Waverley* as a symbol of a romantic adventure that may be put on or off—thus confirming the excursion by which the hero can experience the world of romantic action without actually performing any" (Welsh, p. 161).

14. Graham McMaster identifies this as one of "two or three strongly marked scenes in which the reader is clearly asked to make moral judgements." Graham McMaster, *Scott and Society* (Cambridge: Cambridge Univ. Press, 1981), p. 13.

15. In her study of realism and perspective, Elizabeth Ermath notes that "the mnemonic act of recovery is crucial for perceiving the patterns in events." By the act of remembering, Ermath argues, perceived discontinuities eventually give way to a "hidden order," and realistic fiction promises that "given enough time, enough distance, one can fit any anomaly into its proper place in the system." Elizabeth Ermath, "Realism, Perspective, and the Novel," *CritI* 7, 3 (Spring 1981), 499–520, 514–15.

16. Commenting on this scene, Welsh notes: "The romance, of course, is not over. By 'romance' Waverley means the romantic episode, which . . . is characteristically finite. By 'history' he signifies an equally imaginary construction of infinite future time—a part of the reality by which the hero conceives himself to be supported" (Welsh, pp. 147–48). Levine agrees, commenting that in the novel "Scott turns the romantic past into a comprehensible and recognizable experience and yet sustains romance to the end" (Levine, p. 94).

17. Millgate, pp. 53–54.

18. Brown argues that these survivors have two things in common: "the ability to compromise with the inevitable" and "the ability to forget." I would contend that more crucial is their ability to remember in a new way, one that involves compromising and forgetting but is still a remembering. David Brown, *Walter Scott and the Historical Imagination* (London: Routledge and Kegan Paul, 1979), p. 23.

19. The ceremony of drawing off the prince's boot is the most obvious of these symbols.

20. Fergus also dies, of course, because he is a threat to civil order, but Beiderwell is right to emphasize Scott's discomfort with the manifest injustice of the disparity between the fates of Fergus and Waverley and his dissatisfaction with (though endorsement of) a system of justice in which "[q]uestions of security and the general public good outweigh the more abstract concerns of fairness and human sympathy" (Beiderwell, p. 16). This discomfort is far more serious than his discomfort with the death of romance. For a discussion of Waverley and Fergus as doubles, see Robert Kiely, *The Romantic Novel in England* (Cambridge, MA: Harvard Univ. Press, 1972), pp. 145 f.

21. Cottom notes: "Perspective, memory, and writing all serve to tame sensations and events; they are all civilizing tools that withdraw one from the dangers of immediacy as they withdraw one from action; they are supposed to put an end to disorder." While affirming such civilizing tools, however, the Waverley Novels, Cottom points out, concentrate on exciting in the reader "the very dangers [the tools] are designed to eliminate." Daniel Cottom, *The Civilized Imagination: A Study of Ann Radcliff, Jane Austen, and Sir Walter Scott* (Cambridge: Cambridge Univ. Press, 1985), p. 143.

22. On this point see Millgate, who argues that the novel does not so much reject as transcend "youthful romanticism" and that Scott, far from rejecting the imagination, affirms it as the source of knowledge and wisdom (Millgate, pp. 55–57).

23. For recent analyses of the subtitle, see Millgate (p. 37) and Wilt (p. 27).

24. LuKács, p. 53.

25. This is a point frequently made in Scott criticism. A.O.J. Cockshut, for example, argues that Scott is at his best when he is working within the range of memory, "within about 100 years of his own boyhood." A.O.J. Cockshut, *The Achievement of Sir Walter Scott* (London: Collins, 1969), p. 104.

Wilt comments: "each man's own 'now' is romance time inevitably, as is his great-grandfather's time. His father's time is 'real' time, not 'my story' but 'history' " (Wilt, p. 28).

The Power of Naming: Language, Identity and Betrayal in *The Heart of Midlothian*

Carol Anderson

For a Scottish reader of Scott's fiction, in particular, there can be a pleasurable sense of recognition. His fictional universe has given not only voices and imaginative life, but literally, names, to Scottish culture. Arriving in Edinburgh you step off the train at Waverley station, and perhaps go for a drink at the Abbotsford bar. You can even support a football team called the Heart of Midlothian.

And yet there may linger what Muriel Spark describes as a very Scottish qualification: 'Nevertheless' . . .[1] Why do I enjoy the dialogue of Scots speakers in Scott's work, and then feel, so often, curiously betrayed? Why, as a *female* Scottish reader of Scott do I sometimes feel both pleased and frustrated? Such questions lie behind this paper, which takes up the issue of language in one particular novel.

The Heart of Midlothian is a linguistically selfconscious work; one need only think of the punning exchange between the young lawyers in Chapter 1, which teases out the various implications of the word 'heart.' The plot, too, pivots on linguistic points. At the heart of the novel is an association between language and power, which Scott reveals; he appears to establish sympathy for speakers of Scots, members of the native 'oral' culture, women (strongly associated with Scottish culture in this novel), all those who are linguistically, and indeed politically 'powerless,' suppressed or marginalised in post-Union Britain. However, as is well known, the novel, partly through the account of Jeanie's acceptance at court, and the concluding scenes at Roseneath, ultimately sanctions the Union of 1707.

Another aspect of the novel's debate about language heightens the issues. Through the figure of the 'truth-telling' Jeanie, Scott appears to lend support to her idea of language, which is, as James Kerr puts it, 'grounded in a radically representational notion of how language ought to be used, based on the assumption that there can be a genuine correspondence between word

From *Scott in Carnival*, Selected Papers from the Fourth International Scott Conference, Edinburgh, 1991, ed. J. H. Alexander and David Hewitt (Aberdeen: Association for Scottish Literary Studies, 1993), 189–201. Reprinted by permission of the Association for Scottish Literary Studies and Carol Anderson.

and world, language and reality.'[2] The corrupt use of language at the court in England appears by contrast unworthy. Yet Scott himself is not 'innocent,' either in his use of language or the manipulation of plot. He presents a version of history which is ideologically loaded, and through it can be seen to 'betray' the very ideas, the very figures of his fiction, the very language to which he apparently lends support. Thus in a sense, Scott can be seen as a kind of 'double-dealer,' and this may be one reason why many readers feel dissatisfied.

Language is shown again and again in this novel to be invested with enormous power, not least because, in the words of modern linguists, 'Saying is doing, and utterances are acts, capable of producing enormous and far-reaching consequences.'[3] *The Heart of Midlothian* is full of speech acts that emphasise this: Jeanie might save Effie with a word; the death sentence is pronounced by the Doomster with the word 'Doom;'[4] an act of parliament is passed, to be read in churches (Ch. 18; 188). Characters constantly talk of the power they exert over each other: ' "What signifies coming to greet ower me," said poor Effie [to Jeanie], "when you have killed me?—killed me, when a word of your mouth would have saved me" ' (Ch. 25; 245).

This power of language is emotively expressed by Madge Wildfire when she tells the double-dealer Ratcliffe he is 'a villain out o' hell' (Ch. 17; 175). Ratcliffe, 'conscience struck,' protests: ' "I never shed blood," he replied.' Her answer is bitter:

"But ye hae sauld it, Ratton—ye hae sauld blood mony a time. Folk kill wi' the tongue as weel as wi' the hand—wi' the word as weel as wi' the gulley!"

Her remark strikes home, as Ratcliffe thinks 'And what is that I am doing now?'. He is about to betray Geordie Robertson—though he draws back on hearing Madge's words—and also Madge herself, whom he exploits for her knowledge of song first in the service of the authorities, and then in order to outwit them.

The critic of betrayal, Madge Wildfire, is described by Tom Crawford as 'the creation, almost, of the language itself, of Scots vernacular and Scots-English folk culture.'[5] She contrasts herself with the written word (and the Church) when she tells Reuben Butler 'I am as weel worth looking at as ony book in your aught' (Ch. 16; 164). Her roots in oral culture explain in part the strong emphasis she places on the power of the spoken word. Walter Ong discusses this:

The fact that oral peoples commonly and in all likelihood universally consider words to have magical potency is clearly tied in, at least unconsciously, with their sense of the word as necessarily spoken, sounded, and hence power-driven.[6]

Events of the novel bear out Madge's insight. Words carry the power of life and death.

One significant aspect of language in oral culture is naming. Walter Ong explains that 'Oral peoples commonly think of names (one kind of words) as conveying power over things' (33). Although such a belief may seem naïve to chirographic and typographic peoples, 'names do give human beings power over what they name' (33), an idea reiterated by contemporary linguists.[7]

The significance of names is brought out frequently in the novel in speech acts such as Sharpitlaw's address to Jeanie when he arrests her: 'Your name is Jeanie Deans and you are my prisoner' (Ch. 18; 178). Jeanie also feels fear when she is unexpectedly addressed by name, but by a nameless speaker, on her journey (Ch. 29; 282). For the Cameronians, such as Davie Deans, the mere naming of an act is tantamount to performing it: 'Dance?—dance, said ye? I daur ye, limmer that ye are, to name sic a word at my doorcheek!' (Ch. 11; 110).

Naming is, of course, associated with identity. *The Heart of Midlothian* is full of characters who go by a range of names, suggesting this is a world in which identity is uncertain, or fractured. Effie is Euphemia, but also 'the Lily of St Leonard's.' (Significantly, Jeanie's daughter Euphemia is known as 'Femie.') Staunton has several pseudonyms, George Robertson, Geordie, Gentle George, etc.; Madge's mother, whose real name is Margaret Murdockson, goes by the name of Meg, but also Old Maggie (Ch. 17; 187), Mother Damnable (Ch. 29; 286) and others.

The power of naming is especially significant for Magdalene Murdockson, who has been 'given' her 'popular' name of Madge Wildfire by an Englishman, her ex-lover George Staunton. He has abandoned her to madness, then assumes her identity when it saves his skin. She herself is both sadly and irritably conscious that her name is not really 'Madge Wildfire' (see Ch. 16; 164 and Ch. 29; 303). Her association of naming with power over her identity lies behind her reaction to Jeanie's question about the 'real name' of 'Gentle George:' 'What have ye to do asking for folk's names? . . . Never ask folk's names, Jeanie, it's no civil . . .' (Ch. 30; 300). When persecuted by the local authorities she becomes confused: 'I'll be upsides wi' you, as sure as my name's Madge Wildfire—I mean Murdockson—God help me, I forget my very name in this confused waste!' (Ch. 32; 312).

Rather than arguing, as Judith Wilt does, that 'in this confused waste she has forgotten her gender,'[8] I would argue that Madge's forgetting her name signifies her utter loss of power at this point, her already tenuous sense of identity slipping from her under pressure. Through the presentation of Staunton's naming of and abuse of Madge a powerful point emerges. In the words of a modern feminist, Mary Daly, 'Women have had the power of *naming* stolen from us. We have not been free to use our own power to name ourselves, the world, or God.'[9]

Madge may be mad, yet she conveys a view of her situation. The destructive effects of male power misused in sexual relationships are emphasised in her song to Ratcliffe:

> "It is the bonny butcher lad,
> That wears the sleeves of blue,
> He sells the flesh on Saturday,
> On Friday that he slew." (Ch. 17; 175)

The jilted lover is a familiar traditional figure, but the remarkable violence and bitterness here lend force to the central idea of exploitation and betrayal that reverberates throughout the novel. Its awful meaning in relation to Madge herself is implied by her account of her imagined relationship with the murdered Ailie Muschat, whose blood seeps out of the winding cloth: 'they say bluid never bleaches out o' linen claith' (Ch. 17; 173). For the daughter of 'Mother Blood' (and her mother hangs on 'Moll Blood,' the gallows), death is never far from love, or from fertility. 'Naebody kens weel wha's living and wha's dead,' she says (Ch. 29; 289), very tellingly, for this 'marginal' figure implies all that is repressed in the consciousness of her society (and perhaps of her author).

Madge and her mother, indeed, are figures akin to those described by Hélène Cixous and Catherine Clément, who examine the Sorceress and Hysteric, female figures appearing in some literature written by men, such as Michelet and Freud: 'these men are filters that are less impervious than others to the myths that women, with no cultural function in the transmission of knowledge, could not elaborate themselves until recently.'[10] In the analysis of Cixous and Clément, women are, along with 'neurotics, ecstatics, drifters, hawkers, jugglers, tumblers' (8) outside the symbolic order, and both a product of, and resistant to, among other things 'the domination of the Church.' They are also associated with 'the repressed past' (5).

Like the figures analysed by Cixous and Clément, Madge is an outcast, killed by the Scot-hating mob in Carlisle as a witch or 'sorceress' (Ch. 40; 392–3 and 50; 470). Despised by the Church and society as mad and a 'fallen woman,' she is also both despised and feared for her voice, her language. An officer of the law commands her 'Haud your tongue, ye skirling limmer, haud your tongue, or I'se gie ye something to skirl for' (Ch. 16; 164). Ratcliffe, too, is frustrated by her, for she falls silent just when it would suit him to have her raise her voice:

> "And this mad quean, after cracking like a pen-gun, and skirling like a pea-hen for the haill night, behoves just to hae hadden her tongue when her clavers might have done some gude! But it's aye the way wi' women; if ever they haud their tongues ava', ye may swear it's for mischief." (Ch 17; 176)

Scott illustrates male fear and impatience with this powerful female voice (does the name 'quean' echo queen?), one which offers a threat to linear logic

(Madge is particularly resistant to a 'legal' type of questioning: Ch. 31; 302) and which, in Kathryn Sutherland's words, 'evades the strict economy of the action' through its 'unreadability.'[11] The disruptive nature of Madge's speech gives it affinities with contemporary theories concerning female discourse. French feminists have postulated different ways of viewing women's relationship to language; one might think here of Julia Kristeva's idea of 'the semiotic,' outside of the male symbolic order of language, to which women have access, or the radical and controversial views of feminine *'différence,'* as described by Luce Irigaray.[12]

Feminists argue about the value and validity of defining 'feminine' language; it may be that, as some critics argue, assigning women to a realm of 'psycho-babble' is regressive.[13] Nevertheless, here Scott illustrates the marginalisation of a particular discourse associated with the feminine, implying its power and the ways in which it has been repressed.

Broken up, sporadic and riddling, Madge's discourse also has its own kind of meaningfulness, rooted in oral culture (see for instance Ong, 44), interestingly, since, as recent critics have demonstrated, Scott himself strove to retain links with the oral storytelling traditions.[14] Madge's discourse is 'oral' in its mode of interaction with others, as in its perception of the relationship between literature and life. Madge does not merely suggest the ways in which she and Jeanie resemble the characters of *The Pilgrim's Progress:* for her, they *are* those characters. This may be 'childish,' and yet in the context, it is also poignant, and indeed, for the reader, meaningful. Through the heroism of his 'oral' heroine Jeanie, and also his wild woman, Madge, Scott appears to stress the humanity, and even wisdom, of traditional culture.

And yet, ultimately, these characters are in some sense 'compromised,' rejected or destroyed. The novel concludes with a vision of a peaceful and relatively stable Great Britain; Effie, as Lady Staunton, is sent into exile, and Jeanie, uprooted from her old home, is also in a sense exiled, 'cultivated' into a new life as Mrs. Butler. Madge is killed off; on her deathbed she cannot even answer her name when addressed by it: 'On the contrary, the patient, like one provoked by interruption, changed her posture, and called out, with an impatient tone, "Nurse—nurse, turn my face to the wa', that I may never answer to that name ony mair, and never see mair of a wicked world" ' (Ch. 40; 395).

Madge is associated with a culture which, in Scott's view, belongs to the past. The opening image of the novel, the mail coach bearing letters—written letters—suggests a major historical shift: 'The times have changed in nothing more . . . than in the rapid conveyance of intelligence and communication betwixt one part of Scotland and another' (Ch. 1; 13). The oral culture of Scotland will never be the same again; in Jeanie Deans's time—already past when the novel opens—there were not even coaches in Scotland (see Ch. 34; 336). This image of the mail coach recurs (Ch. 28; 271), emphasising the differences between the past and the new, lettered present. (Perhaps significantly, the post-chaise is a figure of art in *Waverley,* Ch. 5).

On one level, Madge, and indeed Jeanie, represent much that Scott values: he wrote of 'peasants' as bearers of national identity, and thus interesting. They illustrate 'the operation of the higher and more violent passions,' and 'seldom fail to express them in the strongest and most powerful language.'[15] Yet while the peasants and their language are admirable, Scott's choice of words here betrays the limits of his approval, because, as can be seen from his treatment of Staunton and Effie, 'the higher and more violent passions' must be contained if society is to remain orderly. The word 'wildfire' is used by Scott in *Redgauntlet* as an adjective: 'the wildfire blood of the Redgauntlets' (Ch. 17), where it is implied that national identity, to which Scott alludes approvingly in the passage cited above, is dangerous when it turns into *nationalism*. Madge, as a figure of the darker passions of Scottish culture, must be controlled.

The national language is also shown dwindling in power. At the end of this novel, the 'antique simplicity' of language, presumably embodied in Jeanie, and in a different way in Madge (that 'proud lady'), has degenerated to the speechlessness implied in the name of The Whistler, who has no other name, who has never been baptised. Here the 'language of nature' has gone beyond words into mere sound, degenerated to the level of savagery suggested in the figure of the outlaw boy. Yet that boy is released by Jeanie, to his own 'wild' fate, as if Scott, like Jeanie, cannot quite bear to destroy that which he stands for.

Many critics and readers have expressed discontent with the last quarter of *The Heart of Midlothian*. The didactic tone of the conclusion does not appeal to a modern audience; there is something striking, though, about the imagery of crime as 'the ghosts of the murdered,' which 'haunt the steps of the malefactor.' The crimes alluded to one supposes to be those of Staunton and Effie, but who, exactly, are the ghostly dead? Madge is haunted by her dead child, and so, perhaps is Scott; beneath the surface moral may lurk the ghosts of Scott's own imagination, those figures of the repressed which he could not, at the last admit, but which he could not, either, altogether deny.

Scott was embarrassed by, ashamed, even, of his own love of 'the romance of roguery,' which contained elements found in his own novels. Writing of the work of Defoe, which he admired, he characterised the reader feeling 'as a well-principled young man may do, when seduced by some entertaining and dissolute libertine into scenes of debauchery, that, though he may be amused, he must be not a little ashamed of that which furnishes the entertainment.'[16] This passage illustrates the ambivalence which colours his attitude both to sexual women and to the figures of his own imagination, the fictions and the more colourful characters, 'the actors' in them. Thus Madge and Effie must be denied as fallen women, and because they are associated with the imagination and art, dangerously beguiling. There is, for instance, a similarity between the words of Madge Wildfire when she tells Jeanie that she wants to speak 'good words,' but 'then comes the Devil, and brushes my lips with his black wing, and lays his black loof on my mouth' (Ch. 30; 298)—and Scott's own confession about his compulsion for writing: 'I think there is a demon who sits himself on the feather of my pen when I begin to write.'[17]

Yet Scott is not only attracted to, and fond of those 'Dalilahs' (*Heart of Midlothian*, Ch. 1; 21) of the imagination; they are his family, as a much-repeated metaphor of paternity in several of his introductions stresses.[18] He feels responsible and guilty. In the words of Davie Deans 'what will the lightsome and profane think of the guide that cannot keep his own family from stumbling?' (Ch. 12; 117). And, finally, Scott was undoubtedly on some level aware that what Daniel Cottom calls his 'guilty passion'[19] fed 'the public's all devouring appetite for the wonderful and the horrible' (*Heart of Midlothian*, Ch. 1; 20–1). Both the acts of creating his reprehensible creations, and then killing them off, were highly popular and profitable. One can understand a faint guilt—and there is a lot of guilt about in this novel—hovering about an author who used his 'family' in that way (particularly its female members).

There are, then, I suggest, a number of possible reasons for a reader's sense that Scott is in some sense writing against himself in this novel. The idea of loyalty to family is, moreover, not only a figurative one hovering behind the fiction, it is a theme in the fiction itself. There is much emphasis in *The Heart of Midlothian* on loyalty, especially familial loyalty, and on that of the peasantry, even of outlaws and thieves. There is a good deal, too, about the national ties the Scots feel to each other (see Ch. 28; 275 and Ch. 38; 374). Most telling is Jeanie's fear of being held guilty of treason in her culture:

> With the fanaticism of the Scotch presbyterians, there was always mingled a glow of national feeling, and Jeanie trembled at the idea of her name being handed down to posterity with that of the "fause Monteath," and one or two others, who, having deserted and betrayed the cause of their country, are damned to perpetual remembrance and execration among its peasantry.— (Ch. 34; 341)

In a novel which so powerfully presents the passionate Scottish sense of national identity and pride, Scott, by ultimately accepting the status quo at a sensitive moment, might be described as betraying his nation, and guilt at his own disloyalty may lurk in the interstices of his text.

More specifically, it might be argued that Scott does, in fact, compromise his national culture in linguistic terms. For although apparently approving and admiring of the vernacular and the culture on which it draws, Scott is also ashamed of it. Many critics have taken Scott's comments on his characters and their vernacular speech as apolitical, even generous; in discussing Jeanie's interview with the Queen, Graham Tulloch emphasises Scott's wish to show her as dignified:

To make doubly sure no incongruous feelings arise in the reader, he adds that she spoke 'in tones so affecting, that, like the notes of some of her native songs, provincial vulgarity was lost in pathos'.[20]

It may be true that, as Emma Letley comments, there is nothing 'specious' about the *speaker's* pathos; Jeanie is entirely sincere, and her use of Scots aligned with her personal honesty.[21] However, *Scott's* willingness to collude in the assumption of 'provincial vulgarity' at the same time as he apparently refutes it does have something specious about it. Certainly, Scott was negotiating difficult new territory in presenting Scots language to many non-Scots readers, but the remark about 'provincial vulgarity' might well *produce* 'incongruous feelings' in the Scots-speaking reader, rather than quelling them.

Scott's presentation of Jeanie's letters is also challenging (Ch. 39; 378). Although some critics remark on the power of her 'rhetoric',[22] my own view, notwithstanding Scott's explanation that Jeanie does not often write letters, is that the reader is invited to smile in a rather patronising way at both the language and the spelling ('fisycian' for 'physician', for example) and the content ('Gowans, the brockit cow'). The scientific metaphor employed by the young lawyer in Chapter 1 about the 'curious history of mind' is relevant here, for the manner is rather that of a scientist—or a lawyer—smilingly laying out before us the evidence of poor Jeanie's charming naïveté.

Daniel Cottom discusses a passage from *The Fair Maid of Perth,* commenting that it perpetuates a kind of 'sexual manipulation':

Just as a woman is thus compelled by the narrator to agree to her own abuse, so does that narrator try to lock his readers within the delusions of immature eras of history even as he speaks of regretting the imprisonment of his characters within those times. (141)

There is some force to this image of the reader, like the abused woman. Certain categories of reader (female, 'lower class', Scottish) have a special relationship to a text which is problematic in its attitude to Scottishness as well as femininity and class, in terms of the ideological interpretation of history it offers, and in its manipulation of language to that end.

One of the ways in which Scott may be seen to compromise Scots—both language and people—is in his use of names. Scott was well aware of the significance of naming, as can be seen from his essay on Bunyan.[23] Obviously Scott works in an old tradition of naming as a key to character and uses it to some effect in this novel (Magdalene, Meg Murdockson etc.); he is also, of course, a great comic writer, and uses names often to comic effect. The sometimes problematic effects are illustrated, however, I think, in the last part of *The Heart of Midlothian.* Here, the two main representatives of Highland culture are Duncan of Knockdunder and Donacha Dhu na Dunaigh. Both men are called Duncan, implying a narrowness or homogeneity about Highland culture. The first name is evidently supposed to be funny, playing on an image of failure, although the character himself refutes this (Ch. 45; 431). The second name also strives to be comic through use of alliteration. Both seem to me crudely achieved. This is to say nothing of the way in which the Gaelic-English of the two speakers is transcribed, which as Graham Tulloch has shown, makes his Highlanders 'tend . . . to look foolish and ignorant' (256). Even for an impartial reader, I think, the humour may seem heavy-handed and trivialising when one considers the destruction of Gaelic culture that was taking place in the early nineteenth century. The light-weight treatment of history in the final stages of the novel also seems a 'betrayal' of the profound seriousness of the opening scenes.

David Murison has pointed out that in his 'bilingual' approach, Scott tends to associate 'English with what was serious, solemn and formal and . . . the vernacular with the more informal, colloquial, sentimental, and humorous aspects of life'.[24] Although the associations are often 'positive', W.F.H. Nicolaisen points out:

> . . . since many of the more humorous of the 'self-interpreting' names are semantically embedded in Scots and generally apply to minor vernacular characters, their 'self-interpretation' can no longer be taken for granted and requires footnoting comment in standard English, while the characters so named lose an important, immediate dimension and are often seen as quaint rather than vital, as barbarous rather than truly humorous.[25]

I believe there is a valid and important point here about the effect produced by the use of 'comic' names in Scots, although this analysis favours the experience of the English reader over those to whom such names would *not* be impenetrable. The irony is, however, that while even today many Scots speakers would still appreciate the meaning and 'humour' of names such as Fairscrieve or Whackbairn, these marginal figures are, as representatives of their culture, obviously ridiculous, and access to the comic effect is a somewhat double-edged privilege. Susan Ferrier and John Galt also used such devices, of course. But it is surely Scott's more influential practice of associating comic names with Scottish identity that can be seen in degenerate form in the invented names of, for example, J.M. Barrie's Thrums stories. Would you take a character with the name of Jess McQumpha seriously? The tendency is still, disturbingly, alive in popular culture.

For a range of reasons associated with his narrative techniques, critics have accused Scott of 'doubledealing'. Daniel Cottom, for example, has described Scott as 'duplicitous' and a 'double agent' (141), while James Kerr has called him a sometime 'trickster' (17), and Judith Wilt comments on his 'duplicity' (212). Scott was, I would argue, both 'inside' and 'outside' the culture he writes about (see the image of the coach passengers in *The Heart of Midlothian*, Ch. 1); he was also 'a border rider of both kingdoms' (Ch. 40;

390). It is perhaps not surprising that Scott was especially fond, among his characters, of such 'enterprising' figures as Dalgetty in *A Legend of Montrose,* and Bailie Nicol Jarvie in *Rob Roy.* Scott's narrative method may justify seeing in the duplicitous but successful Ratcliffe in *The Heart of Midlothian* a figure akin to Scott himself:

> The doubledealing of Ratcliffe in the matter of Robertson had not prevented his being rewarded, as double-dealers frequently have been, with favour and preferment. (Ch. 19; 200)

Ratcliffe has, notably, evaded justice through his assumption of various identities; when asked his name, he says he has at least twenty (Ch. 13; 136). Throughout the novel he is called, among other things, Rat (Ch. 17; 168), Ratton (Ch. 17; 175), Jim Rat (Ch. 30; 291), and—significantly, in the light of Scott's use of the paternity metaphor mentioned previously—Daddie Ratton (Ch. 19; 300).

In his article on names in *Waverley,* W.F.H. Nicholaisen observes that various characters, including Waverley himself, 'expediently adopt different names as successful disguises. . . . Under the circumstances, anonymity, in contradistinction to namelessness, turns out to be also a form of naming. Anonymity conceals identity; it does not represent a total lack of it' (340). Scott, of course, knew better than anyone the significance of names; he chose to conceal his own, yet as 'the Great Unknown' enjoyed enormous popular success. In fact, anonymity may have contributed to this: 'In the pen of this nameless romancer, I seemed to possess something like the secret fountain of coined gold and pearls vouchsafed to the traveller of the Eastern Tale',[26] and indeed the use of masks enabled Scott at 'the height of his popularity 1816–19', as Kathryn Sutherland points out, 'to increase productivity by publishing simultaneously under two separate identities, as the "Author of *Waverley*", and as the anonymous . . . author of *Tales of my Landlord*' (105). Scott has Jedediah Cleishbotham address the reader at the start of *The Heart of Midlothian,* 'What can a man do to assert his property in a printed tome, saving to put his name in the titlepage thereof, with his description, or designation, as the lawyers term it, and place of abode?' (100). Underneath the teasing mask, Scott makes some real points about the links between naming and identity, yet he himself remained secure behind the visor. Readers, some more than others, may have a dual response to the doubleness of Scott.

To end there would be, nevertheless, a heartless act of betrayal. Frustrating though he sometimes is as a writer, Scott gave a voice to Scottish people in fiction, where one barely existed, and names to the world they inhabited. We owe him a great deal. It would be fairer to dwell on the remarkable richness of Scott's work, and conclude with Hélène Cixous, another (different) kind of 'nevertheless':

I believe in what we call in French *quand même,* the however, the nevertheless, or the still, because there are readers, because there are writers. For me joy is always linked to the possibility of sharing in a work of art.[27]

Notes

1. 'What Images Return', *Memoirs of a Modern Scotland,* ed. Karl Miller (London, 1970), 152. See also Alastair Reid, 'Digging up Scotland', *Whereabouts: Notes on Being a Foreigner* (Edinburgh, 1987), 21.

2. *Fiction Against History: Scott as Storyteller* (Cambridge, 1988), 74.

3. Elizabeth Closs Traugott and Mary Louise Pratt, *Linguistics for Students of Literature* (New York, 1980), 228.

4. Chapter 24; 238: page references given are to the World's Classics edition (Oxford, 1982), ed. Claire Lamont.

5. *Walter Scott* (Edinburgh, 1982), 102.

6. *Orality and Literacy: The Technologizing of the Word* (London, 1982), 32.

7. For example Traugott and Pratt, 11.

8. *Secret Leaves: The Novels of Walter Scott* (Chicago and London, 1985), 142.

9. *Beyond God the Father: Toward a Philosophy of Women's Liberation* (Boston, Mass., 1973), 8.

10. *The Newly Born Woman,* tr. Betsy Wing (Manchester, 1987; originally published in Paris as *La Jeune Née,* 1975), 5. Further references are to this edition.

11. 'Fictional Economies: Adam Smith, Walter Scott and the Nineteenth-Century Novel', *ELH,* 54 (1987), 97–127 (120).

12. One useful account of salient ideas is Ann Rosalind Jones, 'Inscribing Femininity: French Theories of the Feminine', *Making a Difference: Feminist Literary Criticism,* ed. Gayle Greene and Coppelia Kahn (London, 1985), 20–112. Works by Kristeva and Irigaray among others are now available in translation in various editions.

13. For example, see Elaine Millard 'French Feminisms', in *Feminist Readings/Feminists Reading,* ed. Sara Mills and others, 154–86 (154).

14. Kathryn Sutherland; also Marilyn Orr, 'Voices and Text: Scott the Novelist', *Scottish Literary Journal,* 16:2 (November 1989), 41–59.

15. In 'Advertisement' to *The Antiquary,* 1829.

16. 'Daniel Defoe', *Prose Works,* IV; and in *Sir Walter Scott on Novelists and Fiction,* ed. Ioan Williams (London, 1968), 164–83 (167).

17. 'Introductory Epistle' to *The Fortunes of Nigel.*

18. See for instance *General Preface to the Waverley Novels,* 1829, and 'Introduction' to *Chronicles of the Canongate,* 1827.

19. *The Civilized Imagination: A Study of Ann Radcliffe, Jane Austen, and Sir Walter Scott* (Cambridge, 1985), 141.

20. *The Language of Sir Walter Scott: A Study of his Scottish and Period Language* (London, 1980), 303.

21. *From Galt to Douglas Brown: Nineteenth Century Fiction and Scots Language* (Edinburgh, 1988).

22. For instance, Jane Millgate, *Walter Scott: The Making of the Novelist* (Toronto, 1984), 160. Graham Tulloch, however (330–1), has some interesting remarks on Scott's lack of 'realism' in Jeanie's letters.

23. A review of *The Pilgrim's Progress, with a Life of John Bunyan* by Robert Southey, in *Quarterly Review,* 43 (1830), in Williams, 379–406.

24. 'The Two Languages of Scott', *Scott's Mind and Art,* ed. Norman Jeffares (Edinburgh, 1969), 207.

25. 'Literary Names as Text: Personal Names in Sir Walter Scott's *Waverley*,' *Nomina,* 3 (1979), 35–6.

26. 'Introduction' to *Chronicles of the Canongate,* 1832.

27. 'Difficult Joys', *The Body and the Text,* ed. Helen Wilcox and others (London, 1990), 25.

Death and Disappearance
in *The Bride of Lammermoor*

BRUCE BEIDERWELL

Scott's *The Bride of Lammermoor* is bound by a pressing and pervasive sense of death. The first chapter of the narrative proper centres on the funeral of the hero's father. And the hero is, of course, immediately established as one who is doomed by his family's history. Edgar, the Master of Ravenswood, is left at the outset of the tale to contemplate a ruinous past and anticipate an evil future. That future eventually arrives in all its wastefulness. We are left, at the very end of the novel, to respond to the "splendid marble monument" which marks the passing of the last—and most culpable—of the principal characters in the tragedy (Ch. 35; 349).[1]

Given this nearly unrelieved tone of despair, it is hardly surprising that readers were quick to accept and reluctant to give up fictions that long surrounded the composition of *The Bride of Lammermoor* (that Scott dictated it in a delirious state, that he remembered nothing of its telling). Indeed there is some critical insight we may still glean from these fictions. For there is a desperate fear expressed in the *Bride* that is at once both deeply personal and broadly social. On the one hand, the fear may be rooted in Scott's experience as a jilted lover;[2] on the other, it seems clearly part of Scott's vision of historical moment. The matter is one of what I will call *presence*. Readers are disturbed by the failure of death to register a sense of loss in the community.

We often experience death scenes, after all, as dramatic expressions of self—of human worth or personal significance.[3] For example, in *The Antiquary* the fisherman Steenie becomes in passionate emotions that surround his death the occasion for a ceremony that effectively (if only momentarily) levels social classes. It is this substantial feeling of the individual human presence that Mr Ramsay in Virginia Woolf's *To the Lighthouse* relishes in Scott. And Mr Ramsay's enthusiasm clearly stems from the absence of such presence in his own life. His narcissism forces him to fret endlessly over his academic reputation and to seek affirmation unrelentingly from those about him. Perhaps the

From *Scott in Carnival,* Selected Papers from the Fourth International Scott Conference, Edinburgh, 1991, ed. J. H. Alexander and David Hewitt (Aberdeen: Association for Scottish Literary Studies, 1993), 245–53. Reprinted by permission of the Association for Scottish Literary Studies and Bruce Beiderwell.

greatest fear of such characters is that even their own death will not communicate the specialness they feel due themselves—a specialness routinely denied in everyday life.

The action of *The Bride of Lammermoor* represents a series of failed gestures by the hero to establish presence. History denies Ravenswood the context he needs to make himself felt as a son, as a citizen, as a lover, or even as an enemy. What Ravenswood is left with may indeed be less than a series of gestures (which at least implies movement or physicality); he is reduced to something more like postures or futile set speeches (stiff, ineffectual, and at times even faintly ludicrous in a world that moves rapidly about him). It is appropriate that Ravenswood literally disappears when he dies.

We might say that Scott tames Ravenswood's gestures by placing them squarely in the literary realm of romance and having them jar against the settled reality of the established order.[4] Scott employs the language of romance to distance himself and his readers from the hero. In this way Scott comes to terms with his own acceptance of—and investment in—the post-Union, Hanoverian order. But such a domestication does not fully account for the hero's almost total ineffectuality.

In other Waverley novels, romance expresses feelings that translate into some sort of real (even if unwise) action. We need only think of the scene in which Edward Waverley is introduced to Charles Stuart. The Prince abruptly breaks off Fergus's introduction: 'I beg your pardon for interrupting you, my dear Mac-Ivor; but no master of ceremonies is necessary to present a Waverley to a Stuart' (Ch. 40; 293–4).[5] Such recognition plays to a fantasy of self-importance, to a set of romantic notions of the individual self that may have little place in the novel's ultimate resolution. But the desire encoded in this scene powerfully takes shape from Waverley's sense that the real (politically established) world does not truly recognise him. Scott's words make this clear:

> To be thus personally solicited for assistance by a Prince, whose form and manners, as well as the spirit which he displayed in this singular enterprise, answered his ideas of a hero of romance; to be courted by him in the ancient halls of his paternal palace, recovered by the sword which he was already bending towards other conquests, gave Edward, *in his own eyes, the dignity and importance which he had ceased to consider as his attributes.* Rejected, slandered, and threatened upon the one side, he was irresistibly attracted to the cause which the prejudices of education, and the political principles of his family, had already recommended as the most just. These thoughts rushed through his mind like a torrent, sweeping before them every consideration of an opposite tendency,—the time, besides, admitted of no deliberation,—and Waverley, kneeling to Charles Edward, devoted his heart and sword to the vindication of his rights!—(Ch. 40; 295: my emphasis)

If Ravenswood is never seduced into the revenge he vows early on in the narrative, neither is he given the thrill of personal recognition that is part of a successful seduction. Waverley feels that thrill in his encounter with Charles Edward. In comparison, we can observe that Craigengelt (or 'Craigie' as Bucklaw calls him) does not possess the requisite personal qualities or social position to flatter Ravenswood into a purposeful sense of action.

The hollowness of Ravenswood's gestures, of his attempts to make the stuff of romance communicate his sense of self, are in part legacies of his father. Lord Ravenswood's death comes in a 'fit of violent and impotent fury' that is occasioned by the 'loss of a cause'. Scott's word choice makes this sense of diminishment unmistakable. The 'cause' here becomes a legal term as opposed to the grandiose expression of Jacobitical principles. And the death of the elder Ravenswood is announced with a pun on the law: 'death closed the litigation, by summoning Ravenswood to a higher bar' (Ch. 2; 31). Such verbal playfulness keeps the death of Lord Ravenswood from lending substance to his life. It in fact makes his life an abstraction within a complicated system of law.[6]

The funeral that follows similarly devalues Lord Ravenswood. The entire production is out of scale to the occasion. It is too large, too elaborate in comparison to the ever shrinking life it was supposed to honour. Certainly the challenge the authorities make to the lawfulness of the Episcopal proceedings allows for some drama, but the Master of Ravenswood's threats against Ashton and his family seem essentially theatre. The audience to the show may observe and even cheer his words of defiance, but its members also keep a distance from Edgar, and Edgar feels the insincerity that that distance indicates:

> When the last flask was emptied, they took their leave, with deep protestations—to be forgotten on the morrow, if, indeed, those who made them should not think it necessary for their safety to make a more solemn retraction.
>
> Accepting their adieus with an air of contempt which he could scarce conceal, Ravenswood at length beheld his ruinous habitation cleared of this confluence of riotous guests, and returned to the deserted hall, which now appeared doubly lonely from the cessation of that clamour to which it had so lately echoed. (Ch. 2; 34)

The pomp and ceremony that marks the close to Lord Ravenswood's life, then, has little to do with Lord Ravenswood or his son. It serves merely to remind us of the presence the old lord once enjoyed before he is finally 'consigned to the realms of forgetfulness' (Ch. 2; 31).

The system of law that had forced Lord Ravenswood to pursue a cause through agents also enmeshes the Master of Ravenswood. Edgar becomes an abstraction, bound in ways he does not know by paper. The Lord Keeper (whose very character is defined by its insubstantiality) makes 'careful notes' of testimony that places Ravenswood's remaining fortune and personal liberty at his disposal. The language of these early passages must be attended to: Ravenswood's words, actions, his very identity are forcefully defined by the notes Ashton compiles. Ashton reviews the file he has collected on Ravenswood's behaviour at the funeral and concludes: 'These memoranda, properly stated to the Privy Council, cannot but be construed into an aggravated riot' (Ch. 3; 37).[7]

Of course Ashton does not pursue this line of action. Edgar's dramatic rescue of Ashton and his daughter Lucy from the charging bull causes the Lord Keeper to revise his strategy. It also provides Edgar a seemingly grand opportunity to register presence. In the scene of introduction to his enemy he abruptly cuts off Ashton's offers of favour (the only way Ashton has of expressing gratitude) with a ringing announcement: 'Request nothing of ME, my lord ... I am the Master of Ravenswood' (Ch. 5; 62). But even Ravenswood's extraordinary, concrete act of saving his enemy and the 'stern and peremptory tone' it allows him to assume are quickly made insubstantial. His identity remains something for others to shape for their own interests. Ashton immediately begins to construct through paper another Ravenswood—one that still does not regard what we may, for lack of a better term, call the original. After securing medical advice on Lucy's condition, Ashton 'proceeded to revise the memoranda' which he had taken down earlier: 'Bred to casuistry, and well accustomed to practise the ambidexter ingenuity of the bar, it cost him little trouble to soften the features of the tumult which he had been at first so anxious to exaggerate' (Ch. 5; 65). These 'public dispatches' are followed by letters to private persons who oversee Ravenswood's case. Although these efforts do remove one kind of threat against Ravenswood, they reinforce the pervasive sense that his life is not his own. We might note that at this point in the novel, Ravenswood has been wholly unaware of the case that had been constructed against him and then reconstructed for other purposes. All goes on without his knowledge or conscious influence. Nevertheless, he like his father feels the consequences of such shadowy operations.

This diminishment of personal presence is something that may be considered in context of Adam Ferguson's principles of union among humankind. In *An Essay on the History of Civil Society* (1767), Ferguson suggests that man's social disposition may be clearly observed in those simple societies where no one has learned to 'affect what they do not actually feel'. The most profound emotions can only be realised in a social setting. And Ferguson depicts those emotions in language that rapturously underscores their physical expressiveness and effectiveness: "It is here [in the company of our fellow-creatures] that a man is made to forget his weakness, his cares of safety, and his subsistence; and to act from those passions which make him discover his force. It is here he finds that his arrows fly swifter than the eagle, and his weapons wound deeper than the paw of the lion, or the tooth of the boar."[8] But in Ferguson's 'philosophical' reading of history, this felt connection of person to person may well be lost, and with it the feeling of physicality or 'force'. In a 'commercial state' he notes that the individual 'is sometimes found a detached and a solitary being'. Human interaction continues in language and increasingly in written language, but the 'bands of affection are broken'.[9] Such advanced, individualistic societies are ironically the least fully human and the most fully subject to abstract powers of the state.

We might widen the discussion here and consider a specific abstraction that gained power in Scott's time: social/political theorists of the late eighteenth and early nineteenth centuries reckoned much over the meaning of human population figures. Robert Wallace's *Dissertation on the Numbers of Mankind* (1753) argued that Scotland could cultivate more land with more people. And, of course, Malthus's *An Essay on the Principle of Population* (1798) alarmed many with the then relatively uncommon notion of population as a *problem*.[10] The point I wish to make is that such texts involve an act of abstraction that would be unthinkable in the 'simple' world of community and energy that Ferguson describes as elemental to the formation of society. Indeed, the advanced world could well measure its specific losses by the fact that it makes such an abstraction thinkable. Malthus's formula (human numbers increase geometrically while the means of substinence increase arithmetically) counts people in a way that makes a person count for very little. Ferguson's thoughts on population may be seen as implicitly critical of this tendency to think abstractly on human society; his interest in population is essentially moral rather than political or economic. He is not concerned about numbers so much as the way people are numbered (and valued) in civil society. We can sense similar concerns in *The Bride of Lammermoor* as Scott depicts a society that attends to matters of property and money disconnected from personal qualities or social values.

This progressive loss of the necessary social context for sustained energetic expression of self should make us more respectful of what we tend to write off as masculine foolishness in much of Scott. The 'Big Bow-Wow strain' that Scott self-deprecatingly refers to in his work is more psychologically insightful than we often appreciate. When this strain seems most silly it may be functioning most meaningfully. For example, Bucklaw's rather coarse sensibility allows him to draw heavily on Craigengelt for needs that remain unfulfilled in the more reflective hero:

> "I will be d—d if ever I saw French, Italian, or High-Dutchman ever make foot, hand, and eye, keep time half so well as you, Bucklaw."
> "I believe you lie, Craigie," said Bucklaw; "however, I can hold my own, both with single rapier, backsword, sword and dagger, broadsword, or case of falchions—and that's as much as any gentleman need know of the matter."
> (Ch. 21; 219)

A character as uncomplicated as Bucklaw can carry such physical assurance to the field of sport and there take satisfaction within its limits. The hunt preserves for him forms that enable action. It is Bucklaw who wins a 'shout of triumph when [he] . . . with the dexterity proper to an accomplished cavalier of the day sprang from his horse, and dashing suddenly and swiftly at the stag, brought him to the ground by a cut on the hind leg with his short hunting sword' (Ch. 9; 109). Ravenswood, left behind on an inferior horse, feels pained by the recognition that 'his poverty excluded him from the favourite recreation of his forefathers, and indeed their sole employment when not engaged in military pursuits' (Ch. 9; 107).

Significantly, military pursuits are no more available to Ravenswood than sporting ones. Just before his engagement to Lucy, Ravenswood has announced his departure in terms that would suit one as simple as Bucklaw: 'My preparations are already made—a sword and a cloak, and a bold heart and a determined hand' (Ch. 20; 206). But to what cause is Ravenswood so devoted? Surely no cause strong enough to sustain him against the tears of Lucy: 'Each attempt which the Master made to explain his purpose of departure, only proved a new evidence of his desire to stay; until, at length, instead of bidding her farewell, he gave his faith to her for ever, and received her troth in return' (Ch. 20; 207). When Ravenswood finally does find means of 'honourable exertion' it is in service of his uncle, the Marquis, who plays at politics with the same unprincipled dexterity as Ashton (Ch. 25; 267).

Apparently, Ravenswood is too self-conscious, too aware of the limits built into the causes he serves. In some respects, this hero of a dead order—of a time long gone even in Scott's day—seems a surprisingly modern character. I do not refer here to Ravenswood's occasionally moderate and forward looking political statements.[11] Rather I want to stress the feelings behind the very things that mark him as an archaic figure: his brooding gothicism, his bold declarations of revenge, his proud assertions of honour. The gestures that sum up these qualities can all be seen as efforts to fill in some missing emotional space. Ravenswood shifts about from the stance of a seemingly moderate hero to that of a feudal lord because neither of these roles is grounded sufficiently in a widely shared system of value or in a secure political and social order. Nor does Ravenswood possess the confidence to repudiate everything in the grandiose fashion of Byron's Manfred. Nothing, as the servant Caleb seems to know or at least makes comically clear, provides the context necessary for him to establish presence.[12] In this way, Ravenswood seems entirely consistent as he reacts verbally and variously to the confusing world that surrounds him. Perhaps Woolf's Mr Ramsay would be too closely touched by Ravenswood to enjoy reading of him: Steenie's death is more comforting because of the marked emotional impact it has on surrounding characters.

The ultimate destructiveness of Edgar's verbal reactions should also seem familiar to readers of modern novels. Ravenswood often adopts the language of action, but for him language (as in the engagement scene) comes to supplant action. Ravenswood (although no villain and no lawyer) shares many of the dangerous qualities of the ressentient character Richard Weisberg traces in his book *The Failure of the Word: The Protagonist as Lawyer in Modern Fiction*. Weisberg summarises the work of Max Scheler who

... sees ressentiment as issuing from a specific sense of insult, followed first by an onslaught of unfulfilled reactive desires, then by a condition of existential envy of the unchallenged perpetrator, which the subject attempts to vent by lashing out at those closest to him. Finally, an almost organic impulse to mis-judge ... and a constant sense of "being insulted" arise within the ressentient man.[13]

Weisberg argues that the plots of modern novels change with these new char-acters: 'More and more often, whole novels follow the paradigm of perceived insult, thwarted vengeance, and misdirected violence. Protagonists no longer respond simply and directly to real or imagined acts of injustice. Because of their nagging sense of futility, they make guiltless others the butt of their ... fatal eloquence.'[14]

Lucy is, of course, a victim of far more than Ravenswood's eloquence. But she does suffer greatly through the collected force of the suppressed anger that had been apparent in the Master's character from the beginning of the novel. That this anger finally vents itself on the helpless Lucy only affirms what has long been obvious: Ravenswood feels blocked from dealing directly with the sources of the pain that afflicts him.

With this deficiency in mind, it seems fitting that Ravenswood's own death is emptied of dramatic moment.[15] He is given no last opportunity for speech, and no last chance to act. He becomes invisible as he rides to duel with Lucy's brother and is lost in the sands of the Kelpie's flow. Surely he felt invisible before he became so. The feelings of a jilted lover intensify but do not differ from the feelings Ravenswood has contended with from the start—feelings of erasure, of diminishment, of ineffectuality. Scott's *Journal* vividly registers such feelings born from his own youthful experience in love.[16] In *The Bride of Lammermoor* he gives readers eyes to testify to what no one can see: disappearance, not death. Ravenswood's servant Caleb witnesses his disap-pearance from one side, Colonel Ashton from the other. Both meet at the fatal spot and discover a single sable feather—a reminder of the Master of Ravenswood that is somehow dignified by its apt insubstantiality.

Notes

1. Walter Scott, *The Bride of Lammermoor,* ed. Fiona Robertson (Oxford, 1991). Cita-tions to *The Bride of Lammermoor* appear in the text.

2. See Harry E. Shaw, *The Forms of Historical Fiction: Sir Walter Scott and His Successors* (Ithaca, 1983), 219.

3. Garrett Stewart explores the notion that moments of death in novels are moments of intense self-definition. See Stewart, *Death Sentences: Styles of Dying in British Fiction* (Cam-bridge, 1984).

4. James Kerr, *Fiction Against History: Scott as Storyteller* (Cambridge, 1989), 88–101.

5. Walter Scott, *Waverley,* ed. Andrew Hook (Harmondsworth, 1972). Citations to *Waverley* appear in the text.

6. Alexander Welsh's comment that the reality individuals confront in *The Heart of Midlothian* is 'undisguisedly a "construction" of the law' may be considered here in reference to *The Bride of Lammermoor.* See Welsh, *The Hero of the Waverley Novels* (1963; rpt. New York, 1968), 139.

7. See my discussion of the notion of 'constructive treason' in *Power and Punishment in Scott's Novels* (Athens, Georgia, 1992), 78.

8. Adam Ferguson, *An Essay on the History of Civil Society,* ed. Duncan Forbes (Edinburgh, 1966), 18.

9. Ferguson, 19.

10. See the excellent introduction to Thomas Robert Malthus, *An Essay on the Principle of Population,* ed. Philip Appleman (New York, 1976), xi–xxvii.

11. Ravenswood's 'moderation' and consequently Scott's 'optimism' has long been the subject of debate. See for example Robert C. Gordon and Andrew Hook, '*The Bride of Lammermoor* Again: An Exchange,' *Nineteenth-Century Fiction,* 23 (1969), 493–9. Recent discussions on the significance of the changes Scott made in the text of the novel after the first edition have sustained the debate. Jane Millgate contends that the first edition carefully locates Ravenswood's pre-Union historical position and therefore allows us to particularise his tragedy. Fiona Robertson, however, prefers the Magnum Opus as copy text for her recent edition of *The Bride of Lammermoor.* See Millgate, *Walter Scott: The Making of the Novelist* (Toronto, 1984), 172–85; and Robertson's 'Note on the Text' in *The Bride of Lammermoor,* xxx–xxxviii.

12. I am grateful to Tom Dale for pointing out that Caleb essentially parodies Ravenswood's own futile efforts to establish presence.

13. Richard H. Weisberg, *The Failure of the Word: The Protagonist as Lawyer in Modern Fiction* (New Haven, 1984), 26.

14. Weisberg, 8.

15. Fiona Robertson remarks that Ravenswood 'does not so much die as disappear.' See her introduction to *The Bride of Lammermoor,* xxviii.

16. *The Journal of Sir Walter Scott,* ed. W.E.K. Anderson (Oxford, 1972), 315, 375.

The Recuperation of Canon Fodder:
Walter Scott's *The Talisman*

Caroline McCracken-Flesher

Canonization, we have learned, "authorizes" a text. To be canonized, a text must to some degree express the dominant ideology; canonization thus constitutes an ideological recognition of conformity, and a concurrent assumption of "quality." And once canonized, a text will operate as "quality control," denying authority to less culturally conformist works. The canonized text obscures and forces out the texts of otherness—indeed, as our recent professional/political battles have demonstrated, it can be launched like a literary cruise missile to obliterate them.

As generations of schoolchildren have discovered in Britain and the Empire (latterly, the Commonwealth), Walter Scott is one of the English canon's biggest guns, and his works make up a large and heavy pile of ammunition. Salvoes of *Ivanhoe* have been loosed at hoards of trembling teenagers with deadly—one might even say deadening—effect. Legions of *Ivanhoe*'s shell-shocked victims have gazed down the twin barrels of *Waverley* and *The Heart of Midlothian* and acknowledged the novels' firepower by surrendering to their greatness without reading them.

But I would suggest that Scott himself is the primary casualty of the canonical bombardment in which he figures so prominently. How can this be? The answer lies in the criteria that loaded Scott into the canon. When the canon's architects included Scott in their pantheon of novelists, they did so grudgingly and for all the wrong reasons. Their choice had nothing to do with avowed criteria such as aesthetic quality or realism—it didn't even have anything to do with Scott himself. Time and again, we find these self-conscious builders of novelistic tradition invoking Scott as a naive, flawed, yet authorizing precursor for some "better" novelist. For instance, ever digging for the roots of his own genius, Henry James declares after a visit to Scott's home at Ashestiel, "I took up one of Scott's novels—*Redgauntlet;* it was years since I had read one. They have always a charm for me—but I was amazed at the badness of [it]: *l'enfance de l'art.*"[1] Similarly, although less sympathetically,

From *No Small World: New Directions in the Theory and Pedagogy of World Literature,* ed. Michael Carroll (Urbana, Ill.: National Council of Teachers of English, 1996). Copyright by the National Council of Teachers of English. Reprinted by permission.

as he gathers the Pole, the American, the Englishman, and the (manly) Englishwoman from whom he will oddly constitute the "Great Tradition" of English novelists, F. R. Leavis takes a moment to install Scott in the canon—and summarily eject him from it. He writes, significantly in a footnote, "Out of Scott a bad tradition came. It spoiled Fenimore Cooper. . . . And with Stevenson it took on 'literary' sophistication and fine writing."[2] Leavis and James imply that Scott's successors, while owing him some vague degree of provenance, succeed in spite of him, or fail because of him. The hapless Walter Scott is tamped down the canon as a kind of primitive wadding for the really important (Anglocentric) weaponry.

Perversely, then, we might consider Scott not just as canonical ammunition, but as a kind of canon fodder. Although fed into the canon to enhance the ballistic power of superior English authors, the Scottish novelist is there digested into England's cultural stew. However centered in the canon he may appear, Scott resides there for his service to other authors and texts, and to interests not his own. Even though this grudging canonization empowers him, it constitutes him as unremittingly English. He thus languishes disempowered as what he really was, a Scottish Other. To be fair to James and Leavis, however, this process of canonization and consequent homogenization gained momentum along with Scott's popularity as a writer, and it affected even his compatriots' view of his work. In 1838, with Scott only six years dead, his countryman Thomas Carlyle wrote, "So bounteous was Nature to us; in the sickliest of recorded ages, when British Literature lay all puking and sprawling in Werterism, Byronism, and other Sentimentalism tearful or spasmodic (fruit of internal *wind*), Nature was kind enough to send us two healthy Men [Cobbett and Scott], of whom she might still say, not without pride, 'These also were made in *England* [my emphasis]; such limbs do I still make there!' "[3] Carlyle goes on to discuss Scott's national origins in his next paragraph, but the Freudian slip has been made; however Scottish their shared background, Carlyle sees and celebrates Scott in an English context. From its inception, then, Scott's canonization transformed him into an indistinguishable servant of the Empire, even for fellow Scots.

This is the more ironic because, as I will argue, not only is Scott's work in many respects specifically Scottish, it is actively and aggressively so. Moreover, it is constructed in opposition to precisely the kind of cultural cannibalism inevitably exercised by England's dominant culture over Scotland's national literature, and under which Scott's own novels have suffered. Indeed, Scott's novels, if once disgorged from the canon and recoded according to their Scottish cultural matrix, might join with those "Other" texts marshaled under the banner of World Literature that seek to deconstruct the canon as an oppressive instrument and to open in its place a discursive space.

To the canon's harshest critics, and to the staunchest advocates of World Literature as a literature of difference, this may appear an unlikely case. It is to combat such criticism that I have chosen here to argue from an unlikely text, *The Talisman*.⁴ This novel, of all Scott's works, seems thoroughly and uncritically to participate in the discourse of Empire; to all appearances, it little deserves to be snatched from the canon's mouth. Despite the fact that it comprises the elements of an oppositional text, it seems to offer no critique of English mores or even of colonial subjection. For instance, although in *The Talisman* as in nearly every Scott novel, the supposedly central character is Scottish, in Sir Kenneth we find no resistant figure; a Scottish prince in disguise, Sir Kenneth serves anonymously but supportively in Richard the Lionheart's crusading army. Further, although while guarding the English standard Sir Kenneth commits a sin of omission that results in the standard's theft, his crime cannot be seen as even a momentary gesture of resistance, for he immediately subjects himself to English justice, effectively putting his neck under the executioner's axe. Then, although Sir Kenneth escapes subjection/death, he is saved not by his own actions but rather over his objections and by "the enemy," Saladin. Finally, when rescued, he returns to the camp to find the thief, redeem the honor of England, and marry a Plantagenet. Not surprisingly, even the canon's advocates have viewed this apparently simplistic romance suspiciously, but perhaps because of their formal reservations, *The Talisman* has achieved that most dangerous kind of canonization; it has become a high-school text. Not sophisticated enough for adults, it has nonetheless indoctrinated generations of schoolchildren in Britain and throughout the colonies with the romance of empire.

Understandably, then, Edward Said considers Scott a logical target for his critique of Orientalism. Said focuses on the first encounter between Sir Kenneth and Saladin, the conjunction between Occident and Orient. Sir Kenneth comments to Saladin, "I well thought . . . that your blinded race had their descent from the foul fiend, without whose aid you would never have been able to maintain this blessed land of Palestine against so many valiant soldiers of God. I speak not thus of thee in particular, Saracen, but generally of thy people and religion" (39). Taking predictable offense at Sir Kenneth's sweeping generalization and his blindness to specific difference, Said writes, "what is truly curious . . . is the airy condescension of damning a whole people 'generally' while mitigating the offense with a cool 'I don't mean you in particular.' "⁵ For Said, *The Talisman* clearly functions as part of England's arsenal of oppressive, imperialist texts.

Yet the sin of thoughtlessly dismissing cultural difference for which Said chastizes Scott can equally be identified in Said's own text. Just as Sir Kenneth diminishes Saladin by sweeping him into the category of undifferentiated Arabs, when Said seeks to validate middle eastern culture against the imperialist dynamic, he diminishes Scott by sweeping him into a similarly general but dominant category, "the English": "Scott, Kinglake, Disraeli, Warburton, Burton, and even George Eliot . . . are writers . . . for whom the Orient was defined by material possession, by a material imagination, as it were. *England* had defeated Napoleon, evicted France: what the *English* mind surveyed was an imperial domain which by the 1880s had become an unbroken patch of British-held territory" (my emphases; 169). And again: "*English* writers . . . had a more pronounced and harder sense of what Oriental pilgrimages might entail than the French. . . . Romantic writers like Byron and Scott consequently had a political vision of the Near Orient and a very combative awareness of how relations between the Orient and Europe would have to be conducted" (my emphases; 192). Said sees Scott as English even in a comparative context that necessarily foregrounds terms like "British" and "French" to problematize his assumption. Ironically, this advocate for Otherness is fooled by Scott's canonization into committing that cardinal sin within his own system, failing to recognize difference.

And in fact, if we read *The Talisman* by Said's own criteria, not by his interests, it appears a quite Other tale. Despite the text's apparent Englishness and endorsement of English imperialism, when subjected to the light of *Orientalism*, *The Talisman* stands forth not as a quisling imperialist romance, but as a resistant, Scottish tale—as exactly the kind of ethnic and oppositional text Said might celebrate.

Scott wrote *The Talisman* at a moment when he was becoming deeply concerned with the effects of anglicization in Scotland. In 1707, Scotland had joined in parliamentary Union with England to avoid economic penalties— but also for financial gain. After a slow start, in the early years of the nineteenth century, she finally began to achieve her monetary desires. Scott, however, realized that whatever the financial benefits of Union, Scotland's assumption of her neighbor's bourgeois economic goals inevitably subjected her to England's imperialist narrative; Scots stood to lose their remaining national institutions, and even their national identity. In his early novels, therefore, Scott painstakingly constructed two types of narrative for Scotland, one within which she could enjoy the gains of Union, not bringing herself unduly under English scrutiny and losing nothing of her own identity, and another wherein she might retain a separate subjectivity protected from England's colonizing impetus. (As I have argued elsewhere, these narratives are marked by Jacobitism and gender, on the one hand, and socialized Calvinism on the other.)[6] By this strategy, Scott himself managed to remain outside the colonizing economic narrative while yet participating in it. Although he narrated a space for Scottish difference, in so doing he made English money. Indeed, he wrote himself into a knighthood (gazetted 1820). Around 1825, however, Scott began to realize that even this cautiously played game was not worth the candle. First, the financial gains of Union suddenly appeared ephemeral, as bubble corporations began to burst. The predicament of small joint-stock companies that Scott parodied in his introduction to *The Betrothed* and *The Talisman* (published together as *Tales of the Crusaders*)[7] was about to overtake him in his own ill-advised association with publishers and printers.[8] Equally important, perhaps, through his son's service in an English regiment in Ireland, Scott was becoming aware that Scotland had other comparator nations than England, and that—for worse and for better—she might stand categorized with the lowly Ireland.[9] Both these perceptions bear most obvious fruit in Scott's 1826 *Malachi Malagrowther* Letters. Here, Scott responds to a projected English encroachment on the Scottish banking system that he considered would prove financially and nationally damaging by at last arguing openly and vigorously for Scotland's own financial rights, and by appealing to Ireland for support in his opposition. He writes, "What is our case today will be [Ireland's] the instant you have got a little tranquility. . . . I see you grasp your shilela at the very thought! Enough; we understand each other: Let us be friends. Patrick aids Saunders to-day; Saunders pays back Patrick to-morrow. . . . But what do I talk of to-day or to-morrow? The cause of Ireland is tried ALONG WITH that of Scotland."[10] *The Talisman*, then, was written at a moment when financial circumstances were beginning to bring home to Scott that however successful his nation, from England's perspective she was still inevitably Other and inevitably less. Scott, moreover, was beginning to understand that Scotland had chosen her friends ill-advisedly, and that her most effective alliance might be with equally othered nations, like Ireland.

It is perhaps his growing awareness of Scotland's status as Other that causes Scott to struggle in *The Talisman* not to diminish or dismiss difference, but to recuperate and empower it. Indeed, I suggest that through Scott's novel, Scotland as Other stands empowered in itself, and through its conjunction with similarly obscured nations and persons. The distorting light of canonization refracted *The Talisman* to Said as a text wherein Saladin can be seen only momentarily as an individual, but persistently as a relatively insignificant Saracen Other. Said consequently argues that Sir Kenneth and Scott, themselves representative of the Occidental cultural bloc, together see Saladin as "*first* an Oriental, *second* a human being, and *last* again an Oriental" (102). But viewed from a less canonically driven and more culturally conscious perspective, Scott's novel works to demonstrate through the racially, religiously, and geographically distinct Saladin—and to model for a specifically Scottish Sir Kenneth—the positive value of Otherness. However Saladin enters the text, he exits it as no mere "Oriental," but rather as a celebrated, highly visible leader, and one who significantly owes his effectiveness to his difference. He shows, in fact, that otherness may have operative force, that difference may comprise not diminution, but agency, and that Others may work successfully as brothers. Thus Scott looms from *The Talisman* not as an imperialistic oppressor, but as a visionary opening a space for colonized nations, as one who transforms otherness from a position of weakness into an oppositional position of strength.

In *The Talisman*, far from establishing Sir Kenneth as an unproblematic representative of England, or even of Scotland, Scott uses him to explore the conditions of Scotland's contemporary subjection; he takes a long, cool look at Scotland as she stands Othered by the English perspective. Committed to the Crusade, Sir Kenneth nonetheless vigorously denies Saladin's suggestion that he serves Richard or England. He insists on his separate, Scottish identity when he noisily declares, "One of [Richard's] followers I am, for this expedition ... and honoured in the service; but not born his subject, although a native of the island in which he reigns" (35). And in response to Saladin's suggestion that Richard might better have served the cause of Christendom by subduing his Scottish neighbors before turning his ambitions to Palestine, Kenneth exclaims, "No, by the bright light of Heaven! If the King of England had not set forth to the Crusade till he was sovereign of Scotland, the Crescent might, for me, and all true-hearted Scots, glimmer for ever on the walls of Zion" (36). But whatever the vehemence of Sir Kenneth's protest, and perhaps because he constantly emphasizes his Scottish otherness, he stands effectively elided by the English court. Kenneth's assertion of national difference has led his English allies to assume in him that primary marker of otherness, bodily difference. Thus, Richard's right-hand man, Sir Thomas de Vaux, when first he notices Sir Kenneth on his return from his desert encounter with Saladin, cannot immediately identify him, but can categorize him as "a Spaniard or a Scot" (82). Like the Christian Spaniard, Sir Kenneth can serve in the English cause, but like the racially distinct Spaniard, he cannot be considered English. For Sir Thomas, Kenneth verges away from Occidental and towards Oriental. And once located as Other, the Scot stands voiceless, deprived of his function as speaking subject. Kenneth, in fact, is returning from a mission where he has unwittingly served as an empty vessel bearing the words of conspiratorial forces, and now, de Vaux's first instinct as an Englishman and consequently one of the crusade's elite, is to pass Kenneth by without speaking to him. Scott writes: "Loath to ask even a passing question, he was about to pass Sir Kenneth, with that sullen and lowering port which seems to say, 'I know thee, but I will hold no communication with thee' " (82). Given that Sir Kenneth turns out to be a prince of Scotland, David, Earl of Huntingdon, serving anonymously in the crusading forces, Scott offers no optimistic picture of the contemporary Scot's rehabilitation within the Union; even the primary representative of Scottish difference cannot maintain his identity, his role as speaking subject, inside the orbit of English power.

But Scott interestingly takes care to emphasize that Scottish subjection does not arise simply as an inevitable effect of England's hegemony. Instead, he suggests through Prince David/Sir Kenneth that the Scot shares responsibility for his own subjection. Kenneth, after all, has joined the Crusade, and taken the role of follower (wherein, as Saladin points out, he may be confused with "subject"; 35), by choice. Further, as the story proceeds, he takes on the values of the colonizer to the extent that he willingly gives over not just his voice but also his body to English purposes. As a reward for bringing to Richard a Saracen doctor who cures him of fever (Saladin), Kenneth receives the task of guarding the English standard. When he proves derelict in his duty and the standard is stolen, his punishment is death. Yet far from recognizing his failure as a necessary expression of Scottish resistance, Sir Kenneth covers himself with remorse, and subjects himself to English punishment. As Alexander Welsh notes, when Kenneth declares, "I have deserted my charge—the banner intrusted to me is lost—when the headsman and block are prepared, the head and trunk are ready to part company" (170), "not only is Richard prepared to execute the hero, but the hero is prepared to die."[11] Kenneth cannot, and despite Saladin's promptings, will not step outside the English system even to save his own Scottish life; he subjects himself unquestioningly to the terms and processes of English power. By accepting England's honor code, Sir Kenneth accomplishes his own erasure as a Scottish subject—with relatively little help from England. And in so doing, he casts a critical light on contemporary Scots who sought the gains of Union and thereby subjected themselves to English power.

Moreover, Scott stresses that such unthinking subjection to a foreign code achieves little honor for the Scottish subject. When Sir Kenneth worships before a fragment of the true cross at Engaddi, he conjures up two oddly substantial visions. First, a parade of veiled women circles the shrine. As they pass Sir Kenneth, one drops rosebuds at the knight's feet. This, Sir Kenneth acknowledges, is Edith Plantagenet, his one true love, and he forgets the one true cross in order to worship—as befits a Scottish Other—speechlessly at her English feet. After this vision retires, another takes its place. From the floor erupts a misshapen creature, which eagerly displays itself to Sir Kenneth. Scott writes:

> a long skinny arm, partly naked, partly clothed in a sleeve of red samite, arose out of the aperture, holding a lamp. . . . The form and face of the being who thus presented himself, were those of a frightful dwarf, with a large head, a cap fantastically adorned with three peacock feathers, a dress of red samite, the richness of which rendered his ugliness more conspicuous, distinguished by gold bracelets and armlets, and a white silk sash, in which he wore a gold-hilted dagger. This singular figure had in his left hand a kind of broom. So soon as he had stepped from the aperture through which he arose, he stood still, and, as if to show himself more distinctly, moved the lamp which he held slowly over his face and person, successively illuminating his wild and fantastic features, and his misshapen but nervous limbs. (65)

With his tawdry accoutrements and his deformed body, the dwarf parodies knightly nobility, but when he very deliberately reveals to Sir Kenneth his red samite rags, his peacock feather *fleur de lys,* his trusty broom, he stresses his role as the Scottish knight's similitude. Scott here suggests that the Scottish knight, functioning in an English army, can be only a thing deformed, a thing showing grotesquely through the knightly signs to which he has subjected himself. But Scott goes further. When Nectabanus, the dwarf, is followed from the depths by "his lady and his love," an equally deformed apparition named "Guenevra," Scott mocks both courtly romance and Kenneth's aspirations, as Scottish Other, to the unattainable Edith Plantagenet; an alliance between Englishwoman and Scot can occur only in Sir Kenneth's dark dreams or in the persons of these deformed representatives (67). Then most incisively of all, when Nectabanus lures Sir Kenneth from his post guarding the English standard to fulfill a supposed assignation with Edith, Scott brings into question Sir Kenneth's very commitment to the Crusade he espouses. The dwarf demonstrates that Sir Kenneth makes only a deformed, an ineffective, and perhaps even an insincere knight, a knight with a secret, self-serving agenda. For Scott, then, the Scotsman in part subjects *himself* to outside standards, but without much visible gain and at considerable risk. He will not accomplish the alliances he desires; he will prove derelict in his duties to his adopted system; and he will lose, or severely deform, that which he is.

So in *The Talisman* Scott carefully maps the conditions of Scottish subjection to England's colonizing power, not omitting to detail the naivete and complicity of the colonized Scot. Then, with equal deliberation, he offers a way for the Scottish Other to step outside England's malforming concerns, to escape England's dominance, a way, indeed, to convert Scottish otherness into agency. How does Scott accomplish this? When we meet Sir Kenneth, he rides by the Dead Sea, an almost anonymous knight. Years of blows suffered in the course of the Crusade—in his subjection to the English-dominated cause—have practically wiped out his identifying heraldic device. Moreover, the design that looms uncertainly from his shield is that of a couchant leopard, underwritten by the words, "I sleep—wake me not" (14).[12] As a Scot, Sir Kenneth is asleep, with the result that his identity as a separate Scottish subject has been practically obliterated. But Scott now begins to wake the Sleeping Leopard. He starts the long process of Sir Kenneth's re-education as a speaking subject by confronting him with Saladin. This most alien of others can teach the Scottish knight neither to hide his otherness nor to subject it to English power, but to embrace it and to use it, to voice himself across it.

In the heart of the land, at a fountain of clarity and truth called "The Diamond of the Desert," Sir Kenneth meets Saladin (here Sheerkohf, the warrior; later El Hakim, the doctor). As a Scot in the matrix of England and a soldier in the Crusades, Sir Kenneth has studied to suppress difference in himself and in Palestine, so now, not surprisingly, he fails at first to recognize his kinship with this epitome of otherness: the two men do battle before becoming friends. But once Scott has established the friendship between Kenneth and Sheerkohf, he carefully aligns his characters. He compares the two men for how they fight, judge horses, eat and, in a series of conversations, how they believe and love. In every case Kenneth and Sheerkohf stand parallel: each fights well in battle, rides a horse perfect for him, eats appropriately to his needs, is sincere in his religion, respects women. The Scot and the Saracen can be equated. But interestingly, in every case, they are also distinguished from one another. Kenneth, for instance, appears the perfect type of a soldier—from the North. He is "a powerful man, built after the ancient Gothic cast of form, with light brown hair, which . . . was seen to curl thick and profusely over his head. . . . His nose was Grecian. . . . His form was tall, powerful and athletic. . . . His hands . . . were long, fair, and well proportioned." Similarly, Sheerkohf perfectly represents the warrior—for the Middle East: "His slender limbs, and long spare hands and arms, though well-proportioned to his person, and suited to the style of his countenance, did not at first aspect promise the display of vigour and elasticity which the Emir had lately exhibited. But, on looking more closely, his limbs . . . seemed divested of all that was fleshy or cumbersome; so that nothing being left but bone, brawn, and sinew, it was a frame fitted for exertion and fatigue" (24). The men, Scott stresses, while similar, are not the same; their every similitude comprises a difference. That is, Kenneth and Saladin are the same only insofar as they are systematically different; they are brothers in their otherness.[13]

As the more racially and geographically distinct of the two warriors, and consequently as the more experienced and self-accepting Other, Saladin has a series of lessons to teach Sir Kenneth. First, he demonstrates that if one is delineated by dominant powers as inevitably and inalienably different, the best strategy may be not to resist or repine one's designation, but to use it. Because he is racially other, Saladin is almost invisible to the crusaders. Just as Sir Thomas de Vaux couldn't distinguish a Scot from a Spaniard, neither can the invaders individualize Middle Eastern Moslems. Indeed, Sir Kenneth himself initially takes Sheerkohf/Saladin for an Arab, although he is in fact a Kurd. Sheerkohf/Saladin has to inform Sir Kenneth, "For me, I am no Arab, yet derive my descent from a line neither less wild nor less warlike. . . . I am Sheerkohf, the Lion of the Mountain, . . . Kurdistan, from which I derive my descent, holds no family more noble than that of Seljook" (33). But far from being subjected by his erasure, Saladin turns it to his advantage. If his body renders him indistinguishable from the Arabs, and effectively invisible to the crusaders, then he can play different roles without drawing attention to himself. Thus, in the course of the novel, Saladin appears first as the warrior Sheerkohf, then as the physician El Hakim, and finally as himself. In these roles, he manages to negotiate a treaty, cure King Richard, and set the crusading camp to rights. That is, Saladin transforms his bodily difference and its accompanying erasure into mutability and mobility; he uses his body like a cloak of invisibility under cover of which he can direct the course of events.

Second, Saladin shows that there are advantages in accepting one's otherness, as well as in making strategic use of it. Sir Kenneth asserts his national difference, but does not live up to it, instead subjecting himself to English codes; Saladin, by contrast, fully embraces the otherness in himself. Most obviously, he acts in the apparently mutually exclusive capacities of warrior and doctor. As he explains to Sir Kenneth, the roles are necessary if opposite elements in the multiplicity that constitutes the complete man. He comments:

Doth it so surprise thee . . . and thou an approved warrior, to see that a soldier knows somewhat of the art of healing?—I say to thee, Nazarene, that an accomplished cavalier should know how to dress his steed as well as how to ride him; how to forge his sword upon the stithy, as well as how to use it in battle; how to burnish his arms, as well as how to wear them; and, above all, how to cure wounds as well as how to inflict them. (242)

And as the complete man, Saladin manages both to kill crusaders and to cure their leader, in each case directing events toward a treaty in the Saracens' favor.

Third, Saladin reveals that one can use not just the otherness in oneself, but the very principle of otherness. The dominant King Richard cannot moderate his Englishness toward otherness even so far as to negotiate with his own allies. When Scott first introduces the English monarch, he notes that the Crusade is already in decline because of "the jealousies of the Christian princes . . . and the offence taken by them at the uncurbed haughtiness of the English monarch, and Richard's unveiled contempt for his brother sovereigns" (69). By contrast, Saladin embraces even the otherness of death. As a doctor, he acknowledges death and consequently gains the power of life; as a ruler, he accepts his own death, and thus uses his power more advisedly and effectively. In his tent, Saladin reclines under a spear, a shroud, and a banner that simultaneously proclaims his power and its transience. It reads: "SALADIN, KING OF KINGS—SALADIN, VICTOR OF VICTORS—SALADIN MUST DIE" (308). Saladin brings this awareness to play in his crucial closing scene with Richard. He hosts for Richard the tournament in which Sir Kenneth disciplines the real thief of the English standard, and afterwards he himself disciplines the Crusade's conspirators. In the celebrations that follow, not recognizing the possibility of death for himself, Richard challenges Saladin to a duel for Jerusalem or, failing that, a friendly bout in the lists. Saladin refuses for a number of reasons, but one is of interest here. He argues, "The master places the shepherd over the flock, not for the shepherd's own sake, but for the sake of the sheep. Had I a son to hold the sceptre when I fell, I might have had the liberty, as I have the will, to brave this bold encounter; but your own Scripture sayeth, that when the herdsman is smitten, the sheep are scattered" (313). The monarch, in the knowledge of death, must preserve himself as governor. So Saladin lives in death's shadow, and works with it; he realizes that death comes even to kings, but on his awareness he builds careful action. Thus he derives his power from accepting what others fear or—in Richard's case—lack the sense to fear.

And finally, if Saladin shows how to turn otherness into agency, he also demonstrates how to convert its forced silence into speech. Scott repeatedly emphasizes that one of the colonized subject's inevitable and most damaging losses is that of the right to speak. In the context of imperial power, the Other cannot voice himself in a way that may be heard. Richard, as English monarch, fully enjoys the right and the power of speech; his loud voice constantly echoes around the camp. In fact Richard's speech is so effective an instrument that it works not just to establish his dominance, but to fragment the crusading alliance—it unavoidably others even England's friends. Richard's words, indeed, are too powerful; he must constantly call them back. In one crucial scene, he apologizes for his English, monarchical, and overbearing voice, on the grounds that it is an untutored, military one. He cajoles his offended royal brothers:

> Noble princes, and fathers of this holy expedition, Richard is a soldier—his hand is ever readier than his tongue, and his tongue is but too much used to the rough language of his trade. But do not, for Plantagenet's hasty speeches and ill-considered actions, forsake the noble cause of the redemption of Palestine—do not throw away earthly renown and eternal salvation . . . because the act of a soldier may have been hasty, and his speech as hard as the iron which he has worn from childhood. (202)

With these words, apologizing for his dominance by self-deprecatingly allying his word with his sword, Richard hints at the terms of his power, and once more establishes it. The word of English governance, even when retracted, inevitably asserts English control. Saladin acknowledges this when Richard declares, in response to pleas from his women and from Kenneth's confessor that the delinquent knight's life be spared: "Ladies and priest, withdraw, if ye would not hear orders which would displease you; for, by Saint George, I swear—." "Swear NOT!" Saladin intervenes (183). A word of kingly power must not be lightly uttered, for such a word has performative force. As for Kenneth, his word has no power; he serves as a vehicle for the crusading voice and cannot speak even his own name, David, Earl of Huntingdon. By contrast, though even more othered than Kenneth, Saladin enjoys the power of speech. If Saladin is overborne by crusading voices, he has not, nonetheless, given up his own culture's modes of speech; at different points in the story, he speaks as warrior, doctor, and even muezzin.[14] Furthermore, he has found ways to speak as ruler within his own system; he has but to send a sign to accomplish real effects. He tells Sir Kenneth, who is bemoaning the desertion of his own troops: "When I send one [eagle-feathered arrow] to my tents, a thousand warriors mount on horseback—when I send another, an equal force will arise—for the five, I can command five thousand men; and if I send my bow, ten thousand mounted riders will shake the desert" (33–34). Saladin's speech is so powerful that he doesn't have to open his mouth. But more importantly, if Saladin has found alternate forms of speech, unlike the garrulous Richard, he understands the power even of *no speech*. When Richard challenges him to fight for Jerusalem—or even for fun—Saladin withholds consent. Two of his reasons are of interest here. First, he refuses the challenge because he already holds Jerusalem, and would stand only to lose in the encounter. Second, he refuses the contest because, Other though he may be, he can yet resist the lure of inclusion in the dominant culture that lies behind Richard's invitation to participate in the discourse of English chivalry. It is not, then, that Saladin cannot say yes, but that he will not say so. So Saladin demonstrates how to assess a situation dispassionately and how to take control of it; he shows how to exercise and assume power by remaining silent, remaining Other.

Sir Kenneth, however, constitutes for Saladin no promising pupil. He steadfastly refuses to recognize his otherness, holding instead to an English culture which has already rejected him as alien. On the one hand, he insists on his similarity to his fellow knights—against even their indications to the contrary. Despite the fact that he is so constantly Othered by crusaders like Thomas de Vaux, Kenneth constitutes his body as English when he subordinates it to Richard's punishment. A further index to his failure to recognize and act upon his own bodily difference occurs even after he has been saved from death by Saladin. In the desert, they meet a troop of Templars. Kenneth refuses to flee men he calls "my comrades in arms—the men in whose society I have vowed to fight or fall" (236). Despite Saladin's observations that these same Templars are the least honorable of the crusaders and that they will certainly slaughter him along with the Saracens, Kenneth again has to be forced to flee, to separate his Scottish body from men who, while espousing the crusading code of honor, do not in fact adhere to it. Kenneth would prove a martyr to an adoptive code whose own proponents ignore it. On the other hand, if he insists on his similarity with the crusaders, he is equally insistent that he cannot be compared with the Saracens. When he meets Saladin at the Diamond of the Desert, his first instinct, based on Saladin's appearance, is to fight him. Then, when Saladin urges him to flee death and to recognize the Saracens as his friends, Kenneth makes no bones about declaring that such an alliance would be a dishonor. For him, as for the crusaders, the Saracen seems immutably, and negatively, Other. Saladin has humanely and practically argued that "Man is not a tree, bound to one spot of earth, nor is he framed to cling to one bare rock, like the scarce animated shell-fish. Thine own Christian writings command thee, when persecuted in one city, to flee to another; and we Moslems also know that Mohammed, the Prophet of Allah, driven forth from the holy city of Mecca, found his refuge and his helpmates at Medina." But Kenneth replies, churlishly, "I might indeed hide my dishonour . . . in a camp of infidel heathens, where the very phrase is unknown. But had I not better partake more fully in their reproach? Does not thy advice stretch so far as to recommend me to take the turban?" (158). Kenneth is so thoroughly colonized by crusading ideas that he cannot step outside them and cannot even begin to accept a brotherhood based on the Scot's and the Saracen's distinctive otherness. Small wonder, then, that Saladin has to drag him first from the camp, and then from the Templars, to initiate his recuperation as Scottish Other and Saracen brother.

In the course of *The Talisman,* however, Saladin does finally teach Sir Kenneth to embrace his otherness. The Saracen Other who is yet a brother teaches the Scottish knight not simply to succumb to or adopt the crusading culture's view of the world, but rather to act expediently, across his othered body; he teaches him to speak across silence. In the depths of his despair, Kenneth asserts that rather than become a Moslem, he would wish "that my writhen features should blacken, as they are like to do, in this evening's setting sun" (158). Saladin recognizes in this death wish an opportunity both to separate Sir Kenneth from his false brothers and to connect him with his own body, his otherness; thus he transforms the Scottish knight into a Nubian slave. Judith Wilt considers Kenneth's transformation "one final humiliation,"[15] but Scott makes very clear that it is not loss, but gain of identity that is at stake. Saladin stresses that in this black body, "not thy brother in arms, not thy brother in blood, shall discover thee" (247). Kenneth will be separated, by the barrier of his racially distinct body, from his false brothers; what is more, in this othered body, he will finally attain agency: he will be able to explain the events surrounding the theft of the standard. All he has to do is accept himself as other, and model his behavior on that of his brother. As Saladin tells him, "Thou hast seen me do matters more difficult; he that can call the dying from the darkness of the shadow of death, can easily cast a mist before the eyes of the living" (247).

But in this blackened body, Kenneth will be voiceless. His blackness itself will render him thoroughly other, and as such, he will become functionally invisible and mute. Further, Saladin insists that as Nubian slave, Kenneth lacks not just the ability to make himself heard, but also the basic power to articulate. Sir Kenneth, of course, has been subsiding into voicelessness in the course of the text, but now Saladin offers him an opportunity to influence events and achieve identity once more: All he must do is voice himself out of the silence of subjection, by means of that which renders him most visibly subject, his Othered body. And this he accomplishes. With a certain ingenuity, Kenneth communicates in writing and with the help of man's best friend, his dog Roswal. However, it is his body that initiates the train of events leading to the discovery of the thief and to his own recuperation as a distinct, Scottish entity. A Marabout makes an attempt on Richard's life; Kenneth, in his role as slave, sees the fanatic approach mirrored in the shield he is cleaning, and aborts the attack, but in the scuffle, he sustains a possibly poisoned flesh wound. Predictably, Richard's courtiers refuse to suck the poison from such a visible Other—however his actions have served their purpose, and whatever they might cost him. Long Allen protests, "methinks I would not die like a poisoned rat for the sake of a black chattel there, that is bought and sold in a market like a Martelmas ox" (223). But when Richard himself sucks the poison, he sucks away some of Kenneth's black dye, and realizes that this is no Nubian, but some Other, perhaps, even to him, a sort of brother. Of course, Richard, as prime mover in the dominant culture, cannot quite grasp

Sir Kenneth's situation. After the tournament wherein Sir Kenneth has begun the rout of evil and re-established himself as Scot, Richard opines, "thou hast shown that the Ethiopian *may* change his skin, and the leopard his spots" (303). However, Kenneth has not so much changed his skin and his spots as acknowledged them and learned to use them. Sleeping no longer, and speaking loudly through his (Scottish) knightly body, he is now, truly, the "Knight of the Leopard" (303).

According to *The Talisman,* then, the subjected Other has two obvious options: like the early Sir Kenneth, he can accept his subjection, and effectively die as a distinct self, or, like the Marabout who is mirrored in Richard's shield as Kenneth's inverse, he can openly resist, and be killed. But Scott recommends Saladin's more complex and creative strategy. Saladin teaches Kenneth to accept his own otherness, and thus neither to reject the boundary between himself and the crusaders, nor to transgress it. Indeed, Saladin insists on delineating boundaries clearly: he lives under the sign of death; he welcomes Richard to his camp with a shower of arrows that clearly demarcates the English monarch's acceptable space—if the crusaders exceed the room Saladin allows them, they risk death; and even to Kenneth, to whom he claims he is a brother (230), Saladin presents himself not as slavemaster, or physician, or friend, but "as your ancient foe . . . a fair and generous one" (241). Why all this emphasis on recognizing one's difference? First, as Saladin stresses to the resistant Sir Kenneth, "Knowledge is the parent of power" (158). To him, difference realized constitutes the subjected Other's only locus for agency; bodies and boundaries are to be recognized for what they are— and used. Second, if Others can honor one another for their difference, they can truly become br/others; they can multiply their agency against colonial subjection across their varied bodies. And, as Scott demonstrates in his novel, the strategy works. Through his br/other Kenneth, Saladin manages to negotiate a treaty with Richard; through his br/other Saladin, Kenneth manages to operate within the crusading system without sacrificing his identity. The knight who first appeared with arms effaced now blazons forth on his shield a leopard with collar and broken chain; Kenneth has learned to control and exploit his difference, and can now acknowledge and cut the leading string that bound him to Saladin.

And within *The Talisman,* Scott makes it clear that this is his preferred strategy for the contemporary, subjected Scot. At the end of his novel, he projects the talisman, the occulted symbol of Saladin's mobility, into Scotland. Using this little stone in a net bag, Saladin has penetrated the crusading camp and persistently seized life from death. But the talisman's "plop plop, fizz fizz" must be administered according to the movements of the heavens; if the stone is not used enough, or not used aright, the last patient and the physician both will die. Now, Scott casually mentions that Saladin has given the talisman to Kenneth as a wedding present. How do we read this remarkable gift? The talisman requires its operator to recognize death, but to live to heal. The Scot is to flee the death of accepted subjection, but to recognize himself as Other, to deal with death, and accomplish life. Moreover Sir Kenneth, as Prince David, is to perform a kingly cure on his people.

But as I suggested earlier, in 1825 Scott was just beginning to grasp the limitations and the potential in the contemporary Scottish situation. In the years immediately following *The Talisman*'s publication, he learned that his country's problems were more acute, their solutions more urgent. It is perhaps for this reason that after his own financial collapse and the Scottish banking crisis, and after he appealed openly to the Irish for support, he hedged his text about with rather strange supplements. For the 1832 edition of his works, he loaded the novel with prefatory and closing material, some of which is worth particular note. First, in his Introduction, he links the talisman to a curative stone brought back from the Crusades and held by the Lockharts of Lee (3–4). Then, in a footnote, he recounts that the Lee-penny, as it is now known, serves to cure cattle, and that the ungracious Presbyterian Scots have rejected even these cures as potentially diabolic (316). That is, Scott indicates paradigmatically for those who have missed the message that his countrymen need to regain their talismanic power, to accept and to use Otherness, to fight for life in the context of death, and to be agents of their own destiny. Second, in an appendix to the 1832 "Introduction," he quotes George Ellis's retelling of a tale in *Richard Coeur de Lion*.[16] Here, suffering from fever like the king in Scott's own novel, Richard craves pork. With none available, his cooks slay and serve a Saracen, instead. When Richard discovers the substitution, far from resenting it, he uses it to intimidate the Sultan's ambassadors: rather than negotiate with them, he invites them to a banquet at which he serves and eats their relatives. Needless to say, they are only too happy to forget their ambassadorial duties, and to escape with their lives. In this appendix, Scott adds a new urgency to his text; he stresses as far as he can the risks to the unresistant Other: to a voracious, dominant culture, the Other looks a lot like dinner. Just a little cultural cookery will make it digestible.

If Scott's supplements make him seem paranoid, if his text's reinscriptions indicate desperation, the history of his own text reveals that he didn't worry without reason. As we have seen, even *The Talisman*, Scott's carefully modulated consideration of the dynamics of ethnicity subject to colonial power, has slipped easily down the English canon's open maw. But perhaps this article's Saidian Heimlich maneuver can dislodge it, can make the canon cough it up and return it to the discursive space of World Literature—or at least, perhaps it can give the canon a case of cultural indigestion.[17]

Notes

1. *The Notebooks of Henry James*, ed. F. O. Matthiessen and Kenneth B. Murdock (1947; Chicago: University of Chicago Press, 1981), 37.

2. Leavis began more complimentarily, describing Scott as "primarily a kind of inspired folk-lorist. . . . a great and very intelligent man; but not having the creative writer's interest in literature, he made no serious attempt to work out his own form and break away from the bad tradition of the eighteenth-century romance." See *The Great Tradition* (1948; Harmondsworth: Penguin, 1980), 14.

3. Review 51 in *Scott: The Critical Heritage,* ed. John O. Hayden (New York: Barnes and Noble, 1970), 345–73. See especially 350.

4. Walter Scott, *The Talisman* (1825). As we await the Edinburgh Edition of Scott's works, I have chosen to refer to the most easily accessible current edition: 1906; rpt. London: Everyman, 1991.

5. Edward Said, *Orientalism* (New York: Random House, 1979), 101.

6. See my "Thinking Nationally, Writing Colonially? Scott, Stevenson and England," *Novel* 24 (1991): 296–318; "A wo/man for a' that? Subverted Sex and Perverted Politics in *The Heart of Midlothian,*" in *Scott in Carnival,* ed. J. H. Alexander and David Hewitt (Aberdeen: Association for Scottish Literary Studies, 1993), 232–44; and "The Female Body and the Body Politic: Narrating the (Gendered) Nation in Walter Scott's *The Heart of Midlothian,*" forthcoming.

7. This introduction seldom prefaces *The Talisman* when the novel is published separately, but it appears in any complete edition of Scott's works.

8. Scott's son-in-law J. G. Lockhart sounded the alarm in November 1825, although the crash occurred in 1826. See Scott's November 18 letter to Lockhart in *The Letters of Sir Walter Scott: 1825–1826,* ed. H. J. C. Grierson (1935; rpt. New York: AMS Press, 1971), 291–95.

9. See, for example, Scott's April 4 letter to his son, Walter. He shifts blame for Ireland's problems from her poor, Catholic population to her rack-renting and absentee landlords: "The Catholic question seems like to be accommodated [*sic*] at present. I hope though I doubt it a little, that Ireland will be the quieter & the people more happy. I suspect however it is laying a plaister to the foot while the head aches & that the fault is in the landholders extreme exactions not in the disabilities of the Catholics or any remote cause." Parts of *The Talisman* were in press by May 15th of the same year. See *Letters: 1825–1826,* 63 and 113.

10. Scott wrote three letters, each headed *To the Editor of the Edinburgh Weekly Journal, from Malachi Malagrowther, Esq. on the Proposed Change of Currency, and Other Late Alterations, as they affect, or are intended to affect, the Kingdom of Scotland* (Edinburgh: William Blackwood, 1826), 25–26. He addresses "Patrick" in the second, 23–29.

11. Alexander Welsh, *The Hero of the Waverley Novels* (New Haven: Yale University Press, 1963), 217.

12. Scott thenceforward refers to him as "The Knight of the Sleeping Leopard."

13. In his recent book, Bruce Beiderwell adds his voice to those stressing that here Saladin and Sir Kenneth represent the East and the West. He calls Sir Kenneth and Saladin "the two best representatives of their respective cultures' virtues." See *Power and Punishment in Scott's Novels* (Athens, Ga.: University of Georgia Press, 1992), 85. He misses, I think, the fact that each is also encoded as Other.

14. When Kenneth is saved by Saladin/El Hakim from death, their ride through the desert is interrupted for prayer. Scott writes: "the sonorous voice of El Hakim himself overpowered and cut short the narrative of the tale-teller, while he caused to resound along the sands the solemn summons, which the muezzins thunder at morning from the minaret of every mosque" (233).

15. Judith Wilt, *Secret Leaves: The Novels of Walter Scott* (Chicago: University of Chicago Press, 1985), 182.

16. George Ellis, ed. *Specimens of Early English Metrical Romances,* vol. 2 (London: Longman, Hurst, Rees, Orme, and Brown, 1811), 233–46.

17. My thanks go to Ric Reverand, University of Wyoming, for the careful reading and thorough comments that have helped me to limit this paper's controversy to its content, rather than its form.

Index

◆